RENEWING THE MAYA WORLD

Renewing
the Maya World

EXPRESSIVE CULTURE
IN A HIGHLAND TOWN

GARRETT W. COOK

 UNIVERSITY OF TEXAS PRESS

To Edith Cook and Lori Cook,
for countless acts of love and kindness.

Requests for permission to reproduce material from this work should be
sent to Permissions, University of Texas Press, P.O. Box 7819, Austin,
TX 78713-7819.

∞ The paper used in this book meets the minimum requirements of
ANSI/NISO Z39.48-1992 (R1997) (Permanence of Paper).

Library of Congress Cataloging-in-Publication Data

Cook, Garrett, W., 1947–
    Renewing the Maya world : expressive culture in a highland town /
Garrett W. Cook.
        p.   cm.
    Includes bibliographical references and index.
    ISBN 0-292-71224-3 (cl. : alk. paper)—ISBN 0-292-71225-1 (pbk. : alk.
paper)
        1. Quiché Indians—Guatemala—Momostenango—Rites and
ceremonies. 2. Quiché mythology—Guatemala—Momostenango.
3. Quiché cosmology—Guatemala—Momostenango. 4. Cofradías
(Latin America)—Guatemala—Momostenango. 5. Momostenango
(Guatemala)—Religious life and customs. 6. Momostenango
(Guatemala)—Social life and customs. I. Title.
F1465.2.Q5   C66   2000
972.81′8100497415—dc21   99-058459

Contents

List of Narratives

Preface

I began research in Santiago Momostenango, Guatemala, in January 1974. From January through May, I conducted a survey of agricultural practices sponsored by the Agency for International Development and directed by Dr. Robert M. Carmack. During this time I developed basic fluency in Spanish, began to study the Quiché language, and observed Holy Week for the first time. In October 1975 I returned to conduct dissertation research, this time supported by Bob Carmack's Quichean Civilization Project, funded by the National Endowment for the Humanities. I returned to Albany to participate in a conference in late January 1976, and so missed the great earthquake of February. After conducting aid-related work in the Guatemalan highlands with Bob Carmack in March, I returned to Momos to complete my dissertation research, from April through August. During my research in Momostenango, I witnessed Holy Week in 1974 and 1976, Christmas in 1975 and Santiago's fiesta in 1976. Without Bob Carmack's inspiration and guidance there would have been no beginning to this project. My research agenda, an attempt to identify continuities with the *Popol Vuh* in Quichean expressive culture, especially in the cults of Jesucristo and the saints, was his suggestion. It is my fervent hope that this book will finally live up to his high expectations of me and of my project.

I did not find it easy to work in Momostenango. I suffered from periodic bouts of profound depression and culture shock during the first few months of my work. During this difficult time Gustavo Lang, Santiago Guix, Valentín Cuyuch, and Andrés Xiloj showed kindness and hospitality to me as a student of their friend Roberto Carmack. Anacleto Rojas introduced me to the saints in their cold and quiet house, and also to his family. He allowed me the great privilege of sharing a visit with the souls in the cemetery, and showed me the mysteries and beauty of the *calvario*. He and his eldest son, Fermín, offered me friendship. Their invitations to the family homestead in Pa T'uraz strengthened and nourished my spirit when I most needed human contact. Julian Ak'abal, a very bright and cosmopolitan Momostecan with a profound interest in Maya traditions, had worked with a linguist during the previous year. He became my principal language teacher and part-time research assistant. His expertise and advice were invaluable. At length I found an identity as an ethnographer and was ready to pursue my work.

Then I discovered that the leaders of the *cofradías* would not cooperate with my research project. My fantasy of being invited to observe and record esoteric ceremonies was simply not going to happen. Nevertheless, as my self-understanding and understanding of Momos improved, my work began to bear fruit. There were *pasados* who had devoted years of their lives to the *cofradías* and sacred dances who were willing to talk about their experiences and share their perceptions and understandings with me. There were also raconteurs willing to tell me their stories about the beginnings of everything, the founding of the town, and the origins of the saints.

After a long internal debate I have finally convinced myself that my original plan of crediting the contributors to the present work as the authors of their texts is not appropriate. Given the reluctance of the leaders of the *cofradías* to help with my project, and the comments of at least one principal contributor that the neighbors were gossiping about him and perhaps working sorcery against him because he was helping me, it is clear that within the community there were, and presumably still are, strongly mixed feelings about sharing knowledge of the traditions with outsiders. I believe that those who worked with me behaved honorably by my standards and theirs. They were not compensated for the information they shared, which they often said they believed should be given to one who sought it. They gave me permission to tape-record and to publish their words, and I pledged to them that I would accurately report and preserve a record of what they told me. I did not, however, ask permission to credit them as the sources. At the time, my main reason for making the recordings was to compensate for my lack of fluency in Quiché; I did not realize that eventually I would wish to publish translations of long passages. From their willingness to share what they considered to be appropriate portions of their knowledge with me and the larger world I represented, I incurred a debt that I cannot repay. The contributors are introduced in chapter 1, lamentably but I think ethically with pseudonyms.

I completed my dissertation in 1981 but was unable to locate a publisher during the next couple of years. I was too close to the work to read it critically myself, and I was emotionally unable to accept the critiques of reviewers or the monumental revisions that would have been necessary to make it publishable. Following the New York State budget cuts in the middle 1980s, I lost my teaching position at the State University of New York College at Potsdam and spent the next five years supporting my growing family through contract archaeology and museum work. During this phase of my life I had neither the opportunity nor inclination to consider writing a book on Momostenango.

In 1990 a really strange thing happened. John Fox called me at the Saint Lawrence County Museum, which I directed as one of my two jobs, and asked me if I would like to come to Baylor University to help him develop a Maya program. It seemed kind of miraculous when, after a dreamlike visit to Waco—which was enjoying glorious spring weather while bleak, snowy Saint Lawrence County was still in the middle of its mud season—Baylor actually offered me the position. John and I then spent five exhilarating field seasons together in the Guatemalan highlands. He encouraged me, by generously inviting my participation in his more established life of scholarship, to seek a contributing position as a Mayanist. Without John's intervention this book would have existed only as a vague fantasy about what might have been. A chance meeting with Linda Schele and David Freidel at the American Anthropological Association meetings in Chicago in 1992, and my discovery that they were familiar with my work and found it good, finally convinced me that I had something to offer and should attempt this project.

Much had changed in both the world of the Maya and in Maya scholarship between the late 1970s and 1992. In 1981, the year that I finished my dissertation, Victoria Bricker published *The Indian Christ, the Indian King*, which scooped what I had written in my dissertation on the Maya millenarian myth. She wrote with such intellectual brilliance and such comprehensive documentation that my encyclopedic work on highland Maya mythology and its historic transformations seemed to me to be but a pale and pedantic seven-hundred-page footnote to her work. I became a bit depressed about my future as a Mayanist.

During the time that I was conducting surveys of the remains of

nineteenth-century communities along the byways of the Saint Lawrence Valley, the study of the Maya was revitalized. The 1980s and early
1990s saw incredible breakthroughs in Classic Maya epigraphy, the first
brilliant products of the Schele and Freidel collaboration, and the creation of a whole body of exciting work in the conjunctive synthesizing
mode. In 1991, when I began to get caught up on what had happened
in my absence, I saw that my Momostecan data on *cofradías,* dance
teams, and cosmogenic ritual had new meaning in this rapidly developing collective intellectual enterprise. This book is my exploration of
the significance of Momostecan sodalities and their ritual symbolism
for understanding a larger Maya expressive culture tradition.

Financial support for the writing was provided by a Baylor University sabbatical in 1996. I am especially grateful to Wallace Daniel, Dean
of Arts and Sciences at Baylor University, for finding the additional
support that I needed to embark on the final revisions in 1998.

1. Introduction

The bus clanks and grinds down from the cold and barren finger of alpine prairie above San Francisco El Alto, a mountain fastness, a *ju-yup*, where flowering bunchgrass is collected each year to construct the body of San Simón during Holy Week. The rutted dirt road winds down through a misty forest of giant pines and ancient twisted oaks bearded with Spanish moss. Heading north, the bus breaks out of the forest into sunlight, into a world of maize fields, scattered homesteads, and wood lots, a cultivated world or *takaj*. Here Momostecan settlement begins on the southern edge of a great basin dipping gently to the north and northeast. Streams, muddied from milpa runoff, erode gullied shoulders of exhausted land and combine in valley troughs to form the northern drainage of the Chixoy, or Black, River (see fig. 1.1).

The Chixoy, a tributary of the great Usumacinta, defines the Quiché country. Its ancient valley, holding the oldest known Quichean sites near the salt deposits of Sacapulas (Fox 1976, 1987), is the gateway to the mountains from the Western Rivers Region of the lowland jungles where a regional variant of the great Classic Maya civilization flourished. The Usumacinta flows between shaded banks in the jungles defining the Petén/Chiapas frontier. It glides past the ruins of Yaxchilán and Piedras Negras as it drops from the hilly Maya country onto the Gulf Coast plain.

Back on the bus, at the southern end of this great watershed, the ground falls away on the left. Across the valley is a cluster of tan adobe houses with reddish tile roofs straggling up the hillside and along the ridge crest. This is a *paraje*, a tiny settlement amid stepped fields and islands of trees. In the *parajes* a house encloses a patch of earth with mud-brick walls and roofs it over with silvery thatched bunchgrass or

FIG. 1.1. The Maya area, showing Momostenango.
(Redrawn from Freidel, Schele, and Parker 1993, fig. 1.6. Used with permission of William Morrow.)

fired red tiles. When a house is abandoned, the roof tiles are salvaged and the timbers fall in. The walls are eroded by rain. Milpa lives in the house again. The house is made of earth, and the earth is made of many houses. The parents and grandparents who lived in the house are melded into the common dead, a community of the dead counted and measured in generations and centuries of the dead, a world of the dead that vastly outnumbers its living children.

From up on that ridge back, one could see the church of Momostenango, vague and soft with distance, where the valley broadens to the north. It is large and cold inside. It is a house of cold, often filled with murmured prayers. It is the home of faded wooden saints lining the walls in niches and glass cases. Little clumps of supplicants in poor ragged clothes, bare callused feet padding along the cold concrete floor, raise candles before the glass cases, tapping lightly on the glass doors. Shoulder bags of cracked vinyl or woven brown and white wool, sweat-stained straw hats or narrow-brimmed gray or brown fedoras, and colorful cloth-wrapped bundles wait for them on the pews. The church, built on the old cemetery after the original church collapsed in the earthquake of 1906, is said to cover catacombs. Sacramento, the main altar, is located "above the hair," over the heads of the dead. If the priest allowed it, the floor would be carpeted with pine needles, a forest of glowing candles and flowers, whenever certain holy days arrived.

The great portal of the church opens to the west, facing the steep slope of a high plateau that looms over the little town. A rutted track curving off toward the distant Pan American Highway runs up and over this western ridge with its feathery skyline of pruned pine trees. Each tree is scarred from the harvesting of resinous sap. A few miles from town on this road is the entrance to Pueblo Viejo, also called Ojer Tinamit, the old town, the site of the ruins of Chuwa Tz'ak. There, perhaps six hundred years ago, a valiant war captain, an *ojew achi'*, from the Nim Jaib, the Great House lineage at K'umarca'aj, the Quiché capital, established a stronghold, a *tinamit*, and claimed the surrounding country as the estate for his lineage segment.[1] From the *tinamit* he and his younger brother would control several local *chinamits*,[2] land-based communities something like feudal fiefdoms, each of which was headed by the patriarch of a locally powerful lineage segment. The sons and brothers of the *ojew achi'* would marry local women, cementing the *chinamits* into a chiefdom, an *amak* centered on the *tinamit*. In time their sisters and daughters would marry local men.

The warriors from the *tinamit* would fall upon neighboring communities, screaming like jaguars and blowing conch shells. Captured warriors would feed the *cabawil* whose mouth was opened in counsel and prophecy when smeared with blood, a hungry god that embodied their unity and power and gave them victory in war. What happened to that *cabawil?* Has it been forgotten, or is it still remembered in some collective dreamworld? Is the *ojew achi'* remembered by his descendants, or by the descendants of his victims, the tribes that he subdued six centuries ago?

After the Spanish conquest the Franciscans came to Chuwa Tz'ak and established a hermitage. Within a few decades an earthquake toppled it. A new center was established where the town center, the *cabecera* known as Momostenango, is located today. For four hundred years, though, most of the population in the territory that is today the town of Momostenango lived on large multilineage communal estates, *parcialidades,* headed by *caciques* (chiefs) descended from the aboriginal *chinamit* lords.[3] A *parcialidad* took the name of its patron saint. It maintained a god house for its patron and celebrated the saint's day. How were these *parcialidades* and their saints related to the *chinamits* and *cabawils* that preceded them? What happened to them, and how are they related to the *cofradías* (religious confraternities) of this century?

At about the same time that the new center was being established at Momostenango, an unknown native author "in this place called Quiché," the new settlement to which the population of the original Quiché capital Utatlán (K'umarca'aj) had been transferred by the victorious Spaniards, lamenting the loss of the original Council Book of his people, tried to fix the Quichean cosmogony and history in written form (see Tedlock 1985: 71). Using the characters of the new Spanish alphabet, he recorded the text that we know today as the *Popol Vuh.*[4] Thus a substantial piece of the Quichean tradition, at least as it was known to the elite at K'umarca'aj, was fixed, frozen in time, recorded it seems as an alternative to the fixed, written biblical tradition (D. Tedlock 1986). Then, gradually, literacy declined, along with the power and privileges of the *cacique* class. Ancient documents were retained, guarded as sacred objects and evidence of status but less and less accessible to their guardians as sources of information. Yet an oral tradition continued in the Quiché mountains. History, which we might call mythology as it was not critical and was no longer written, was told around family fires, told by grandparents to their grandchildren, their replacements in this world. At births and at wakes, at weddings and at family gatherings, stories were told. Mythology was lived and enacted in initiations, rites of renewal, and dance dramas, and from time to time in nativistic uprisings. What was this mythology, the story held close to the collective heart of the conquered people? What story did they strive to live, struggling to make lives for themselves and their descendants, struggling to honor and placate the owners of nature and the generations and centuries of the dead's souls, and struggling to make sense of a world transformed by a new kind of warfare, by ethnic castes, communal labor obligations (*encomienda*), plantation labor, and evangelization? How did the story change?

In the sixteenth and seventeenth centuries local Maya cultures, adjusting to forced population movements, major epidemics, and the imposition of the Spanish colonial order, "crystallized" within the colonial order into local variants of colonial Indian culture and became traditional or conservative.[5] What complexes from the colonial tradition have survived the destruction of the *parcialidades,* as well as the modernization of Guatemala's economy in the nineteenth and twentieth centuries, as a recent or modern Indian culture emerged from the devastated colonial order in Momostenango?[6] Are there Maya premises at the heart of late-twentieth-century Costumbrista culture?[7] What mythos dictates Momostenango's stories about itself? These issues are addressed below in an investigation of tradition in Momostecan expressive culture.

Other visitors have described Momostenango (Huxley 1934; Schultze Jena 1954; Carmack 1966, 1995; Tedlock 1982), and so it has gradually become known, revealing itself in depth and detail, yet always holding something back. A few elements in the existing portrait need highlighting as context for my attempt to illuminate a little part of what has remained obscure.

Momostenango is a typical highland township or *municipio* (fig. 1.2). It seems to be very much like Chichicastenango, for example. In the typical western highlands pattern, it has its own local culture at the *municipio* level (Tax 1937). The population, numbering over forty thousand in the mid-1970s (it has nearly doubled since then), is allocated among a town center with four *barrios* and about thirteen official

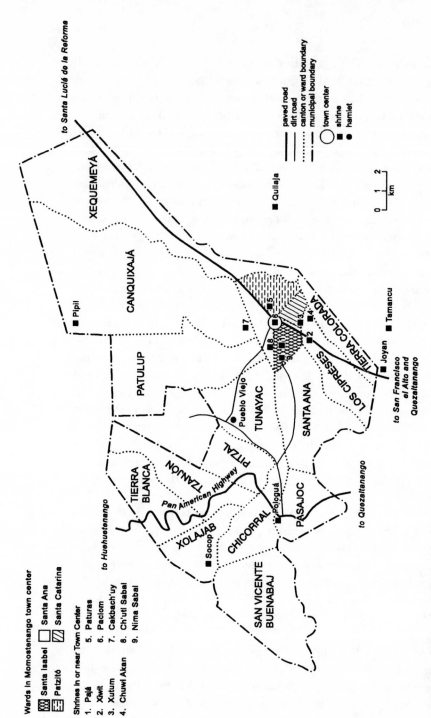

FIG. 1.2. Map showing twentieth-century Momostenango.
(Redrawn from Tedlock 1982, map 2. Used with permission from University of New Mexico Press.)

aldeas that correspond in most cases to traditional territorial divisions called *cantones*. Each one is divided into local hamlets (*parajes*) named for a physical feature nearby, some historical event, or a founding lineage (Carmack 1995: 295–296).

The official local government in the recent past has been dominated by acculturated Indians from the town center who have formed political alliances with the town Ladinos and blocs of rural traditionalists (Carmack 1995: 311–313).[8] The municipal government includes an elected council and a mayor (*alcalde*). These positions are generally held by acculturated Indians, though village politics and perceptions of technical competence have resulted in some ethnic power sharing. *Ladinos* ("Latins," the Guatemalan term for mestizos) usually hold the positions of first councilman and secretary-treasurer. As in other highland Indian towns, Momostenango also has a subservient "Indian" administration called the *auxiliatura,* composed of officials appointed as representatives of the *principales,* the elders who actually administer local affairs in the rural administrative divisions (*aldeas*) and the wards of the town center. With a separate office in the municipal palace headed by the Indian mayor (*alcalde indígena*) or *síndico segundo,* the *auxiliatura* includes the *alcaldes* and their subordinate officials in each hamlet and is responsible for overall supervision of the *cofradías.* The *principales,* the governing board of elders, are retirees (*pasados*) from the *auxiliatura* who have held the rank of *alcalde* in an *aldea* or of *síndico segundo* in the town center. In the 1970s it was estimated by one such elder who had served as *síndico segundo* that there were about 250 *principales* in Momostenango (Tedlock 1982: 37).

Momostenango, like other large highland towns, has a very large market once a week. This *día de plaza* is on Sundays, with a second large market on Wednesdays. On Sunday the town literally fills up as country people come in to sell a pig, a chicken, or some eggs and to buy some plastic shoes or a new straw hat, and as merchants come from Quetzaltenango and Guatemala City to participate in the blanket market.

There are about twenty *cofradías* in the Momostenango Catholic church. In the 1970s the Catholic community was divided—it seemed nearly down the middle—between Costumbristas who practiced the traditional Christo-pagan religion and members of Catholic Action, a theologically reformist and, by rural Guatemalan standards, socially progressive movement headed by the Catholic priest and numerous catechists. In the 1970s Mormons and Seventh Day Adventists made up small but influential communities in the town center and were joined by several less influential Protestant missions. Pentecostal churches, led by local reborn charismatic preachers, were just beginning to appear.

Like other highland communities and the Guatemalan national culture, Momostecans make castelike distinctions between Ladinos—who are few in number but dominate the local economy—and Indians.[9] A "civilized" group of entrepreneurial Indians, most of them involved in the merchandising of locally produced textiles, represent a kind of mediating category and have been competing with the Ladinos to dominate Momostenango throughout the twentieth century.[10]

There are some factors that make Momostenango unusual and need to be considered as background to the issue of Momostecan mythology and traditionalism. While rural Momostecans are skillful, dedicated farmers and most try to meet their families' subsistence needs, the limited land base and degraded soil have made this an impossibility for many in recent decades. A blanket-weaving industry with roots in the early colonial period became important by the eighteenth century (Carmack 1995: 69) and today is definitive. Momostenango is known primarily for its blankets. About one-third of the male producers in Momostenango are primarily farmers, while another third are primarily artisans. About half of the artisans are weavers (Carmack 1995: 257). This is an important factor in considering traditionalism in Momostenango. Its commercialism is typical of the core zone marketing network in the highlands. Communities economically dominated by artisans and merchants are generally more traditional and more typically peasant in orientation than are proletarianized wage-oriented peripheral communities (see Carol Smith 1978; Carmack 1995: xviii).

Another unique circumstance is Momostecan militarism (see Carmack 1995: 171–219). During the unsettled liberal period, a Ladino *caudillo* (regional political boss) formed a militia in Momostenango. It gave him a power base for regional domination, but also provided a framework for social and economic advancement for Indian men. The militia sided with the losing conservatives after the fall of President Ubico, and it never revived after the October revolution of 1944 (Carmack 1995: 219). However, it was a significant element in the creation of the local acculturated or "civilized" Indian sector. Momostecan militarism, as well as the related support of conservative leaders at the national level, has helped to buffer Momostecan traditionalism and its carriers from interference by the typical authoritarian militarist regimes of the post-Arbenz period.

Finally, perhaps as a consequence of the political struggle within its traditional sector, Momostenango never developed the interlocked civil-religious hierarchy that is commonly seen as a central element in highland Maya community structure. Momostecan *principales* are veterans of service in the *auxiliatura*. Very few have filled posts in the *cofradías*. A critical historical study by Chance and Taylor (1985), discussed in more detail below, suggests that a political hierarchy based on a central and powerful *cabildo* (municipal corporation) with a separate *cofradía* system was the dominant pattern in Mesoamerican communities, including those of the Maya in Chiapas, during the colonial period. This was replaced by an interlocking civil-religious hierarchy with individualized sponsorship of fiestas only as a result of the collapse of the *cacique* class and the later collapse of communalistic Indian economies in the republican period. Perhaps the commercialism and militarism of Momostenango have fostered the retention of core institutions in a social and political system that has made fewer and later adaptations to the forces of modernization than have many smaller and more remote villages that might superficially appear to be more traditional.

IN THE TIME OF THE GREAT EARTHQUAKE: THE FIELDWORK AND ITS SETTING

Back in the time of President Laugerud García, just before the great earthquake, a young man and an old man were talking. They sat on tiny hard wooden chairs opposite each other at a little wooden table in the doorway of a one-room adobe house across a gullied track from a stand of scrub oak and scattered giant pine trees. On sunny afternoons like this the house was shaded by the tall, straight pines growing across the road. The old man, Don Domingo, was a diviner and daykeeper who had for many years performed offerings for his clients on the four sacred mountains surrounding Momostenango. He had grown frail and had nearly lost his eyesight, and was now only able to follow his calling at shrines in the town center. He had time to talk and much to say. He was demonstrating how his *vara*, his collection of scarlet *tzité* beans and rock crystals, were sorted and counted to do a divination. This demonstration was taking place in the open doorway because his failing eyesight required light, but also because the neighbors were talking about his working with a foreigner, telling him he shouldn't reveal anything. He felt that it was best to work openly together in plain sight.

The young man was a gringo, a foreigner from New York, a student of Don Roberto Carmack, who had lived and worked in Momostenango in the previous decade. The young man struggled to find an identity in his fieldwork and a clear way to follow. He enjoyed his visits with Don Domingo, who seemed accepting and was eager to share his wisdom and knowledge.

Now and then people passed on the road, often barefoot, though some of the men wore sandals or oxford-style shoes with a hole in the front for their toes to stick out. They all carried loads. The women carried baskets on their heads, or the large blue and white striped plastic pots that had recently become popular, balancing the load with gentle pigeonlike movements of their necks. The men carried bundles on their backs with tumplines, the forehead straps hidden by weathered straw hats or rain and sweat stained fedoras. The old man was always greeted politely, the passerby's hand raised before the face, palm inward, the head inclined slightly. They greeted him with a gently voiced "Tat" ("Sir" or "Father"), somewhat drawn out with the pace of walking and breathing on the steeply sloping road: "Ta-a-at." Then three men passed, dressed in dark suit coats and white shirts and wearing shoes and shiny new straw hats. One carried a staff of office, another kind of *vara*. They also saluted Don Domingo politely as they passed. The instant they went by, Don Domingo leaped up from his seat and, leaning on the table, stuck his tongue out rigidly at their receding backs. His face was twisted in a grimace. Then he sat down again with the nervous little laugh that the gringo student was coming to associate with any mention of *brujería,* the use of offerings and invocations or sorcery to injure one's enemies.

"That was the secretary. He especially has been telling me I shouldn't talk to you. I told him it is a sin to withhold knowledge from one who requests it. You are only learning good things from me. It is my responsibility to teach you these things."

He paused for a moment, reflecting. The secretary, like Don Domingo, was a Costumbrista, yet there were other obstacles to Don Domingo's living his ideals.

"Then take those in Catholic Action," he said. "The sacristan is ill.

He was hit by lightning. Perhaps this is his punishment for not allowing us to perform *costumbre* [rituals or traditional customs] in the church.

"Now I will tell you the truth. Look at all the people in the church [during mass], only catechists, men and women; these are those of Catholic Action. Look what happens when one burns a candle. 'Witch [*Brujo*],' they say. When incense is burned, 'It is the witch,' they say. The truth is that this is not witchcraft, these are *costumbres* before God.

"In the first days there were no places for burning, there were no churches, no *calvarios* [cemetery chapels]. Then everyone just knelt down where they did their *costumbre,* and they knelt like this [he knelt to demonstrate], you see? Then, when it was the time of Carnaval, then it was time to be smeared with ashes. When Carnaval came around, then sometimes people prayed, 'God our Lord, God the Son, God the Word, God the Holy Spirit in Glory, and you the Virgin: Blessed are your holy names.' Yes, this is the subject. The people today do not believe it. They all say it is witchcraft, yes. This is not witchcraft, because there was a time when there was no *calvario*. Then when it entered, when the conquest entered, when Tecum was totally erased and the Spaniards entered, then all these things began. They raised up the barracks, the jails, everything. They raised up the church. They ordered the construction of the *calvario*. And thus it went, and so the Costumbre [syncretized Maya-Christian religion] is being forgotten.

"They are foolish to give up a religion that existed before the Spaniards came and made the churches. They throw away their *varas* or leave them at Pasabal [outdoor shrine in the *barrio* Santa Isabel]. They destroy the *winel* and *warabal ja* [the two altars of each minimal lineage or *alaxik*]. This can lead to death or ruination for a family, to alcoholism. They call us witches [*brujos*] when we are only practicing the ancient customs before God."

In the 1970s it was Catholic Action that opposed the syncretized religion of the Quiché traditionalists. Then in the 1980s and 1990s it was evangelical Protestantism, especially Pentecostalism. Many, like Don Domingo, felt sadness and confusion over the attack on their way of life, made sometimes by their children and grandchildren. History repeats itself. In one of the versions of the life of Jesucristo told by Costumbristas in these Quiché mountains, the children are taught to pray by Jesucristo, and their prayers cause their parents to fall on their faces, unable to move. According to one account of the founding of Momostenango, Diego

Vicente, a colonial period *cacique,* grew rich by keeping a *cabawil* in a cave. Because of its craving for human victims, it was finally destroyed by people from the community, including Diego's own sons.

Thus some were reluctant to introduce me to their deeper wisdom and esoteric knowledge. Perhaps I was a missionary. Some feared for my safety should I seek to obtain supernatural power without a calling and initiation. I was told the story of a gringo from New York, about my age, who had visited the community a few years earlier, and who had sought knowledge of hidden things. He lost his mind. Only an initiated daykeeper could be taught some things. Yet they welcomed a sympathetic listener who was interested in learning what Costumbre meant to them, perhaps especially in this time of trouble and change.

The Costumbristas, facing growing opposition, had to clarify for themselves what Costumbre meant and defend it intellectually in the debates raging in their communities and families. A leader of the more acculturated Costumbristas in the town center once explained that the thirteen numbers used to designate days in the ancient divining calendar represented Jesus and the twelve apostles. The following pages convey the words of Momostecan traditionalists. What they wanted me to know was not always what I originally set out to learn, and was not always clear to them. Within their words are many clues to the meanings of a complex world that I continue to understand in greater depth, including some clues that I have not recognized as clues, which will hopefully spark connections for others that I haven't made. As Don Domingo understood it to be his duty to convey knowledge to one who sought it, I believe I have a duty to pass this knowledge on to a broader community that will hopefully discover additional meanings that have eluded me.

By the mid-1970s not even the dispersed hamlets in highland Guatemala were homogenous peasant villages unified by the milpa cycle, a gerontocracy, offerings to protective ancestors at hilltop shrines, and calendrical festivals at a god house. Yet within the villages there were communities, sometimes complacent majorities and sometimes embattled minorities, that continued to represent and embody that ideal as their preferred alternative. Those who have lost their ties to the land and to local places and maybe even to their own ancestors need some other kind of philosophical and emotional moorings, and there are many who choose to live in a world of wider horizons. The traditional institutions embodied in a Costumbrista community include accommodations to and perhaps even some vehicles for oppression. The Maya are moving to inhabit several divergent futures, and in the 1970s a number of competing options were emerging in Momostenango.

Yet a sympathetic and perhaps romantic tendency to treasure the ideal of community life, as well as the wisdom of another culture, was my principal personal reason for going to Momostenango. In my heart, intuitively, I believe that much of what is found in Costumbrista institutions did exist, as Don Domingo argued, before the Spaniards came and built the churches. I believed this when I first encountered Momostenango in the mid-1970s. I believed it when I was writing my dissertation between 1979 and 1981, and I continue to believe it today. This intuition leads me to conclude that there is much that archaeologists and epigraphers trying to decode the physical remains and the written texts left by the ancient Maya can learn from their descendants.

When contemporary community narrative thematically parallels ancient historiography and myth, I believe that it demonstrates the survival of systemic patterns in Maya culture (Vogt 1964) at an ideological level. In spite of five centuries of colonialism, oppression, military occupation and externally imposed cultural engineering—five centuries of creative and adaptive and sometimes also desperate and violent responses by the Maya—some themes have persisted. As I hope to show, this is neither amazing nor is it based on some mystical essentialism.[11] The colonial cultural crystallization established a very conservative pattern that retained selected elements of pre-Columbian social organization and ritual in the newly organized Indian pueblos of highland Guatemala.[12] As social and economic investment in these "new" patterns grew, they became increasingly resistant to change.[13]

By relating the words of Momostecan experts to several centuries of Western observations, descriptions, and interpretations of the Maya, it is possible to discern the outline of a systemic Maya cultural pattern in the mythology, ritual, and theology of these natives of highland Guatemala. The expressive culture of the Costumbristas of Momostenango is an ongoing attempt to formulate and to convey a worldview that is continuous with the past but that also makes some kind of sense, within a Maya frame of reference, of experience lived in Guatemala. My task in the field as I saw it was to collect information that might help to reveal both the underlying intellectual principles of the Costumbrista tradition within Momostenango, and the process by which the tradition maintains and renews itself.

My focus was on cosmogony and on how the religion was expressed in collectively organized manifestations, such as festivals, dances, and street theater. My fieldwork aimed to produce Malinowskian descriptions of what Anthony Wallace refers to as communalistic cult institutions, the rituals of Jesucristo and the saints.[14]

Unlike several of my peers, I was not initiated as a daykeeper. I never kept a sacred divining bundle of *tzité* seeds and rock crystals or performed calendrical offerings and divinations. To my combined disappointment and relief, the Maya calendar priests with whom I worked did not perceive that I had this calling, and I didn't seek it. I had no initiatory rebirth. I sometimes felt that I was transported into another reality simply by my immersion in a Maya world, but I did not perceive my inner state as relevant to my research. I worked systematically to accumulate a glossary of the key terms that the Costumbristas used to encode the main conceptions in their religious life. With the help of a paid research assistant from the community, I collected, transcribed, and translated numerous long texts: myths, histories, biographical episodes, exegetical commentaries on expressive culture, and operating manuals for the cult institutions of some of the saints. My lack of a Costumbrista initiation meant that some doors were closed to me, that some kinds of knowledge would not be revealed. It is my hope that this work, with its different orientation, concentrating on *cofradía* and dance team lore, and on the *pueblo*'s enacted cosmogonies, the performance of the myths of Momostenango, will both complement and supplement the fine ethnography of Quiché daykeeping, divination, and shamanic initiation by Barbara Tedlock (1982) researched in Momostenango at the same time. It fills in some missing details necessary for a complete portrait of traditionalist Quiché religious expression in the mid-1970s, the *costumbre* of Momostenango.

A COLLECTION OF TEXTS

Breath on the Mirror, Dennis Tedlock's (1993) excursion into Quichean culture and its history and meaning, recounts conversations, events, and dreams through the artistry of an introspective first-person telling. In the introduction, Tedlock explains that he could have presented texts with commentaries to try to convey the native's point of view, but he chose a more imaginative and personal approach. I am unable to tell the inside story of my encounter with Guatemala, the Maya, and Momostenango. It has been the great adventure of my life, but is too personal and revealing, and in some ways too dreamlike, to share comfortably. My Momostecan journal is full of letters that I wrote and then didn't mail because I didn't want my family and friends to worry that I was in such confusion or despair or experiencing such unaccountable ecstasies. The story that is told here, like most other ethnographic works, is a safely intellectualized and rationalized redaction recounting my observations of events and the words of the natives. In the 1970s I didn't imagine a new kind of ethnography where my personal experiences and thoughts as I encountered Momostenango would be relevant data, and I didn't make the systematic notes or observations that would allow me to reconstruct them. This work therefore adopts a prosaic and traditional approach. Momostecan ritualists here speak directly, though in a context of imposed narrative structure and commentary to provide for effective and topically organized communication. They do not conduct dialogues or conversations with a thoughtfully introspective and reflexive investigator. We certainly had such conversations, but I could not reproduce them now except as a work of fiction. I understood my job to be the depiction of Momostecan culture rather than a depiction of fieldwork or of my thought processes. I will try to explain what the words that I recorded and observations that I made when I was twenty-eight and twenty-nine years old have come to mean to me now in the sixth decade of my life. At the time that I recorded these words, I didn't usually know what they meant to me. Of course, they will always hold greater significance than just what they mean to me.

Robert Carmack had sent me into the field to make a study of the cult of the saints in Momostenango, which he believed had more Maya content than had come through in ethnographic accounts in other communities. I was tremendously frustrated by the recalcitrance of the elders, the *c'amal be* (lit., "road guides") who were the heads of the *cofradía*. They sent me on wild-goose chases, invited me to nonexistent meetings, and ultimately discouraged me completely from pursuing the participant-observation strategy with which I started. I could not allay their suspicions. Perhaps I looked like an evangelist. I had formed a close personal relationship with the sacristan, who had been an ally of several Catholic Action priests and who was therefore seen as an adversary by many Costumbristas. They managed their own "service of the foreign saints" by excluding prying foreigners and even local Ladinos. Yet after residing in the village for six months, I had developed rapport with several elders who were no longer active participants in the system, and they were willing to share their memories and understandings of *cofradía* service and sacred dances with me and have them recorded for posterity.

The following work, then, is constructed around the contributions of these Momostecan experts, participating in a floating symposium on the expressive culture, mythology, and ritual symbols in their community. The participants are here introduced, with indications of their areas of expertise, though using pseudonyms as explained in the preface. Julian Ak'abal, my paid research assistant, had converted to Mormonism but was personally very interested in traditional Momostecan culture. He was literate, had worked with a linguist during the preceding year, and knew how to transcribe Quiché using the Summer Institute orthography that I was familiar with (Fox 1973: 15–18). I have retained this orthography in the Quichean words or phrases that I employ from my field notes and transcribed texts.[15]

The individuals introduced here allowed me to record our interviews on tape, with the understanding that this would result in a more accurate and truthful record than notes and my memory, and granted me permission to use the information in writing on the history and customs of the town. In editing I have replaced the names of persons mentioned in their accounts with pseudonyms and have omitted redundant passages or sometimes rearranged the order of a presentation to improve the flow of information; otherwise I have not changed their testimony. Some interviews were recorded in Spanish. I later transcribed these myself and translated them into English. Others were recorded in Quiché. These were transcribed and translated into Spanish with the help of Don Julian and later translated into English.

Francisco Vicente

Don Francisco was in his sixties, a *principal* in San Vicente Buenabaj who had served as the *chuch kajaw* (a priest-shaman acting for a corporate group) of his *aldea*. He was the leader of his patrilineage, a *cacique* lineage descended from the quasi-mythical founder of Momostenango, Diego Vicente, and a successful farmer with large landholdings and a large flock of sheep. As a young man he had been instructed in local history by an older relative, whom he described as an important defender of the *pueblo* in a series of land disputes. I have not reproduced any of Don Francisco's long texts in this book, but he was the source of the story of Diego Vicente and the *cabawil* that is referred to several times in this work, traditional narratives of Jesucristo, and a commentary on the Devil's Dance that we observed together in December 1975 after he provided me with a lesson in Quiché-style drinking. We also had some very informative conversations about death and the souls of the dead. The texts were all recorded in Spanish.

Domingo Castillo

Don Domingo was an *aj mesa*,[16] seventy-six years old, nearly blind, and starting to become frail when I began working with him at his son's house. He had been *alcalde* of the most prestigious *cofradías*, Patrón Santiago and Corpus. He was philosophical. His wife had died seven years earlier. As he faced the end of his own life, I believe that he enjoyed the opportunity of communicating what he had come to understand about the human condition and his extensive knowledge of prayers and rituals and divination. We spoke of mortality, the major shrines, the count of the holy days, *cofradía* service, and crosses and San Simón. Don Domingo had sponsored and performed in the Conquest Dance, dancing the part of Tecum for 26 years, and he introduced me to his son Miguel, who was preparing to perform in the dance in 1976. The interviews were conducted in Spanish but included some prayer texts and invocations given in Quiché.

Miguel Castillo

The thirty-eight-year-old son of Domingo Castillo, Don Miguel participated in the first two interviews with his father. Immediately after the fiesta, during which I had been privileged to witness and produce a photographic study of the Conquest Dance, we had a long interview at his little shop in which he described and interpreted the dance. Don Miguel was a merchant whose business sometimes took him as far afield as Nicaragua and Costa Rica. Nevertheless, he had performed in the Conquest Dance for a total of eighteen years: nine performances as

Pedro de Alvarado and, before that, nine performances first as Aj Itz Chiquito and then as Aj Itz.

Vicente De León Abac

Don Vicente, a man in his fifties, was a ritualist of *aj mesa* rank and had served as *síndico segundo*. His ancestors, whom he referred to as militarists, had played a role in the native militia that figured importantly in Momostecan politics during the first quarter of the twentieth century. He was the source of a major myth text called the Origins of Costumbre (see Cook 1981: 654–677, 1986: 142–143), a text elicited when I asked him if he could explain why a mass was performed for the town officials at Chiantla each year, or anything else about the origins of Costumbre in Momos. He said that he had learned it from an ancient book at the pilgrimage site of San Jorge.[17] This myth text was recorded in Spanish.

Pablo Itzep

Don Pablo was a weaver who was sixty years old at the time of his interviews, and pleased that he was about to turn sixty-one. That would mean that he could no longer be called for *cofradía* service. He had served twice in the *cofradía* of Niño San Antonio, the second time twelve years after the first time and several years before I interviewed him. Only he and the *nima chichu* ("great lady"; the leader of the women in the *cofradía*) still remained alive from his last period of service. He provided rich descriptions of serving the Niño and many insights into the motivations and fears of the *cofrades*. The interviews were recorded in Quiché.

Pedro Contreras

Don Pedro was a weaver with the vitality of a man in his forties, though he might have been older. He had served as *alcalde* of the *cofradía* of San Francisco and was currently the *alcalde* of the *cofradía* of Santa Cruz.[18] Because both of these *cofradías* participated in a pilgrimage to El Palmar during Holy Week each year, he was able to present a wonderfully detailed and well-informed account of it. He also narrated a life of Jesucristo and described the anxieties and dangers of *cofradía* service. The interviews with Don Pedro were recorded in Quiché.

Florentino Ixbatz

The testimony of Don Florentino and his son, who resided in the *aldea* Xequemaya, were recorded in Quiché. Don Florentino, a man in his fifties, was an *aj mesa* who had served many clients. He had participated for a time in Catholic Action and experimented for eighteen months with Protestantism, and so had developed familiarity with the Bible and with the anti-*costumbre* ideology of these Christian movements. He was suffering from several medical problems: excessive watering of the eyes, crippling pains in one foot, and a face twisted slightly to one side that appeared to be from a minor stroke. He felt that these were the result of witchcraft being worked against him by enemies. A doctor told him there was no cure for his illness, but if he "believed in the idols" he should continue in *costumbre* so he would not get worse.

The main focus of our discussions was the Monkeys Dance. He had served as *chuch kajaw*, performing offerings and prayers for the dancers. He had been trained by his predecessor to call the spirits of the animals from C'oyabaj (the dance shrine; lit., "Spider Monkey Stone"). He had also served as main sponsor (called *autor*) six times over a period of about twelve years. If his health and life permitted, he hoped to sponsor the dance three more times to complete a *novena* (an obligation to perform nine times). His son, a man in his early twenties, had danced in several roles, most recently as one of the Monkeys. Our interviews also covered Don Florentino's practice of divining and the role and obligations of being an *aj mesa*.

Juan Ixc'oy

A weaver in his sixties, Don Juan had served for eighteen years as the *deputado*[19] in the *cofradía* of Santiago, and would still have been serving had he not been removed by the town officials for washing the images' faces without permission and causing damage to the paint job. He had also performed as a dancer in several dances, but especially the Tzulab (Grasejos) Dance of Holy Week. Because he believed that his family had been victimized by witches as a result of a dispute over land purchased by his parents, he had been motivated to pursue a lifelong series of defensive ritual obligations. Four of his brothers were dead, and his only living brother was blind. He had been spared because of his service to Santiago and the *Cristos* of the *calvario*. He provided detailed Quiché-language descriptions of the *costumbre* associated with Santiago and San Simón and a lengthy commentary on the Tzulab.

ORGANIZATION OF THE WORK

The next four chapters describe the expressive culture tradition performed in and by the sodalities (i.e., *cofradías* and dance teams) of Momostenango in the 1970s. The description is based largely on extensive texts transcribed from interviews with the Momostecan experts introduced above. In part 1 (chapters 2 and 3), the social and political aspects of the institutionalization of the expressive culture are described and analyzed. This analysis identifies several significant episodes in Momostecan historiography—especially the colonial transformation of *chinamits* into *cofradías* and the centralization of the *cofradías* in the twentieth century—that conditioned the social forms that embody the expressive culture and its themes. The expressive culture is here contextualized by the social organization and documented social history of the village.

In part 2 (chapters 4 and 5), central symbols and themes in the expressive culture are described and analyzed in the context of the performances and native explications of three enduring Maya cosmogonic complexes: (1) the raising of an *axis mundi* (chapter 4); (2) world transformation as the coming of a new sun (chapter 4); and (3) the vegetative regeneration model at the heart of Holy Week (chapter 5). This is thick description (Geertz 1973) using ethnographic observation and native exegesis to offer an interpretation of the meanings of the dominant ritual symbols (Turner 1977) in the expressive culture performed by Momostecan sodalities.

In the conclusion (chapter 6), Momostecan evidence for historical continuity of forms and meanings in the cultural performances of Quichean sodalities is summarized, and its significance for understanding Maya ideology is investigated. Here some issues related to characterizing and understanding Maya cultural continuity are raised and explored. As a service to those who prefer to avoid the distractions of someone else's speculative intellectual constructs while formulating their own, or who don't share my fascination with issues of cultural persistence, I have tried to reserve my speculations concerning culture history for this chapter, though I doubt that I have entirely succeeded.

PART 1. THE INSTITUTIONAL CONTEXT

2. Religious Sodalities of Momostenango
The Communal Cult Institutions

SAINTS AND SODALITIES

In the midwestern highlands communal ceremonies are, with few exceptions, under the care of the civil religious organization. The communal rites are basically Catholic in origin with no appreciable pagan content. —Tax and Hinshaw, 1969

How would the missionary priests and Maya catechists organizing Catholic Action in the western highlands in the 1970s have reacted to this statement? The main preoccupation of the *cofradías* in Chichicastenango was the propitiation of their ancestors and the *cofrades* who had come before them (Bunzel 1952: 249; Schultze Jena 1954: 38), hardly a Catholic emphasis in the cult of a saint. In Santiago Atitlán some saints' images are the embodiments of ancestral protective spirits called *naguales*—community founders, lightning men, mist men, rain men, earthquake men—who retreated to the mountains leaving the images and sacred bundles behind (O'Brien 1975: 42–43). Maximon is a very peculiar "saint" with no Christian counterpart of any kind left to the village by its late-nineteenth-century prophet Francisco Sojuel (Mendelson 1959).

Most of the Momostecan saints originated in Spain, but what is Spain? Spain is a distant city from which ultimate authority and its local symbols, the saints and the ancient land titles, emanated. Spain is the Tulan of post-conquest mythology. Water from Spain gushes from a rock face in Momostenango even in the dry season. This is where Santiago watered his horse; one of his altars marks the spot. Santiago is the Morning Star. The Baby San Antonio, a Momostecan saint who, like Maximon, does not exist in Catholic hagiography, is a fertility god whose miraculous image was found in a cave. Unlike the other saints, San Antonio is a Santo del Mundo (Saint of the [Holy] World).

Jesucristo was a trickster whose pursuit by enemies established the world order. From Wednesday through Saturday of Holy Week, while Jesucristo lies powerless on a table in the *calvario* and his altars are closed, foul-mouthed lascivious contraries, the Tzulab, dance in the streets. San Simón, the Momostecan version of Maximon and an archetypal Ladino patron in his Momostecan incarnation, is seated at his paymaster's table in front of the church. This is not the outline of a Catholic complex. It is the telling of a Maya story, revised and revised again in response to five centuries of Catholic evangelism and oppression under colonial and neocolonial regimes.

This chapter describes the ceremonial cycle, focusing on the saints and Jesucristo, and investigates the social organization and histories of the *cofradías* and dance teams, the sodalities that perform the cycle.[1] The remainder of the work explores the symbolism and meanings of some key ritual complexes and the stories they enact.

THE SODALITIES AND RITUAL COMPLEXES

Cofradía and dance team performances are conjoined in several major complexes articulated to the Christian calendar and performed in honor of specific sacred images. The Easter festival in the town center (*cabecera*) marks the beginning of the rainy season and planting time, and honors the two Cristos kept in the cemetery chapel (*calvario*) as well as San Simón. Santiago, the patron saint, and his secretary, San Felipe, are honored in late July when the roasting ears are ripe and there is a heightened danger of damaging storms. At Christmas, which comes just after the harvest as the dry season sets in, María Concepción, San José, and the Niño Jesús are honored. A fourth major complex, associated with a Momostecan saint called Niño San Antonio, occurs in August, the mating period for the sheep, and involves two fiestas in a distant *aldea* and many visits to private houses for *paraje*-level festivals. In similar "traveling saint" complexes, Santiago and San Felipe also leave the *cabecera* each November to visit the rural *cantón* Pueblo Viejo, in the *aldea* Tunayac, as well as the *aldea* San Vicente Buenabaj. All of these major festivals include the coordinated performances of *cofradías* and dance teams.

A "complex" refers here to a bundle of institutions associated with a specific named sacred image (a saint) or set of related images that occur together as part of a public event, like Holy Week. An institution is an organized system of activities that fulfill a defined and legitimized purpose, its charter. It utilizes concrete capital and is staffed by personnel whose roles are governed by ideal norms or rules (Malinowski 1944: 47–52). "Cult institutions," are sets of religious rituals sharing a general goal, rationalized by related beliefs and supported by a single social group (Wallace 1966: 75). Wallace (1966: 86–87) has identified individual, shamanic, and communal types of cult institutions. In the communal type, an organized group of nonspecialists perform calendrical or occasional rituals on behalf of a larger social group. The major sodality complexes listed above are classic examples of communal cult institutions, though in hiring *chuch kajaws* they include shamanic cult institutions.

When an organized priesthood carries a universalistic religion, or the cult of a state, it embodies an ecclesiastical type of cult institution (Wallace 1966: 87). In Momostenango this ideal type would be represented by Catholic Action or by some missionary Protestant churches, but it is marginal to the Costumbristas. *Cofrades* attend mass, serve the priest in various capacities, and celebrate saints' days by filling roles within communal cult institutions, thus freeing the larger community from the need to participate on an individual basis in cult institutions of the ecclesiastical type.

Nancy Farriss (1984: 10) identifies three subsystems within the religion of the colonial Yucatec Maya: private negotiations with lesser spirits (Wallace's individualistic and shamanic cult institutions), corporate support of local tutelary deities or saints (communalistic cult institutions), and an elaborated cult with a universal and all-encompassing notion of divinity (the ecclesiastical type). During the colonial period the first level, defined as superstition by Spanish clergy, was not strongly opposed and much of it survived. The second, at the "Weberian community level," was defined as idolatry by the Spanish. Being public, it was actively opposed which led to syncretism. At the third level, Maya universalistic theology disappeared when the Maya elite were submerged in the peasantry and replaced by Christian monotheism in the national culture (Farriss 1984: 288–289).

In Momostenango, sodality rites refer to spirits of the dead and local nature spirits (*dueños*), as well as to the tutelary gods that are now called saints. As Farriss' model suggests, these are local deities, though their types are replicated in other villages. However, the Costumbrista Holy Week complex in Momostenango, also organized and functioning at the "Weberian community level," embodies a universal cyclical cosmogonic interpretation of the world order and its regeneration. This is based on a Momostecan interpretation of the Jesucristo of the ecclesiastical cult as a sun and maize god, whose life is the embodiment of a cosmic cycle that is beneficial to humanity. Similarly, the Holy World (Dios Mundo) is represented in a variety of animistic forms, but is understood by some as a pantheistic single entity of multiple manifestations. Thus, as one Momostecan raconteur explains it:

> *The serpent, the deer and other things are owned by El Mundo, and he sends them to places and gives them orders.* But the serpent, the deer and other things are Santo Mundo because Santo Mundo comes in various forms. . . . El Mundo is invisible but he comes in many forms. *El Mundo lives in the mountain, but he also lives in the earth, he has many fincas [plantations].*

> (Saler 1960: 111, emphasis mine)

In other words, the forced post-conquest restriction of indigenous Quichean religious institutions to forms that are individualistic, shamanic, and communalistic has not restricted Costumbrista theology to local animism.

Sacred dances are clearly attested to as pre-Columbian institutions, though these are poorly understood. None of the dances performed in Momostenango has survived in aboriginal form, though central symbolic elements in two of them, the C'oyob (Spider Monkeys) Dance and the Tzulab (Contraries) Dance, have aboriginal origins, and the dance teams have distinctively Maya charters and patterns of recruitment and organization.

Although the existence of aboriginal antecedents for the *cofradías* of Mesoamerica is recognized (e.g., Wolf 1959; Carrasco 1961; Mendelson 1967; see also Rojas Lima 1988: 190–191), accepted wisdom has generally interpreted them as syncretized versions of religious sodalities introduced from Spain during the colonial period (Reina 1966; Tax and Hinshaw 1969). They have been interpreted as elements in the civil religious hierarchies (Tax 1937; Cancian 1967) that are definitive for traditional colonial closed corporate communities (Wolf 1959). However, evidence from several Mesoamerican regional co-traditions suggests that the civil religious hierarchy dates from the nineteenth century, and that *cofradías* were different during the colonial period (Chance and Taylor 1985).

The Quichean *cofradía* had an aboriginal antecedent in the cult of a *cabawil*, an idol or god image of stone or wood that served as a tutelary god or patron deity. In the 1970s Momostecans reported that *co-*

fradías there had once represented hamlets (*cantones*) in a one-to-one correspondence, and that the *cantones* had originally been *calpules* or *parcialidades* (Cook 1981: 61). Hill and Monaghan (1987) have since shown that in Quiché-speaking Sacapulas pre-Hispanic *chinamits* became colonial *parcialidades* and then *cantones*, each of which still maintains a *cofradía* in honor of a patron saint.[2]

THE *COFRADÍAS*

Origins of the Momostecan Cofradías

Quiché speakers probably entered the Momostenango area beginning around 1000 A.D. and coexisted with Mam speakers until the territory was incorporated into the expanding Quiché polity centered at K'umarca'aj (Utatlán) in about 1400.[3] At the time of the Spanish conquest, Chuwa Tz'ak, a fortified outpost of the Quiché capital, K'umarca'aj, dominated the territory. This *tinamit*, whose ruins remain at Cantón Pueblo Viejo in the *aldea* Tunayac, was the administrative and defensive center of a larger community, an *amak*, composed of *chinamits*,[4] endogamous landholding communities subordinate to the lord at the *tinamit* and headed by partially exogamous elite patrilineages.[5]

At the time of the Spanish conquest, the Nijaib lineage, one of the ruling lineages in the Quiché confederacy, controlled Chuwa Tz'ak. The local branch was headed by Francisco Izquin Nijaib, who held the title of *ah pop*, and his brother Juan, with the title of *calel* (Alvarez Arevalo 1987: 39, 42).[6] However, the conquests that established their rule were a joint endeavor led by both the Nijaib and Cawek lineages (Recinos 1957: 71–76; see also Nijaib I in Carmack 1973; Alvarez Arevalo 1987: 27–37), and the role played by the Caweks and lesser elite lineages in settling and administering Momostenango remains unclear (Carmack 1995: 40).[7] Tensions between the Nijaibs of the Momostenango region and the Caweks controlling the Quetzaltenango valley to the south are documented for the period just before the conquest (Carmack 1995: 42).

The *Popol Vuh* identifies the Nijaibs as descendants of Jaguar Night whose patron god (*cabawil*), received at Tulan, was Awilix, while the Cawek lineages, descended from Jaguar Quitze, had Tojil for their patron (Tedlock 1985: 171, 197). Tojil was hidden on a mountaintop and

Awilix in a canyon in the liminal period before the first sunrise (Tedlock 1985: 178–179, 365). Modern oral tradition of the Vicentes, descendants of the Nijaibs,[8] says that Diego Vicente, a colonial *cacique,* found Santiago on a mountain near the "City of Spain," while Diego's sister, Anna María Vicente Masariej, located Santa Isabel, another important colonial period patron deity, at a streamside.[9] These contexts suggest both the Postclassic hilltop and canyon associations in the hiding of the *cabawils* and the hilltop (*ujuyubal*) and stream or spring side (*uja'l*) elements in contemporary Quichean altar complexes.[10] Colonial ideology preserved the sense of the *Popol Vuh* by discovering the new patron gods in traditionally appropriate contexts following the rising of the Christian-Spanish sun. The identification of Tojil with Santiago in Momostenango is lent support by Santiago's association with winds and storms, his role as a patron in war, and his identification with Venus as Morning Star (Nima Ch'umil).

In Momostenango today two lineages, the Vicentes and the Herreras, both claim to have been the original owners of Santiago. By the early to middle 1600s, the Vicentes had moved their center of power to a western highland area and had adopted the Virgin of the Conception (María Concepción) as their patron. Other elite lineages, possibly led by the Herreras who today dominate Pueblo Viejo, the *cantón* where the ruins of Chuwa Tz'ak are located, had displaced the Vicentes there and at the new town center of Momostenango, and had wrested control of Santiago and Santa Isabel from the Nijaib descendants.[11] This colonial period struggle between the Vicentes and Herreras suggests a continuation of the earlier regional struggle between the Nijaibs and Caweks. The Herreras have not been linked to their pre-conquest lineage (Carmack, personal communication). If the Herreras are Cawek descendants, they would have had a stronger traditional claim to Santiago, the Tojil replacement, than did the Vicentes. This would mark this episode as a continuation of a pre-Hispanic local political struggle within the indigenous elite, utilizing a traditional symbolic Quichean idiom.

As the Spanish policy of congregation resettled families more centrally in the Momostecan territory, a hermitage (*armita*) was constructed at Chuwa Tz'ak in 1540. Santiago was probably introduced as the patron saint at Chuwa Tz'ak at about this time by Francisco Izquin Nijaib. The new *cabecera* or town center, Momostenango proper, superseded Chuwa Tz'ak by 1587 when a convent was established there and the municipal corporation (*cabildo*) was officially organized. Nevertheless, during most of the colonial period there was little centralization. Social and economic life was organized through nearly autonomous rural landholding units, the *parcialidades.*

Parcialidad *Cults or* Cofradías?

Chinamits came to be called *calpuls* or *parcialidades* but remained essentially what they had been: territorial units headed by elite lineages who controlled access to collectively held lands and maintained a cult for a patron image on behalf of the other lineages in the community (Fox and Cook 1996). In the 1600s Momostenango was composed of six *parcialidades* (Carmack 1995: 56–57, 79). Four are well documented and were located in what is now the central area of the municipality. Santiago's territory included the area where the *cabecera* is located today. Santa Ana, Santa Catarina, and Santa Isabel (containing Chuwa Tz'ak) were located nearby. All had individual *encomienda* responsibilities. The names of Santa Ana, Santa Catarina, and Santa Isabel have been retained as the names for three of the four wards of Momostenango. The fifth, headed by the *cacique* Vicente lineage that descended from the Nijaibs, lacked *encomienda* duties and was located in the higher country to the west. Its patron saint is not identified by Carmack (see fig. 2.1).

Today, in the chapel of the *aldea* San Vicente Buenabaj in this western highland area, there is an ancient portrait of the most important of these Nijaib descendants, Diego Vicente, in which María Concepción is shown floating above a church in the background. The Vicentes' oral tradition holds that Diego was forced to leave Santiago and Santa Isabel behind when he left Momostenango, bringing María Concepción with him to Buenabaj. The *aldea* San Vicente Buenabaj probably was the *parcialidad* María Concepción in the seventeenth century. The *parcialidad* Señora de la Limpia Concepción was involved in a documented land dispute with San Carlos Sija in the eighteenth century (Carmack 1979: 207–208), and Sija stole the image of María from Buenabaj in the nineteenth century.

As noted above, Diego Vicente's sister is linked to the image of Santa Isabel, the patron saint of the seventeenth-century *parcialidad* that contained Chuwa Tz'ak. The colonial linkage of Santiago to Catarina and Isabel was still embodied early in this century, when during Lent of

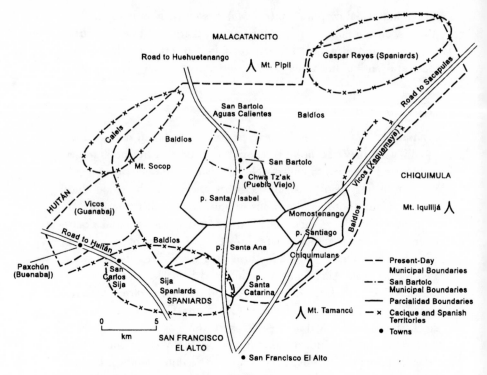

FIG. 2.1. Map showing seventeenth-century Momostenango.
(Redrawn from Carmack 1998, map 9. Used with permission of University of Okalahoma Press.)

each year a ritualized journey was made in which Santa Isabel and Santa Catarina were brought from the town center to visit Pueblo Viejo, the *cantón* containing the ruins of Chuwa Tz'ak, thus temporarily reconstituting the primordial situation of the foundation period. An account by an Herrera elder (see below) indicates that since 1925 this visit has corresponded to the fiesta of Santa Catarina in late November, a harvest time deemed more appropriate for a fiesta by its Herrera sponsors.

However, in the 1920s Santa Isabel was given to Buenabaj (or some say stolen by Buenabaj) to replace the María stolen by Sija. Santiago is also reunited each November with Santa Isabel during her fiesta in Buenabaj in a reconstitutive rite of renewal similar to the one in Pueblo Viejo. The *cofradía* of Santa Isabel in Buenabaj is unofficial because it is not supervised by the Momostecan government or parish priest and lacks a colonial period silver pole-top standard. The Vicentes, having already lost at least three images over the years, will no longer allow Santa Isabel to visit Santiago at Santa Catarina's fiesta in Pueblo Viejo. Thus two *cantones,* Buenabaj and Pueblo Viejo, which were until the end of the nineteenth-century *parcialidades* headed by *cacique* lineages, have retained symbolic recognition of their historical status under the compulsion of tradition. The official *cofradía* of Patrón Santiago in Momostenango continues to symbolically reenact and reconstitute the older, decentralized system with these sacred journeys. The *cabildo* imposes its authority by granting permission each year and requiring from the *principales* of Buenabaj a document agreeing that they will allow Santiago to return to Momostenango.

I believe that the sixth *parcialidad* was, like that of María Concepción, located in the highlands west of the town center in what is now Pologua.[12] In 1710, a plot of three *caballerías* (336 acres; 136 hectares), which later became the *cantón* Pologua, was purchased from the neighboring town, San Carlos Sija, by Momostenango on behalf of the *cofradía* of San Antonio, which had provided most of the funds. The *cofradía* raised livestock on this large estate until it was incorporated into Momostenango as an *aldea* during the liberal reforms of the 1870s (Carmack 1995: 68).

The seventeenth-century Cakchiquel people, speakers of a related Quichean language who occupied land southeast of the Quiché proper (see Hill 1992: 93–95), had both *guachibal* saints and *cofradía* saints. A *guachibal*[13] commissioned by a *parcialidad* head was maintained by his patrilineage. A *parcialidad* could contain several *guachibals* belonging to its lineage segments, but it also had a *cofradía* in honor of its official patron saint. *Cofradías* were endowed with land and livestock by local Maya elite families, but staffed by commoners who managed the endowment and used the proceeds to support the fiesta.

During the eighteenth century the number of *parcialidades* expanded as new landholding units were incorporated by traditional elite and new entrepreneurial elite families, a creative adaptation to the Spanish-imposed land tenure system that Carmack refers to as the creation of "progressive clan-based *parcialidades*" (Carmack 1995: 80) and Rojas Lima (1988: 61–67) calls "indigenization" of the *cofradías.*

In late-eighteenth-century Guatemala, then, there was a complex array of sodalities with a variety of economic and social functions. These included officially recognized *parcialidad* cults called *cofradías,* as well as unofficial *parcialidad* cults that were usually referred to as *guachibals* but sometimes called *cofradías*. In addition, administrative centers like Momostenango proper had official Indian *cofradías* under direct clerical control, as well as *hermandades,* or Spanish-criollo *cofradías* (Rojas Lima 1988: 57–69).

Liberal reforms after 1871 weakened or destroyed the collective land bases of the *parcialidades,* which had also come to be known as *comunidades. Cofradías* had to be supported by private donations rather than by endowments or estates, leading to the sponsorship pattern characteristic of cargo systems in Mesoamerica today (see Chance and Taylor 1985). In Momostenango some communities continued into the twentieth century as *comunidades* or *parcialidades* in name and still had cults for their patron deities. These cults, maintained by private citizens in their own homes but often supported by donations from a *paraje* or other remnant of an indigenized *cofradía,* were now known as *guachibals* in order to distinguish them from *cofradías,* the cult organizations of saints belonging to the entire pueblo and housed in a central location in the cathedral or *calvario.* In spite of these changes, though, the term *calpul,* originally a synonym for *chinamit* and later used to refer to a *parcialidad*'s chief during the colonial period, has survived in the Momostecan *cofradía* system as a term for a *cofrade.* The *cofradías* in totality are referred to today as *oxlahu' chop',* the thirteen teams, referring to their original identification with the thirteen *cantones* or *calpuls* of Momostenango.

In the 1920s a local Ladino, Teodoro Cifuentes, who had risen to power as a regional *caudillo,* completed the construction of the present cathedral, gathered in the saints, and began the process of centralizing the *cofradías.* He also reorganized the Santiago festival to make it into a true Guatemalan (i.e., Ladino-style) *fiesta patronal.*[14]

Another round of centralization of the *cofradías* took place in the 1950s and 1960s.[15] During this period three of the most distant *aldeas,* San Vicente Buenabaj (*cofradía* of Sacred Heart), Tierra Blanca (*cofradía* of San Luis), and Tzanjon (*cofradía* of Santa Bárbara), citing hardship, requested and were granted permission to drop out of the *cofradía* system in the *cabecera.* The Sacred Heart *cofradía* was transferred to Tierra Colorada, and Santa Bárbara's positions were assigned to the *aldea* Santa Ana and the *cabecera.* Pitzal, which had provided the *cofradía* of Jesús, passed it to Xequemaya. Some *cofradías* now have members from more than one territorial unit; San Antonio Pologua's members are from Los Cipreses, Santa Ana, and Tunayac, while Santa

Bárbara, Virgen Guadalupe, and San Francisco members are from Santa Ana and the town center. A pattern of correspondence between a *cofradía* and an *aldea* still exists, though, with, for example, Santa Cruz and Jesús from Xequemaya, and San Miguel and San José from Santa Ana.

Numerous *cantón*-based unofficial *cofradías* were probably maintained until the Cifuentes round of centralization; for example, one for Santiago among the Herreras in Pueblo Viejo, one for the Niño San Antonio in the *aldea* Pologua, one for an image of Santa Ana in the *barrio* (former *parcialidad*) Santa Ana, and another for Santa Catarina among the Chanchabac lineage in the *barrio* Santa Catarina. The decline of the Santa Catarina cult is documented in oral history found among the Chanchabacs living on the eastern edge of the town center, and is provided in the following account.

The Origin of the *Comunidad* Chanchabac
by an anonymous Chanchabac elder

The original Chanchabac [i.e., the founder of the narrator's clan (*alaxik*)] was named Francisco. He had three houses, one in the town center, one in Los Cipreses and one in Santa Catarina.[16] He also had three women: María Calel, Catalina Pasa', and Isabela Coxak.[17]

Francisco was a rich man and had an estate with many animals in the area now called Cho Puerta. He was threatened by thieves, so he sent two mules loaded with silver to the president in Guatemala, and in return he received soldiers to guard his land. He was a *principal*, but he was not one of the militarists.[18] When Don Francisco came to the *barrio* Santa Catarina, it was a virgin wilderness. He brought the image of Santa Catarina with him. We do not know where the image was before this.[19]

The first man to have the image was Don Francisco. The image was originally kept in Jardín Viejo where the school is today, and there was a *porobal* [an altar complex where burnt offerings are made] for the image there. In the time of our fathers, we asked to have the image moved to its present location where we all live now. These lands of ours used to belong to the image. We were a *comunidad* [*parcialidad*] in those days, but they have been divided up among us.[20]

We used to give a fiesta for the image in November. It had no fixed date but was given on a Sunday. It lasted for two days, with marimba, shawm [*chirimía*], Tzulab Dance, and rockets. Donations were requested from the neighbors to help defray the costs. The image was not brought to the church, but the whole fiesta took place here at the house. The house was a regular *armita* in those days. The image had its own document in a leather cover, but no one has seen it for many years.[21]

Don Francisco lived for 150 years. He had a son Miguel, and he had a son Francisco, and he had a son Tomás, and he had two sons Tiburcio and Francisco. The living elder Chanchabacs are all their descendants. The seventh generation is now coming to manhood.[22]

Patrón Santiago was removed from a private Herrera house to the new church in Momostenango in the 1920s. It is unclear whether Santiago had been removed from Herrera control to an official *cofradía* before the colonial church collapsed during an earthquake in 1906, but the Herrera custodianship during church construction suggests that, if so, the Herreras remained centrally involved in the *cofradía*. Note the final line in the account below, implying that Santiago left the *parcialidad* Herrera in about 1920.

Santiago and the *Parcialidad* Herrera
by an anonymous Herrera elder

There was a church when the image was first here,[23] but it had fallen down and the image was in a hut [*ranchito*]. At night when it rained it was brought into a neighbor's house for shelter.

Diego Vicente founded the pueblo of Momostenango and ordered the building of a church. The original church was in the place where the two-story part of the municipal palace now stands. Sixty years ago [i.e., circa 1915] the image was kept in my grandfather's brother's house in the town center, but it was not well cared for. The chickens roosted over it. So in the time of General Teodoro Cifuentes, he ordered that the *cofrades* take it to the church. It left the *parcialidad* Herrera and now it is Patrón of the pueblo.

The ethnographic present of about 1976, the perspective for the following description of the *cofradías*, represents a system that acquired its major features in several phases. The early colonial period transformation of *cabawil* to saint and of *chinamit* to *parcialidad* was followed by centralization and the creation of modern *cofradías* in the late nineteenth and early twentieth centuries, with probable crisis periods or cusps of change in the 1870s and the 1920s followed by a systematic opting out of participation by outlying *aldeas* in the 1960s and 1970s. In the mid-1970s the "traditional" system of Costumbrista *cofradía* institutions that had crystallized early in this century was under attack by the Catholic Action movement.[24]

Within the traditional Costumbrista culture of Momostenango there are *cofradías* for most of the saints in the church, but only two—Niño San Antonio and Santiago—stand out as being important to the Costumbristas. On most days, forests of candles burn in front of them. Both saints were the centers of significant *parcialidad* or *parcialidad*-like cult organizations during the colonial period, have origin myths, and are involved in ritualized annual returns to places where they were originally kept within the municipality. They are the only Momostecan saints mentioned by name in a detailed Momostecan creation account recorded in El Palmar (Saler 1960: 110–112) and in the very different Origins of Costumbre text recorded in Momos (Cook 1981: 654–677). If aboriginal themes and ritual patterns are to be found in the Momostecan *cofradías,* they should exist in connection with these two images.

The Costumbristas also focus much ritual attention on two colonial period images of Jesucristo, called Corpus (an entombed Christ) and Capitagua (a crucified Christ), that are kept in the *calvario* or cemetery chapel. While their histories are undocumented, it is worth noting that a *cofradía* of Vera Cruz existed in the *cabecera* prior to the eighteenth century, and that another called Santísimo Sacramento was added in the eighteenth century (Carmack 1995: 78). Vera Cruz almost certainly pertained to the crucified Christ called Capitagua, and Sacramento is an archaic term still used by *cofrades* for Corpus. An account of entering the service of Capitagua through the *cofradía* of Santa Cruz is presented in this chapter. Additional texts pertaining to these images and the Holy Week complex are presented in chapter 5.

Ethnography of the Cofradías

A *cofradía* is a group of four men who put on the annual fiesta for the image of a Catholic saint.[25] They occupy ranked positions in a hierarchy: *alcalde, deputado,* and first and second *mortoma.*[26] Each *cofradía* is augmented by a women's team composed of two ranked positions: *capitana* or *nima chichu* and *chuch axel.* The highest-ranked woman's position is ranked below the lowest-ranked man's position. All of these personnel are designated as *aj patan* (burden carrier). In order to spread the financial burden, a few important *cofradías* supplement these positions with a second *alcalde,* a second *deputado,* third and fourth *mortomas,* and an additional *chuch axel.*

The *alcalde* bears the brunt of the expenses for the fiesta and attends weekly mass and a meeting in the convent courtyard after mass. *Alcaldes* are excused from menial chores like sweeping the church or cleaning the cemetery. In *cofradías* that make an annual pilgrimage to the coast for flowers to decorate the church and cemetery during Holy Week, the *alcaldes* remain in town while younger junior *cofrades* undertake the initiatory journey.

The *deputado* often remains in the service of an important image for many years, becoming expert in its *costumbre* and lore, thus paralleling the role of secretary in Chichicastenango, who acts as a trustee of tradition (see Bunzel 1952: 249). A *deputado* of Santiago, for example, served for eighteen years, and one *deputado* of Santa Cruz is said to have served for forty. Often it is the *deputado* who performs *costumbre* for the image or who supervises the *costumbre* of a hired *chuch kajaw.*

Mortomas run errands, carry ritual paraphernalia, and serve drinks and cigarettes at *cofradía* functions. The wives of the *cofrades* prepare the food eaten at meetings. The *chuch axels* do not perform these functions or participate in ritual meals with the *cofrades.* They are served drinks at the saint's annual nightlong celebration, but smaller drinks than the men are served. In *cofradía* visits to private houses for special fiestas, the owners feed the *cofrades,* but the *chuch axels* are expected to bring their own food. In some *cofradías* they wash the saint's clothes, but in the *cofradía* of Corpus, where the clothing is of special potency, the *cofrades* do that too and the women wash the glass case.

The images of the saints are kept in the church or the *calvario* chapel, but each *cofradía* keeps a house, or *armita,* for meetings and meals, as well as for the image's fiesta. The *alcalde* provides this house, usually by renting a vacant house in the *cabecera.* The saint is carried in procession from the church to the *armita* and back again for the fiesta on a litter (*anda*) by the *cofrades,* who wear flower crowns. The *alcalde* leads, carrying the silver *cofradía* emblem on top of a staff. The *chuch axels* flank the procession. With their bowed heads modestly covered by red and blue or red and green plaid shawls, they carry bouquets with glowing candles at the center. The procession is ordinarily accompanied by a drum and either a wooden flute or a *chirimía*. At the fiesta a marimba or violin provides music for dancing. The costs of hiring musicians and paying for food and drink, firewood, skyrockets, incense, and candles are common fiesta expenses for all the *cofradías*. Regularly recurring *costumbre* at the image's sacred places (*ra'wa'sil rech Tiox*) varies greatly according to the number of altars and their burning schedules, and may require the hiring of a calendar priest (*chuch kajaw*). Outgoing *cofrades* pass on the lore to the novices in return for traditional gifts of liquor and tobacco.

The veterans and their replacements celebrate the annual fiesta together at the *armita*. Following the meal there is a "social dance" (*zarabanda*),[27] which lasts all night. After breakfast they return the image to the church, where flower crowns are passed from the outgoing to the incoming *cofrades*, who kneel facing each other in front of the main altar. The *chuch axels* then perform a similar ceremony, exchanging flower necklaces. Thus begins a new year (*cac junab* or *c'amo junab*) in the service of a saint. The Momostecan *cofradías* and their fiesta dates are shown in table 1.

During the week before Christmas, in a ceremony called La Posada, all the *cofradías* literally run around town with the images of María and San José seeking lodging at stores and houses. The important miraculous images—Santiago and Niño San Antonio in the church and Corpus and Capitagua in the *calvario*—have large numbers of altars and very complex schedules of *costumbre* that continue throughout the year. These images also figure in visitation by the faithful during major *pueblo*-level fiestas, requiring fasting and all-night vigils by the *cofrades*. Santiago (always accompanied by San Felipe) and San Antonio are transported to distant *aldeas* in arduous sacred journeys. Several *cofradías* are jointly responsible for making sacred journeys to El Palmar in the Boca Costa region to collect flowers and greenery during Lent and Holy Week. Thus the service varies according to the image being served.

In 1976 the twenty-one *cofradías* were listed in the traditional order given in table 1. The first three, Señor Resurrección (Corpus), Santiago, and María Concepción have the highest status. A directorate,

Table 1. *The* Cofradías *and Their New Year Ceremonies, 1976*

Cofradía	Fiesta Date	Location
Señor Resurrección (Corpus)	Corpus Cristi	*Calvario*
Santiago	July 24–31	Church
María Concepción	December 7	Church
San Antonio Xepom	July 31	Church
Santa Cruz	May 2	Church
San Francisco	October 3	Church
Cristo Crucificado		
(also called Capitagua, Capitao)	Fourth week of Lent	*Calvario*
Virgen Dolores	Sixth week of Lent	Church
La Columna (San Pedro Galuna)	Carnaval, Saturday	Church
Santa Ana	July 26	Church
Santa Bárbara	December 3	Church
San Luis Gonzago	June 20	Church
San Miguel	September 28	Church
Jesús	Second week of Lent, Friday	Church
San Nicolás	September 9	Church
San Antonio Pologua		
(Niño, Niño San Antonio)	June 13	Church
Virgen Rosario	October 6	Church
Corazón de Jesús	Corpus Cristi	Church
San José	March 18	*Armita*
Virgen Guadalupe	December 11	Church
Señor Sepultado	January 27	Church

Note: The twenty-one *cofradías* were listed in this "traditional" order by the sacristan. However, the seating order given by *cofrades* places Santa Cruz and Santa Bárbara in fourth and fifth places as members of the *c'amal be* (directorate).

called the *c'amal be*, is composed of the *cofrades* of the first three plus Santa Cruz and Capitagua (Cristo Crucificado). The *c'amal be*, headed by its five *alcaldes*, meets briefly after mass in the convent yard every Sunday with the *alcaldes* of all of the *cofradías*. It is responsible for supervising *cofradía* activities, including nominating replacements for vacancies in the *cofradías* from the town center, a role played by the local *principales* when an open position belongs to one of the *aldeas*. A *cofrade* must go to the *c'amal be* rather than the *alcalde* of his own *cofradía* to be temporarily excused from service. He is represented to the *c'amal be* by a member of one of the five of his rank. For example, a *mortoma* of Galuna might go to a *mortoma* of Corpus to ask to be excused from mass because of a medical problem in his family. The *c'amal be* also supervises sacred undertakings like the Holy Week journey to the coast to get flowers to decorate the cemetery, or the construction of the image of San Simón by the *cofradía* of Santa Bárbara.

Yet the *c'amal be* and the entire *cofradía* system is overseen by the parish priest and controlled by the *auxiliatura*. When property is transferred from those leaving (the *pasados*) to those entering (the *nuevos*)—for instance, the costumes or jewelry belonging to an image—the transfer is supervised by the *síndico segundo* and other officials, not the *c'amal be*. The municipal government, acting through the *auxiliatura*, has required that the *cofradía* of San Antonio confine its visits to *aldeas* within Momostenango, and requires a signed document from the *principales* of Buenabaj agreeing to return Santiago to its official *cofradía* after the fiesta of Santa Isabel. The *deputado* of Santiago was removed in 1976 when he inadvertently damaged the appearance of Santiago while trying to wash the image's face. It was the *principales*, acting under the authority of the *auxiliatura*, and not the *c'amal be* that removed him and reorganized the *cofradía* to include Catholic Action members.

Momostenango differs from the classical Mesoamerican cargo system (Tax 1952; Cancian 1967) in that *principal* status is conferred only on the basis of service in the *auxiliatura*. Prestige accrues to those who have served in higher *cofradía* posts, but it does not translate into wider authority or political power.[28]

There are three separate Costumbrista hierarchical systems in which service—in each case designated by the term *patan* (a burden) or *cargo*—may be undertaken: hierarchies of calendar priest-shamans, *cofradía* positions, and positions in the *cabildo* governance structure. There is no formal rotation of positions between hierarchies. Careers may be pursued in each one independently but, it seems, not in both the sodality and *cabildo* hierarchies. The elders who are retired from the *cabildo* hierarchy are the true *principales* or *ajawib*. They name those who will enter the various posts in rural governance and the *cofradías* and constitute a self-replicating board of directors for the community.

Chance and Taylor (1985) argue persuasively that the interlocking civil-religious hierarchy and related pattern of individual sponsorship of fiestas are both nineteenth-century responses to political and economic changes in postcolonial Mesoamerica. In Momostenango, this involved the collapse of the *parcialidades* and centralization of the *cofradías* as described above. The organization of the overall system in Momostenango into two branches without interlocking rotation seems to be, in part, a modern legacy of the centuries-long struggle for power between the elite *cacique* lineages of the *cantones,* who once controlled most of the saints, and the urban *cabildo* authorities, whose alliance with Teodoro Cifuentes let them gain control of the saints during the period of centralization described above. The *cacique* descendants then either withdrew from *cofradía* participation in Momostenango and re-created local unofficial "indigenized" *cofradías* (the Vicente option with Santa Isabel in Buenabaj), or opted out of the *cofradía* system altogether and attempted to create an independent power base by participating in Catholic Action (the Herrera strategy in Pueblo Viejo, Tunayac, or the Chanchabac strategy in the *barrio* Santa Catarina). Class, status group, folk-urban tensions, and kinship politics are all involved in these complex and poorly understood political dynamics acting in Momostecan social history. Perhaps the colonial period pattern in which the decentralized *cofradías* were staffed by dependent commoners under *cacique* leadership made *cofradía* service unattractive to the emerging urban elite of the nineteenth century.

Individual motivation to participate in the sodalities by Momostecans is more clearly articulated than the underlying political and social dynamics. Why do some remain in a costly higher post for years in spite of inconvenience and expense? The following accounts describe the *cofradías* as institutions, explore the relationship between the *cofradías* and the *auxiliatura,* describe recruitment, and explain the transmission of lore within the *cofradías.*

Entering the Service
by Pedro Contreras

There is a cost of eighty quetzals or more in the year's service,[29] so the people would rather be a councilman or *alcalde* in the *auxiliatura,* because then they do not have to spend money. But it comes out the same, because the *cofrade* does not have to spend as much of his time. The *auxiliatura* has to serve by *quincenas* (two-week shifts), while the *cofrade* only loses two days per week, and even on those days he can get some work done at home after the mass. But we get screwed on Christmas Eve when the Posada runs for nine days. We leave home at three in the afternoon, and San José and María come out at seven. So for nine nights we have to go with the images to visit houses and ask for lodging, and after this there is a mass. We do not get done till nine or nine-thirty in the evening. When a *cofrade* lives close by, its not so bad, but we [coming from Xequemaya] have to sleep here in the center for nine days.

So now the flower is being sent to the entrants of San José and María: 4 Quiej [day in the 260-day divining calendar] is the day for this. In four months they will receive the cargo [i.e., assume responsibility]. This is for *capitana* and *axel* [first lady and her assistant]. The *alcaldes* flower goes later.

When I entered [Santa Cruz] I talked to the one who was leaving. I gave him fifteen *octavos* [pints of liquor] to teach me everything. If I didn't do this, he wouldn't teach me anything, as this is the custom. For the firewater (*aguardiente*) everything comes out. He told me everything, item by item, even where I should sit in the church. First, Aj Señor [he of Señor Resurrección or Corpus], Santiago, María, Santa Cruz in fourth place with the *deputado,* then Aj Bárbara. It goes in order, and if one is absent the place remains vacant. It cost a bottle of six *octavos* to learn this and two packs of cigarettes. If one doesn't pay, one receives incomplete information.

Fortunately, my uncle had been in the *cofradía,* so I went over the material with him. He found that I was missing something. Before I go to make offerings at the image's altars, I have to go to the *calvario* with the materials and light candles before the image and pass over the souls.[30] I had to pay him six *octavos* and two packs also. I will not do the same. I won't refuse to talk because my companion is a poor man and can't pay. It's as in the guardhouse. When one is relieved he must pass the weapons to his relief. You don't ask for *guaro* [*aguardiente*] to do this, nor do you ask for cigarettes.

The first image I served I didn't know you had to pay, and so they didn't tell me the *costumbre.* This is bad. You should try to help your replacement. The outgoing group told me to meet them at the *armita* at a certain hour, but when I came they weren't there. I spent the day looking for them. They were in a store and saw me pass and didn't call to me.

Later I asked, "If you wanted *aguardiente* why didn't you tell me?"

They laughed at me. I scolded them and said I should learn the *costumbres* or I am undone. So they said, "All right, six *octavos* and two packs of cigarettes."

So I gave six *octavos* to the *alcalde* and six to the *deputado*.

They said, "OK, tomorrow at six in the morning we will show you the altars." This was when I entered San Francisco. So they showed me the *porobal* in the *riscos* [eroded badlands area in the *barrio* Patzité]. But they were bad people reluctant to help me. They told me of six candles for the flowers in Holy Week, three for here and three for El Palmar. You go to Paklom and Joyam, and then on to the coast.[31]

Then, when one is leaving [finishing his year's service] he has to give six *octavos* and a pack of cigarettes to the thirteen teams to tell them, "Look for my replacement" [*Catsucuj alak nu caxel*].

They say, "We will think about this. We will meet and find your relief."

When the flowers come to the new one, he has been told in advance. When the day arrives, the outgoing *deputado* brings the flower to the new one, the *calpul*. The new one is prepared to receive [the flower]. This is on the day Ajmak. But before he was told to be ready, maybe on 3 Ajmak or 4 Ajmak, or 3 Aj, 4 Aj [divining calendar days]. These are days to receive the flower, these are the days of the image.

When they came to me they said, "Alo-o-o-w . . . [announcing themselves from a distance outside the house]. We have come to give you this flower."

If one doesn't want to receive it, one must make an excuse, but the *cofrades* then say: "It's not our fault, we were sent, nothing more."

When the flower arrives we must have a table prepared and pine boughs on the floor, and a candle of two cents and a clean cloth on the table. The silver *cofradía* emblem is placed on this cloth with the candle burning before it while the *cofrades* drink their coffee. This is at nine at night. Also there is incense on the table and flowers.

They entered the house and said, "Here is your flower, we have come to leave it with you."

"All right," I said. "Come in and sit down."

So then they told me to call my family, and all of us knelt on the floor before the silver, the representation of Santa Cruz. I asked to be blessed in the coming year and that my family be blessed as well. I asked that nothing happen to me, that my work go well. After this we prayed Our Father and crossed ourselves. Then we served them coffee and bread, but some people don't do this. In fact some rebellious people just throw the flowers on the floor. They say, "What good is this flower? We want to go in the *auxiliatura*." [Here he laughs.]

In the old days we had to serve the Ladinos—they were people. Then we also had to serve the image, which is a representation of God, and this protects us. This service is with goodwill.

I went with my *mortoma* to bring flowers to his replacement. He invited us in. He said he wouldn't serve and that he would bring the flowers to the *auxiliatura* that same day.[32] So [my *mortoma*] didn't tell him anything. When I received we drank *guaro,* and they told me to prepare a *pop* [woven grass mat], two large pots [of food], and a woman's shawl. They said to prepare plastic buckets with three dozen cups of coffee, and [to bring] three dozen plates and two small tablecloths and one large one. These are the materials used when one receives the year's service. The pots with four lugs cost 2½ quetzals each. We borrowed the other materials. We had to prepare six *arrovas*[33] of maize and twenty-five pounds of meat. The pots we still have, but the meat is gone. [He laughs.] Oh, and thirty *octavos*. This is for the fiesta of the new ones and their families, and also the *síndico* and staff have to be invited. Thus they know I am a *cofrade* and the *síndico* will protect me. They told me I had to feed the thirteen teams with coffee and bread, but I only served coffee. It cost too much. God protected us. We have all been fine. After I had served for only fifteen days came the clothes washing, another expense.

The meal for the new ones is given at the *armita* with the families of the new ones and the *síndico.* The images with much *costumbre* have to invite the *síndico.* After the lunch the *síndico* warned me that if I didn't complete all my responsibilities I would go to jail.

The following account of the ouster of *cofrades* from the *cofradía* of Santiago illustrates the politics that are involved in control of the *cofradía.*[34] This complex situation produces counterintuitive results. The Catholic priest, who is antagonistic to Costumbre, defends one of the most traditional Costumbrista *cofrades* against the Costumbrista

principales, while they replace the knowledgeable Costumbrista ritualists in the cult of the most important saint with new ones from Catholic
Action. Within a few years of these events, as the strength of Catholic
Action grew in the *cofradías,* the urban *cabildo*-allied Costumbrista faction that had removed the *cofrades* built an *armita* in the *barrio* Santa
Isabel and created an *hermandad* (Ladino-style confraternity) for Patrón Santiago. The dissolution of the Costumbrista *cofradía* then set
the stage for the creation of a new sodality much freer from interference
by the priest or his catechist allies, though perhaps with loss of traditional sodality lore whose line of transmission was broken.

Tradition and Politics in the *Cofradía* of Santiago
by Juan Ixc'oy

I didn't pay a *chuch kajaw.* I went to do *costumbre* myself, but those
who are in [the *cofradía*] today have to pay a *chuch kajaw.* I worked
for eighteen years with the Patrón and never paid anything for a
chuch kajaw. I wouldn't have left the *cofradía,* but I committed an
offense [*nu mak*].

The son of the sacristan [a Catholic Action member] asked us,
"Why don't you clean the image's face, because you are the *cofrades,*
you have the right."

What happened? My friend the *alcalde* Don Santiago Ajxup was
drunk at the time and didn't tell me yes or no. So I called the two
mortomas.

"It would be good if we cleaned the lord, yes," the sacristan
told me.

And what happened? I didn't go to notify the authorities. This is
what I didn't do. Then I went to Xela [*Xela Ju* (Under Ten), the
Quiché term for Quetzaltenango] and bought a forty-cent soap.
When I returned I tried it with this, and the dirt was removed. And
I did only this. And later the *principales* came and told me that I
touched it, and that I didn't respect it. But I didn't do anything. I
only washed the face.

Later the padre said to me, "Maybe you can paint it."

But I didn't know how. I didn't even know what kind of paint
to use.

[Question:]

And if this hadn't happened, you would not have left the *cofradía*?]

[Don Juan answers:]

No, I would not. The *principales* said I should leave. They said I'd had a long time. So, fine. [He laughs here.]

The *principales* went to the padre and asked him to sign a complaint to send me to jail, but he wouldn't sign it. So they only told me to leave the *cofradía*. The bishop came to see the image, and they removed all of us, but I didn't go to jail.

When I left the *cofradía* all the *principales* gave me dirty looks, but I had done nothing. I left a lot of very good things with the Patrón, not like the overrated junk of San Antonio, good things of value. [I left] fifteen blankets with quetzals, two chests filled with fine blankets and rugs, good stuff, one or two dozen rugs of various classes.

When I came in he had nothing, but because of my *costumbre* Cecilio Ajtun said, "We'll assemble his wardrobe." And we did it.

The Patrón had a visit to Tierra Colorado, and Sebastián Itzep came and said, "Let's give him his blankets to go on his visits but not very fine ones; those are for the big fair [i.e., Santiago's fiesta at the end of July], they would only get dirty on visits." They can't be washed because then they would begin to look old.

* * *

Now there are new *cofrades* [Catholic Action members], and now they have come to us for help. There is much work for the palanquin in the fiesta, and the new *cofrades* don't know how to adorn it. They asked the Ladinos, and they said that they didn't know how either, so they came to us *pasados*. Only my son and I know how to do it. We will do it if we are paid, because we are not in the service now. Even before my son was paid to do it. I don't know how much we will be paid.

* * *

I have been hearing what's happening to the new ones. They say there is no money for *costumbre*. The *deputado* is an Ak'abal [family or clan name]. The *alcalde,* from the *barrio* Patzacón, is Catholic Action. All of them are of Catholic Action. They only pay a *chuch kajaw*. They've hired Ramiro Ixc'oy as *chuch kajaw*. The fiesta [in the *cabecera*] will be a sign if things are OK or are bad. . . .

It is only rarely that we have to use our own money to pay *costumbre*, though. Usually donations take care of that. Those who are in now, though, won't reach into their pockets when the donations are all gone. That is why they always fail.

The *cofrades* went to the *auxiliatura* and said they were out of money—what should they do about *costumbre*? If they don't complete it, there will be a sign at the fiesta. I will have to do my *costumbre* before I go to adorn the throne.

We have to say that we are going to touch the image, that we are going to adorn the throne. My son makes the throne. My first year Javier Poptún did it, but he won't do it now for the new *cofrades*. I used to put the papers in place, but some women came with me and cut the papers. My son did it by himself. It's his job. He knows it.

* * *

Last year I went with the new ones to show them the altars, and to say that I no longer had responsibility there. This is done by all *alcaldes* and *deputados* when they leave the service so nothing will happen to them. This can't be done at the Paklom. The ancient altar is in Pueblo Viejo behind the church. Also, the new ones have to be presented. Before I went to do my farewells the Patrón troubled me in my dreams, but since I have gone he leaves me alone. I knew in my dreams that the people would ask us to decorate the throne [the palanquin]. In my dreams a man came on horseback and entered the patio of my house. I knew it was the Patrón.

"With your permission."

"Come in, sir."

"I have a commission for you [Quiché *at;* like Spanish *vos,* an informal "you" used to designate a junior or social inferior], that you will repair my shoes for the fiesta. You will do it."

"Who knows?"

"You will."

"OK."

"I've told you in advance. I'll be expecting you."

So I explained the dream to my son, and we realized it meant that we would do the decorations again this year. Maybe we had lacked in *costumbre* because then always there is a sign. When we lacked in *costumbre,* he would always come in my dreams and tell me to fix his feet in the stirrups of his horse. I would warn the *alcalde* to do his *costumbre* because I knew that mine was all right. In my dreams

I see him and his foot is out of the stirrup, so I go to fix it; then he says, "Ah, now I'm all right."

Thus the Patrón is well known for getting what he wants. I have seen this.

When someone is not focused entirely on the enterprise, when they have second thoughts about the burden they have agreed to carry, when they are resentful of the expenses of service, then they are of two hearts (*quieb ru c'ux*). This can lead to insanity or death and is one of the greatest dangers of service.

The Danger of Being of Two Hearts
by Pablo Itzep

We *cofrades* just guard the image. We do not think of home or wife, we just concentrate on the image, because this is what happened to a companion of ours, a *mortoma* of two hearts. The first *mortoma* was told to bring cups for drinks, but he stayed in the corridor. They told him again and he went, but he stayed in the kitchen with the women. They went to see if he had lost his mind. They sent an assistant to find out. They found the *mortoma* hiding behind an oven. He had to burn a candle before the image and ask forgiveness.

* * *

If one walks with faith, then it is good in the service, but with two hearts one is likely to die. Sometimes all die, *mortomas* and women, all of them. Only the *nima chichu* and I are still living. Who knows why? [thoughtful pause] [It's] one's destiny.

My father was in Galuna, and told me to accept when I was asked, but Galuna has very little *costumbre*, while [the *cofradía* of] the Niño has a lot. A *compadre* had been in the Niño and advised me to be very careful of the *ropa*. [The Spanish term *ropa* (clothing) is used, but actually this reference includes cloaks, bonnets, and other clothes as well as jewelry and children's toys.] It was very difficult because we didn't know how to write. The clothing is all numbered, but we just tied it up in bundles. Too bad that we weren't in school.[35]

We lost four little horses from his toys and had to replace them, little silver horses at fifty centavos each. These have to be bought from a Sapultapeco [native of Sapultapec], and luckily we found one in Chiquimula. The real danger, though, is with the clothing: some

capes are worth one hundred to two hundred quetzals, and one
could be in debt to replace one.

* * *

I was afraid I would be called to serve again until last year. After age
sixty you are not called and I will be sixty-one tomorrow, so I have
escaped. I was worried because now I know the *costumbres* and
I was afraid that they might want me.

* * *

The day of *rawas* ["the shrine"; i.e., the time for visiting a sacred
shrine] a woman came. She was in good health. The second day she
got sick, and the third day she died. Maybe she was of two hearts.
Maybe she had arguments or discord in her life. It doesn't matter
how many candles, or how many *copales* [one burns]—the saint is
very dangerous [*delicado; itzel ri santo*].[36] The woman was a kitchen
helper, not a *chuch axel.* Maybe she had another man in addition to
her husband. It is a trap for one. I had a friend who served María
[Concepción] and Santiago, but the Niño was more *delicado* [dan-
gerous]. Santiago, after all, only has four altars.

Now the altars of San Antonio: first the Paklom, Ujal Sacramento,
Pasabal, Nima Sabal, then thirteen additional altars. The *alcalde* or
his *chuch kajaw* must burn six to ten dozen nodules of copal incense.
Also fifteen to twenty bunches of candles. If this is done properly
then nothing will happen to the *cofrades,* but if not then calamities
are on the way.

Last year the *cofrades* lost one of the silver chains but later found
it. It would not have been lost if the *costumbre* had been good. The
alcalde lost his mind. He lost his road among the ravines because of
this, but later it was found. This happened because they didn't remember all of the dead *cofrades* since the foundation of the *cofradía*
with *costumbres.*

The dead must be called on the day Ajmak and given *pom* [copal
incense] and candles. The *chuch kajaw* must beg their pardon for
the fact that the present ones do not know enough; he must ask their
protection.

* * *

Chi quiwi animas [above the souls; lit., "at their hair the souls"] is
a place in the middle of the *calvario* where all the *cofrades* of San
Antonio go with candles on 2, 3, and 4 Ajmak. [The *nima chichu*
goes too, according to Julian Ak'abal, my research assistant.] They

go to ask pardon of the souls of the dead, of all the generations [*mais*] of San Antonio, of all those who began it, because they were maybe more powerful and more accomplished.[37] They were the founders of everything.

So we do it. We have no need for a *chuch kajaw,* but we bring an *aj bix* ["speaker"; i.e., someone to chant from the missal].

"It's not our fault if we can't complete everything," we say. "We were selected to do this."

We ask pardon, nothing more. The dead watch us and listen to us. If we do right they protect us, and if we do wrong they curse us, so we say "jun mai" [one generation] and so on.[38]

Now this is the same as the *auxiliatura.* How many have died? One who cannot master this is in trouble. Before, the old men had their benches, and the old women had their mats where no one else could sit. But now the children sit where they please—thus respect is lost. Before, the *cofrades* spent eight, ten, or even twelve years so they knew the *costumbre.* Now it is one year. The souls of the dead see this difference, they see the loss of *costumbres* before God.

When those who are leaving pass the burden to those coming in, they say, "It's your business whether you complete the customs or not. We have completed our service."

The entrants must get nineteen *octavos* of *guaro* [liquor] to give those who are leaving [the service] when they are shown the altars while they are on the road—five *octavos* here in the center, five in Pasajoc, and nine in Pologua. Also, they are given two quetzals in Pologua.

My business went well when I was a *cofrade.* When we finish our service we ask that the Mundo [Holy World] come and protect us. We are happy then. We ask the Mundo to protect us, and if the *costumbre* is well done nothing bad will happen all year. [In his translation, Julian Ak'abal notes that this is a ceremony at the Paklom.] Our *chuch kajaw* had been a *cofrade* of San Antonio.

I was called to the *síndico* and told that I was to be the *alcalde* of San Antonio, and that I should prepare, because the next day was the shrine [*rawas*] of the image. We were shown the altar for which we had to give six packs of cigarettes. Also we had to get the firewood ready in Pologua for the fiesta that was one month later. The trees were twisted and very hard, and it was hard work for the four of us. The trees were given by their owners because then the saint would be miraculous for them. The firewood was brought to a house, a big house where the cooking would be done for the fiesta. This was hard work, because the firewood was far from the house. Now they buy the firewood. It is only five quetzals for the load, and they only have to make arrangements for [delivery to] the house.

The *cofrades* confront, placate, feed, entertain, and try to understand, by the reading of signs, dangerous powers whose support is indispensable to community welfare. Thus, in the ritual or expressive domain they duplicate the practical role of the *auxiliatura* and its directorate of *principales*, who mediate between the community and the dangerous external powers of the Ladinos and the government. The *cofrades* are a ritualized or symbolic counterpart to native governance, through whose enterprise the Holy World is made manifest, and rendered homage.

Those who remain in their posts for longer periods, and master and hand down the complicated traditions, are motivated by personal bonds of patronage with the saint they serve and by fear of the envy of witches, most commonly manifested as sicknesses, from which they are protected during their service. Longer periods of service, then, have an aspect of "sickness vocation." This is clear in the accounts of dancers and dance sponsors in their parallel but less formally organized set of religious sodalities.

Here is the opposite side of the functionalist coin that has been the chief currency in explaining service in *cofradías* as part of a leveling mechanism that converts wealth into prestige and dissipates it, maintaining relative economic equality.[39] *Cofrades* and dancers assert that they became wealthy as a result of their service—not prior to it. Their service freed them to act boldly in purchasing new land, often with borrowed money, or to expand their businesses.[40] While serving in a Momostecan sodality, some are freed to undertake entrepreneurial activities that they would not consider otherwise, since they would incur envy or cross potentially deadly rivals. The cargos of the saints not only serve to legitimize wealth-based stratification after the fact, but also may stimulate it.

THE DANCE TEAMS

Momostecan dance teams have not been described as institutions, and only scanty information exists on Quichean dances.[41] The sodalities, *cofradías,* and dance teams alike perform in honor of the saints, maintaining the communities' relationship with these supernaturals. Recruitment in the dance teams, though, is emphatically based on the desire of individuals to form personal protective alliances with tutelary spirits, and dancing is voluntary. The dances are not formally overseen or controlled by the *auxiliatura.*

Organization and Scheduling

Dance teams perform at major saint-focused festivals. The dancers of the *cabecera* are the Grasejos or Tzulab of Holy Week; Conquest dancers,[42] Moors, Mexicans, Vaqueros, and Monkeys of Santiago's fiesta; and the Devils at Christmas. The Tzulab Dance also takes place at *aldea* fiestas for Cristo Crucificado and the Niño San Antonio. Mexicans also dance for the Patrón when he visits Pueblo Viejo in the *aldea* Tunayac. The Conquest Dance, a reenactment of the Spanish conquest of the Quiché, and the Moors Dance, a depiction of the wars between the Christians and Moors in the reconquest of Spain, are called *K'akatak xojoj* ("war dances"; lit., "red dances"). The Mexicans and Vaqueros depict bullfights, death, and conflicts over inheritance. The Monkeys Dance is a version of the Deer Dance (see Paret-Limardo 1963) with two elements, the usual skit pertaining to hunting and its rituals, as well as the unusual descent of paired animals from the top of a pole erected in the front of the church. The Devils Dance depicts naked, growling, silver-and-gold-painted manlike beings with horrid faces, horns, and tiny wings. One elder explained that the dance depicts Xibalba, a people from ancient times who went naked and did not bury their dead.

Each team of twenty dancers performs every other day. Two such teams take turns day by day sharing the rental fee for one set of costumes. The Devils and Tzulab lack a written script. The Tzulab perform traditional skits, interspersed with improvised clowning and joking. The other dances all include characters with spoken lines to learn in sometimes archaic "flowery" Spanish. The lines are in old books guarded by their owners, who are paid to teach the dancers. The books are passed from father to son, as is frequently the case with the dancing itself. Perhaps similar patterns governed the ownership and transmission of pre-Hispanic dances and instructional manuals.

Sponsorship underwrites *costumbre,* musicians, and the dancers' meals during practice sessions at the sponsor's house. It is contracted as a *novena* (vow of nine performances) by the sponsor with the image in whose honor the dance is given when the image is at its fiesta at the *cofradía* house. The sponsor and any cosponsors are also responsible for recruiting the dancers. In return, the sponsor can expect to live long enough to fulfill the obligation and to prosper, but to suffer dire consequences if he does not complete the promise. The dancers make similar contracts for nine-year runs with a similar expectation of supernatural protection. If a dancer cannot complete his obligation, he may substitute a son or other member of his patrilineage as his replacement.

The sponsor begins with a list of those who have outstanding time in their *novena*s as dancers and then reviews applicants for any vacancies. In some cases active recruiting is necessary, and many dancers await signs in their dreams before agreeing to perform in a particular year or for a new sponsor. Sponsors make traditional payments of liquor to dance leaders and male transvestite dancers, but otherwise dancers are unpaid. They are responsible for securing their own costumes and for paying to learn their lines.

The dance teams are voluntary associations, unlike the *cofradías*. There is no guild of dancers, no formal hierarchy of dancers or sponsors, and no legal sanctions if a dancer or sponsor reneges on his vow. In any particular team, though, the sponsor is accorded respect and deference and dancers who know all the steps and the story line direct the action. Roles with more spoken lines confer prestige, and some individual dancers develop reputations for their skill and, in the case of Monkeys Dance animals, their bravery.

The following excerpts provide descriptions of the organization of the dance teams. Special attention is paid in later chapters to the story lines, ritual symbols, and general exegesis of the Monkeys Dance and the Conquest Dance (chap. 4), and of the Tzulab (chap. 5).

The Conquest Dance
by Miguel Castillo

There are seven practices in the year, and a novice must be taught his part. Last year we had five practices, but we did not do the dance because the dance sponsor fouled up. When he fails we all fail, since he must pay the musicians and everything. We all make contributions, but he bears the greatest expense. We dance for free, as a devotion, a promise, but the musicians must be paid and given their meals. We make a vow to the Apostle Santiago, and must do nine years. If we miss a year we must do it again, but for nine more years if we have the patience. As I said, my father danced for twenty-seven—no, twenty-six—years.

Catholic Action members will not dance. Some dancers join Catholic Action and drop out without completing their turn. We can't always be sure from year to year if we will dance. Sometimes one is called on to be a councilman or other municipal officer, then he can't do both, so we wait till after the municipal elections in October. After the election, the people know if they will be free in the coming year.

In November the public signal is given. The *chirimía* is played before the church to announce that a Conquest [Dance] will be given the next year, and those wishing to dance can make their arrangements. Sometimes the dancers are in a family, father and son, but not always. It is according to the desire of the son. The children [two little princes, two Malinches, and two Aj Itz Chiquitos] are sent by dancers who do not dance that year.[43] They send their kids in their place because it is cheaper. The parts of Malinches have been done by girls for as long as I remember.[44]

The Tzulab
by Juan Ixc'oy

I have brought the dance out seven times from my house, but only in Holy Week. I began fifty-six years ago as a dancer, but have only been a sponsor seven times. If one wants to be a sponsor at one's house, it takes patience for they swear continuously. Even though one is the owner of the house, they will abuse him unless they think they are treated right. They do not ask advice. They have bad words in their heads and they say them without fear.[45] I do not like it, but I am patient because it is my obligation.

When someone brings out [sponsors] a Tzulab[46] performance the dancing starts at his house, but it comes down to the plaza in front of the church. A man who owns an image and wants a fiesta for it brings the image to church Saturday. Then Sunday after mass, the Tzulab dance in front of the church and go back to the house with the image and dance there in the afternoon.[47] For this the dancers have a nine-day fast. It is the same if a dance is organized at a house for a visit by Niño San Antonio. In the *cantones* in January for Esquipulas, and on into Holy Week [the week leading up to Easter], there are fiestas at private houses with Grasejos.

When I began to bring it out I had many dreams, I dreamed many signs. I dreamed I was in the cemetery. I was kneeling near the image [the crucified Christ kept in the *calvario*] and groveling up to it. The image spoke to me. "Remember me." I grew tired of these dreams, so I went to a diviner [*aj vara*] to find out their meaning.

"They are telling you that a calamity is impending. You should dance or bring out a dance again. If not, something will happen. You will die."

I was robbed of fifteen quetzals from my shirt pocket at Sam Pras,[48] and so I came back here with my arms folded [i.e., in a helpless or hopeless situation], without any money. So I went again to the *aj vara*, and he said it was because of those dances and that it would get worse if I didn't comply. As a result I began to bring it out at my house, but I did not know how many days to observe. I had to learn the *costumbre*. Then I began to bring it out. I had to keep the forty days because it was in Holy Week. The Tzulab of Holy Week and Saturday of Glory have to keep forty days. This begins when the first flowers come on the first Friday [of Lent] and continues until Easter Sunday. The Tzulab for dances at private celebrations at individual houses have to keep nine days.

* * *

When I bring out the Grasejos here at my house I am not the *chuch kajaw*, but I do my own separate *costumbre*. I clear my road so that there are no difficulties. If I don't do this I will end up in jail, because this happened to me once. Although this is only Tzulab and not very important, nevertheless it has its certain meaning. Once I brought out the Tzulab at my house and I didn't do the *costumbre*, so I was brought to jail. There I was in jail in my costume, and one of us had been beaten by the rest of us. I was called to the drugstore and asked if I had seen the injured man. I was told we didn't have the right to kill each other and fined ten quetzals for his treatment.

Because of the difficulty of the *costumbre*, people are not very eager to bring it out. It really takes a lot of patience. No one wants to be the bull because he is bothered a lot. Also the Tzulab say bad words, so that a person with a bad mouth is called a *tzul.* The woman has no name. She is called Xinula [Ladina], and the husband is called Mu's [Ladino].[49]

Also the woman [Xinula] has *costumbre,* because he [the dancer] must put on a woman's clothes. The woman is given six *octavos.* It is said, "Here it is because you dress as a woman [*injalbal awij*]." The sponsor of the dance gives this because no one wants to come out as the woman. In Los Cipreses and Santa Ana together, there is only one man who likes to do this. The woman also carries a whip. Every day Xinula receives six *octavos.* The husband also gets six *octavos.* "Here, this is for your steps," he is told.

No one wants to do this either because it is very difficult, so this pair is of the same level. The Nabe Mu's [First Ladino] is in charge of the woman and the first line. There is also an Ucab Mu's [Second Ladino] in charge of the second line. The sponsor also gives the Nabe and the woman their lunch. No one else knows what they know. Others may try to lead, but they make mistakes.

The Nabe Mu's is our teacher. Others don't know the steps. However, when the time comes that the Mu's makes a mistake he gets a beating too. They cry out, "Nawala! Nawala!" ["Think! Think!" but using the formal or polite form] when he gets hit. There is no lord over them when their day arrives!

Who knows the origins of this? The sound of the marimba is heard in Spain. The red dancers [*k'akatak xojoj* in the Moors and the Conquest Dances, the dances that depict war] do not hear it. The Tzulab is more agreeable to God because of the sound of the whip behind, because the whips whistle behind them. They are dear to God because of the lash.

The Monkeys
by Florentino Ixbatz

There is a man with a book on the story of the Monkeys.[50] He knows the names of the dancers. There are ten dancers with rattles in addition to the ten animals.[51] If I live, next year we will bring out the Monkeys [Dance].

* * *

I have been sick forty days. If God gives me permission I will go to the *armita.* If not, I will do the *novena* here in my house. During this *novena* it will be asked that the dancers fulfill their promises. Because the *novena* [he uses the Spanish word *novena* though he is speaking Quiché] is *costumbre* of the ancients, I go along with it.

The first of November [All Saints' Day] is the first organizing meeting. If we have thirty or thirty-five names we only lack a little, because we are forty, twenty each day in turn. After the meeting we begin the *costumbres* at the four mountains [four sacred mountains that surround Momos at the idealized cardinal points]. The practice pole is erected at the sponsor's house to practice six times in two days of practice.

On the seventeenth of July we go to bring the costumes. On the eighteenth we have adoration of the costumes with marimba and violin, and with dancing and drinking all night.[52] On the nineteenth we begin dancing at the house in costume, practicing tricks. On the twentieth the other team dances. The dance is better at the house of the *autor* [producer] because all *costumbre* has been complete. Sometimes, because of drinking too much, things are neglected in town. There is too much confusion, too much to do, loss of control. Here everything is orderly. It is better.

* * *

It's easy to find Lions, Jaguars, and Monkeys. What is hard to find are the *segales* [the ten dancers with rattles mentioned above]. When the animals have taken their turns on the rope, they go out into stores and the market and beg for money and dance for the people. Once a gringo was watching the Jaguar come down and went to the *autor* and said, "Call the Jaguar." So he did and he gave him five quetzals.[53] Another time a different gringo liked the performance of a Monkey and gave him one peso [equivalent to one quetzal]. The tourists like it more here because the dancers perform without a safety belt. At other fiestas they are fastened to the rope. That's nothing.

There was a dancer one year who always came drunk to take his turn. I cautioned him that it was not only his life, he had children. Also, if he was injured it would increase opposition to the dance, but he kept it up anyway. One time this Jaguar was so drunk he didn't remember going to do his performance, but halfway down the rope his mind returned. He heard a voice warning him to be careful or he would fall. It was the *costumbre*. We may have to replace him because he drinks so much. The Lion and the Monkeys do their part; they don't drink. Those who don't drink are those who like the Patrón best. They depend on the Patrón.[54]

* * *

On the twenty-third [of July] the marimba is played at the *armita* [*cofradía* house of Santiago] to announce that there will be the Monkeys [Dance] the next year.

There are problems when it is brought out. The day of the Patrón is Wucub Ajmak [7 Ajmak]. A fellow was looking for me on this day, a boy from Los Cipreses, and he came to the *armita* to talk to me. This guy said he wanted to contribute one hundred quetzals to bringing out the dance, but didn't want it publicized. He didn't give anything as it turned out. I told him all the dancers contribute some, so if you want to help, twenty-five quetzals is plenty, but he insisted on the hundred, then gave nothing. Another man, a Poroj [his surname, a clan affiliation], offered twenty-five quetzals—no, he offered fifty—but he gave nothing. This Poroj has been around asking if we are going to do the Monkeys [Dance] next year, but I tell him I don't know to put him off as he is a liar.

I said, "If you want to do it come to my house with a bottle of *aguardiente* and join us."

He wants to enter as First Jaguar, but the boys in Xequemaya that have been doing this and paying the *costumbre* don't want another to enter, except as second sponsor, and that way he could help.

We've had offers that totaled 138 quetzals and we never saw a cent before God. They aren't to blame because their mouths are borrowed by the Patrón. This is so we will be encouraged, and at the last minute we are stuck with the bill. Once for five years we didn't bring it out because of the cost. A Chiquimulteca warned me that something would happen. So we didn't do it, and look at what this Poroj told me—he deceived me.

"And what difference does it make to you if something happens to me?" I said. "You're from Santa Ana and I'm from Xequemaya."[55]

So I was mad. I got home and divined with my cards to find out who was responsible for this. The answer: the Patrón. So I asked if people that had offered money would really help. The answer: no. And it was true—it was the voice of the Patrón.

* * *

The deceased owner of the Monkeys Dance book had a son and he taught him the *costumbre*, also the names of the marimba tunes, but he forgot it all. Bernardo Domínguez taught me about the *costumbre*. I have been *chuch kajaw* for twelve years, and have done the Monkeys *costumbre* six times, once every other year.

This [1976] is a year of *costumbre*. We advise Patrón Santiago of our intention to dance on the twenty-third [of July]. The *chuch kajaw* visits the Patrón at the *armita* [*cofradía* house] and says, "Father [*Tat*], we are going to bring out the Monkeys [Dance] this coming year. We ask for your help," and the same is done again on the thirty-first [at the end of the fiesta]. After this, on the twenty days numbered one and the twenty days numbered six, *costumbre* is performed all year, to ask that all the dancers stick with their promises to dance.

After this is done, then the practice pole is erected at the sponsor's house in January. Then they have a meeting there. And when they practice there they do the same *costumbre* as at the church [during the fiesta].

To be a Jaguar, a Lion, a Monkey, you have to observe sixty days [of sexual abstinence and *costumbre*]. This runs from the third of June to the third of August. From the third of June you are bound and must burn a candle each day.

A Jaguar now deceased, Antonio Pelicó, had his own personal *costumbre* starting the first of July and running for nine days. He did tricks on the rope that were terrific, the only one who could do them. He would lie on the rope with his arms out to the sides holding the rope between his ankles.

Those who are false with *costumbre,* the strands of the rope open and bite them—they come down injured; their pants get torn and they are cut on the thigh. To protect against this, they burn their candles and there is a *chuch kajaw*. The *costumbre* of the old-timers was forty days before the fiesta without drinking *guaro* [liquor], and also no sleeping with women during these forty days. Thus they avoided discord and remained content.

The rope bites us [*Cutijo ri colop*] if we don't complete the *costumbre*. Once a Monkey came down and his chest was bleeding. The *chuch kajaw* asked him if he had slept with a woman.

"No? Well then, why?"

His teammates scolded him. But it turns out that the Monkey, Lion, and Jaguar all had talked to a woman on the road. One was cut, one lost his crown, and one dropped his mask. This was their fault [or sin (*mak*)], the *chuch kajaw* was not responsible for this. None of this happens if you complete the forty days, if you keep faith with the *costumbre*.

The first year I brought out the Monkeys [Dance], something happened to me. I was sitting at the base of the rope, holding it between my legs with a blanket on top. Suddenly my whole body began to ache as if I had been splitting firewood all day. I really wanted a beer, and I began thinking how this would happen every day.

Then a man came and said to me in my dream: "You are missing something. You have not called together the *chuch kajaws* who have died in your *costumbre* under the pole. You lacked a *bomba* [an exploding skyrocket used to indicate the phases in a communalistic ritual] when you arrived at the house of the first *autor*, and a bomba at the house of the second *autor*. Because you didn't do this you are very tired. And also *costumbre* of the four mountains was lacking, and the expense for this should have been from your pocket. If you do this you won't feel tired. This is why this weariness was sent."

Also the man told me how many guys there are who want to do this *costumbre* but can't.

"You called the *mai* [the generations of the dead], but you didn't acknowledge all the years that have passed since the beginning of this."

And when I woke up I was frightened by this dream. So this is why the dancers were hard to find, because I had neglected this *costumbre*.

> Cuarenta chi tataib, cuarenta chi chuchuib
> [Forty men, forty women]
> cuarenta chi alabom, cuarenta chi alitom
> [forty youths, forty maidens]
> caxajow cakan, caxajow quicab
> [dancing their legs, dancing their hands]
> caxajow qui K'ij, caxajow calaxic
> [dancing their days, dancing their descendants]
> xe rakan u cab, wa' apostol Santiago.
> [under his feet, his hands, this apostle Santiago.]

And why do we do this? For the fiesta of the Patrón. Beneath his arms we dance. And for the heart of our food, the heart of humanity, the heart of the *chiles,* the heart of the salt, the heart of the earth, the heart of coffee, the heart of silver, the successful business. And thus it is concluded.

The dancers come up to me and pat my shoulder. "Don Tino," they say.

"Yes, I'm Don Tino."

"But we have to see the *costumbres,* sir."

"My pants are well tied [i.e., *costumbre* has been performed]."

After this *costumbre,* the weariness left me.

Also it happened to me with this bad foot of mine. The costumes came and I didn't want to go with them because of this foot, but they said I had to go. So I said OK. So I rode my horse to C'oyabaj ["Spider Monkey Stone," a shrine] and did the *costumbre* on the twenty-first, and believe it or not, on the twenty-second we went to get the pole. My foot was now fine! The captain [Santiago is a war captain] gave me strength for the fifteen days, but a week later the pain returned. So maybe this year I will be able to go with him, and if not then I am defeated. But now this year my mouth twisted. I went to a doctor. He said it is rheumatism. I don't know if it is this or if it is witchcraft.

Thus are the courses of *costumbre* of the Monkeys. And the pole: when they bring it, it is not heavy because it hears the *costumbre.* A boy, a Monkey, sat on the pole, mimicking my *costumbre,* doing as I do. Then he was taking his turn on the rope and suddenly he slipped down. Not because he was ignorant, nor was he drunk, but suddenly he almost fell, he was hanging by his hands. When he came down we asked him what happened. He blamed me for not completing the *costumbre.*

A companion had an *ilbal* [a divining crystal] and consulted it and said, "It is not the fault of the *chuch kajaw.* It's yours. What did you do? Pay your fine!"

So he gave a liter of beer to the *chuch kajaw.* His own friends scolded him for making fun of the *chuch kajaw.*

And the *costumbre,* how it represents itself is as a woman. And in the middle of the sixty days, in a dream a pretty girl appeared to me and told me, "I want to marry you, put your woman aside, I want you."

So I said, "OK."

We went to the town hall, but the justice was not there, so we came back to the house. When I woke up I was lying in bed. And in another dream a woman came and wanted to marry me. We were talking when I awoke. It was the nineteenth of July, so I went to do the *costumbre*. Thus it is that I complete the *costumbre*. Maybe the dancers don't, but I do. Thus is the *costumbre*, having a candle every day for the sixty days and no arguments with the wife—contentment, happiness, so the *costumbre* is acceptable. And this is how it is. If a *chuch kajaw* fights with his woman, the *costumbre* is not accepted.

It happened once that a man was having an affair with the wife of a Monkey. In this case the punishment falls on the lover, not on the Monkey. He now finds himself in the Holy Justice [cemetery]. *Costumbre* is just like a religion.

* * *

The Catholic Action people in Xequemaya have said, "Why do you do this? You should lead the people on a good road, not to perdition."

But in the years when I do the Monkeys [Dance] the milpa is good, and the neighbors see this and so are jealous. I believe this [envy] is the basis of their criticism.

[Don Tino's son speaks:]

We shouldn't do it for a while, and they would see that our milpa is good anyway.

[Don Tino continues:]

No, they are right, this is why the milpa is good [to Julian, who is a convert to Mormonism] whether you believe it or not. In the first year of the Monkeys [Dance] we had really good ears of corn and I bought this land where I live now. When the owner came and offered me this land, we were practicing the dance and I said, "Look, I am paying for this. I don't have money to buy land."

I have offered masses to Patrón Santiago instead of the dance, but he didn't want this; he wants the dances. Believe it or not I was sitting here in the house playing with my beans [divining with *tzité* seeds] while the Monkeys were practicing. A man came to talk to me and asked me to buy his land. I said I couldn't because of the costs of the dance. After the fiesta he offered it again. I asked for three days to think. He offered ten *cuerdas* [1 acre or 0.44 hectare] for two hundred quetzals. I was worried about his brothers, but he said they had sold it to him. My father was still living, so I went to ask him what to do. The owner was going to sell to David Méndez [a Ladino], so my father said buy it. I borrowed the money from Pablo Zarate with a lawyer in Xela and bought the land.

A week later the man's four sisters came and demanded fifty quetzals each or they would take the land, so I paid to avoid a scandal. Fifty quetzals for each signature on the document. So I ended up buying fifty *cuerdas* but it cost me eight hundred quetzals. [The lawyer's fees and interest on the loan contributed an additional four hundred quetzals.] And who gave me this? It was a present from the Patrón. This is what I have earned from him. The next year the same thing happened again. And just yesterday a man offered me twelve good flat cuerdas, and I am bringing out the dance this year. He [Santiago] has given it to me. And he wants three hundred quetzals.

I received this opportunity from Patrón Santiago because I sponsored the Monkeys [Dance]. The neighbors asked, "Why wasn't the land offered to us? Why did the owner offer it to a man from the other side of the mountain?"

The Monkeys [Dance] was brought out four times in the old house, now twice in the new house, but the *costumbre* and marimba must still be done at the old house, because it started there in the beginning.[56]

Each time I brought out the Monkeys [Dance] [*xinwesaj C'oyab*] I bought a new field, all because of the Patrón. Now I am sick, but I want to do it again next year. If the Patrón gives me strength I will go to the *armita* on the night of the twenty-third with incense to announce it. It has to be done nine times, a service of eighteen years. I have only completed six so far. When the nine are done someone else will take over.

SERVING JESUCRISTO AND THE SAINTS

The absence of an interlocking civil-religious hierarchy in Momostenango may be related to the prolonged struggle for power between the rural-based native elite (*caciques*) who originally sponsored the commoner-staffed sodalities, and the newer urban elite that now controls the *auxiliatura,* and so oversees the *cofradías* but does not staff them. The *cofradías* and the dance teams are important to this urban *cabildo*-based Costumbrista faction as a symbol of Momostecan tradition, but they do not participate in them. A relatively small number of dedicated *cofrades* and dancers in each generation take on multiple *cargos* and often remain in a position for many years. Many of the *cofradía* leaders are also dancers, rotating between dancing and *cofradía* service in ritualist careers that often last for four decades and sometimes longer, but which do not confer political authority or *principal* status.

For these dedicated ritualists, service to their deceased predecessors (*primeros*) and the saints is a series of ordeals fraught with initiatory symbolism and the search for personal supernatural power. Those whose personal ritual is adequate and who serve an image and the *primeros* with total devotion, being of one heart, are rewarded with life, health, and prosperity. The service of a saint as *cofrade* or dancer is a test of personal *costumbre,* courage, and commitment. Ritual purity— not just sexual abstinence but harmonious relations with the spouse and relatives—is required during periods when *rawas* [shrines] are visited, and prior to and during any performances.

Two *cofradías,* traditionally staffed by leaders among these highly motivated ritualists, serve the most miraculous images in the church, Santiago and Niño San Antonio. These *cofradías,* and no others, transport saints to distant *aldeas* for fiestas and visit private homes for family or *paraje* festivals. These images were the tutelary gods of *parcialidades* during the colonial period, and were probably only brought fully into the centralized *cofradía* system in the twentieth century. The following chapter documents the cult institutions of these traveling, visiting saints, whose sodalities and festivals are most clearly derived from the *parcialidad* complex. The symbolism of cosmogonic tree raising and of millennialistic transformations of the world depicted in the Monkeys Dance and the Conquest Dance in Santiago's fiesta are discussed in chapter 4. The third major sodality-based complex honors the images of Capitagua and Corpus. These two *cofradías* have been in the *cabecera* at least since the eighteenth century and may be older. The Holy Week complex linking the sun and maize and embodying a universal Maya myth of cyclical vegetative regeneration is investigated in detail in chapter 5.

3. Traveling Saints

The colonial Cristos in the *calvario,* together with Santiago and the Niño San Antonio in the church, are the most miraculous images in Momostenango. Only Santiago and San Antonio are transported to festivals in rural hamlets. These sacred journeys return them to their colonial period homes, or to the temporary keeping of the descendants of corporate groups that once maintained their cults, and Santiago is reunited with saintly companions from the distant past. The journeys are ordeals for the *cofrades,* and provide opportunities for dozens of local festivals at private houses in *parajes* and *cantón armitas.* In this chapter the traveling saints, their ritual complexes, and their sacred journeys are described. The Cristos and their cult are presented in chapter 5.

NIÑO SAN ANTONIO

Sometime in the sixteenth or seventeenth century the image of a baby, today known as Niño San Antonio, made a miraculous appearance in a small cave or grotto in the high cold plateau west of Momostenango. The *cofradía* of San Antonio was raising livestock for fiesta meals by the 1680s, and purchased Pologua, where the baby had been found, as grazing land in 1710 (Carmack 1979: 197, 207). Its large estate marks the eighteenth-century *cofradía* as a typical *parcialidad*'s patron saint cult. The image called Niño San Antonio, or El Niño, or more rarely San Antonio Pologua, is now kept in the church in Momostenango in its *camarín* (a small glass and wood box about three feet by two by two) on the left-hand side of the nave near Santiago and San Felipe. Its *cofrades* now come from Los Cipreses, Santa Ana, and Tunayac, as Pologua no longer participates in the *cofradía* system.

The image is small, about the size of a real baby. It reclines against a pillow wearing an ornate embroidered and sequined cloak with little seed pearls and mirrors stitched on and a hat like a bishop's miter, so only its face can be seen. A small knob on the head, hidden by the hat, is the top of a shaft that runs through the Niño's body and was used, prior to the miraculous appearance, to fasten the Niño to the Bible held by a large image of Saint Anthony of Padua still standing in its own case in the church (table 2).

There are always many candles burning on the shelf in front of the Niño, showing it to be the most visited image in the church. It is said to be the richest image, owning large numbers of cloaks, ornaments, kerchiefs, baby's toys, and mirrors kept by the *cofradía*. It also owns a flock of sheep pastured in Pasajoc, the distant *aldea* where the hamlet of Pologua is located. The *cofradía* was very wealthy in the past when the image's flock was large. They used to bring the image to towns outside of Momostenango for fiestas, and to operate a liquor concession. The *auxiliatura* has kept close watch on the *cofradía* since the 1950s, partly out of fear that the image would be stolen on one of these trips and partly because it was believed that the *cofrades* were making too much money with the image.[1] Today the flock is reduced, and an inventory of the image's possessions is made by the *auxiliatura* each year in order to make sure that none have been lost, stolen, or sold by the *cofradía*. The image is no longer allowed to leave the municipality without special official permission. Many *cofrades* rate the Niño as the most *delicado* of all the images in Momostenango because, with eighteen altars, it has the most *costumbre*.

In one Momostecan myth text, Santiago was established as captain of the whole world by the Principales del Mundo, but only the Niño was designated a Santo del Mundo.[2] When the primordial Principales were naming the *cantones* and instructing the Momostecans, they finally came to Pologua. They promised the Momostecans:

" . . . *You are going to find an image, but a precious one. It is king of the good cattle, lambs, and rams. It is going to be found in a little while.*"
"*But where will we find it?*"
"*In Pologua. It will be seen in a few days. We will bring forth a San Antonio del Mundo. Now it is nearly formed. We are going to bring out a San Antonio del Mundo.*"

Table 2. *Saints in the Church of Momostenango, 1976*

	(EAST END)	
Señor Resurrección	Santiago Mayor	María Concepción
Virgen Guadalupe (painting)	"Sacramento"	Señor Resurrección
	Altar Rail	

Patrón Santiago San Felipe		
San Francisco (alcove) San Antonio de Padua		Virgen Rosario Virgen Guadalupe
Corazón de Jesús		San Luis
Niño San Antonio		San Pedro
		San Juan
Holy Family with San Juan, Virgen Dolores, Santa Ana	"Pa qui wi' ri Tiox Animas" (At their hair the Holy Souls)	Virgen Dolores Magdalena Señor Sepultado
Cofradía emblems		Side door to convent
Santa Ana		San Miguel Angel
Virgen Rosario		Jesús de la Merced (Maya image)
San José		
Santa Bárbara		San Antonio Xepom
Virgen Dolores (Ladino image)		Jesús de la Merced (Ladino image)
San Juan Bautista and baptismal font		Monte Calvario
	MAIN DOOR (WEST END)	

Note: Saints' names reflect Costumbrista usage.

And it was true, because now we have it with its sheep and goats,
rams, cattle, horses, and all. It is the king of all kinds of horses. That
is the king San Antonio del Mundo, San Antonio Pologua, San Anto-
nio de Padua as it is called. Because then, San Antonio, there he is in
the heavens, and there is [also] San Antonio del Mundo. The major-
ity of the people have come to see San Antonio, to know San Antonio.
The San Antonio who is in heaven is separate, and there is a San
Antonio ordered and revealed as San Antonio del Mundo, and this is
true. (Vicente De León Abac)

The image of Pologua is considered to be miraculous, and once each
year is brought from the town center to the highland sheep-raising *al-*
deas to bless the flocks during their mating season.

Late in the last century, or early in this one, the Niño disappeared
from the church several times, only to reappear on a hill near the town
center which today bears its name, Loma San Antonio. A Ladino who
owned the land in question may have engineered these appearances to
try to sell his land as a shrine location or to make money through a
concession stand. Neither the location of these appearances nor the
memory of the events figures in today's cult institutions concerning the
image. However, the Niño, like the Patrón, is believed to be capable of
this type of independent locomotion, a belief correlated with their
unique roles in ritualized journeys.

The Niño's fiesta is in Pologua in August, one month after the Patrón's fiesta in the town center. In the highlands of western Momostenango, this cold rainy period is the time for the harvest of peaches, potatoes, and early maize. It is also the rutting season for sheep, and it is
as lord (*dueño;* lit., "owner") of domesticated animals that the image
figures most prominently.

On August 15 the Niño is brought from the church to the *cofradía*
house. On the sixteenth it is escorted to the edge of town near the altar
complex, Pasabal, by all the *cofrades* of all the *cofradías*. The image is
accompanied by a violin and carried by its eight *cofrades*. It passes back
and forth between the *aldeas* of Tunayac and Santa Ana, the home-
aldeas of most of these *cofrades,* during the long trip to the *aldea* Pasajoc and finally to the *cantón* Pologua. On the way, houses are visited
and the image may be offered drinks by the faithful. Gifts of clothing
and money are also made. The image "sleeps" in the same houses each
year.[3] In addition to visiting houses during the fiesta trip, the Niño is

also brought to corrals to bless the sheep. In return for this blessing, the owner gives the Niño a good, fat, healthy sheep which becomes part of its flock. During this fiesta time, thirteen altars in Pasajoc are visited.

On August 22 the image arrives at the official ceremonial center of the *aldea*, the little hamlet of Pasajoc, for a fiesta on the twenty-third. Then, on the twenty-fourth, it is off again for the short trip to Pologua, where the main fiesta takes place. It remains in Pologua for the fiesta from the twenty-fourth until the twenty-sixth. After the fiesta in Pologua, the image is brought to visit its flock at night. While sheep are mating in the corral, a shepherd boy dances among them with the Niño to the music of a violin to ensure their fertility. The skins of any sheep that died during the year are presented to the Niño and later sold by the *cofradía*. The flock is counted. The ceremonial meals of the *cofradía* are justly famous in Momostenango for the richness of the mutton soup that is served. On August 27 it returns to Momostenango via Xolajap, Pitzal, and Tunayac, visiting houses on the way again. The trip ends on the thirtieth or thirty-first when the image returns to the church. In addition to this yearly fiesta round of visits, the image is brought to private houses for fiestas on the days Ajmak, Aj, or Quiej.[4] The days Ajmak and Aj are also the days for *costumbre* at the image's altars. A former *cofrade* describes the trip to Pologua and the pattern of visiting associated with the Niño in the following account.

The Fiesta of the Niño
by Pablo Itzep

The image is brought to the *armita* by the *cofrades* accompanied by the *síndico segundo*. There is an altar in the *armita*. There are thirteen altars in Pasajoc. The image has a total of eighteen altars with *costumbre* on the days Aj and Ajmak. I don't burn [make offerings], so I had to pay a *chuch kajaw* to do this. When the image goes to visit, we put its chain of pesos on it. This is its mystery [*secreto*]. Ah, who knows what it's worth in quetzals? Now the altars of San Antonio: first the Paklom, the Uja'l Sacramento, Pasabal, and Nimasabal. Then there are thirteen altars in Pasajoc.[5]

The thirteen teams [*oxlaju' ch'ob;* i.e., all of the *cofradías*] and the officials of the *auxiliatura* have to go with San Antonio to Pasabal. The image rests on the road while the *alcalde* goes up to the first altar and the thirteen teams and the *auxiliatura* return to town. It goes this way with *costumbres* to Pologua. This *costumbre* is for the road. There is another at Nimasabal almost on the ridgetop just before the Santa Ana boundary. Then in Santa Ana the formal visiting begins.

The *alcaldes* of the *aldea* meet us when we arrive at the *aldea* border, and they stay with us during our entire time in the *aldea*. The house owner meets the image at his property line and escorts us to his house. One person may own nine or ten houses, then the image has to visit them all. When we are asked to visit a private citizen, we stay the entire night. On the way to Pologua we stay for only two hours.

When I was a boy the image came to visit my uncle. We shouted and cried for joy because we had a good life, and the image had given it to us. In those days the *cofradía* had a little stand with beer, *guaro* [liquor], and so on. It was like a fiesta when the image came. They didn't have to pay the priest one quetzal to remove the image in those days. Now there is no *guaro,* there are no candles sold or copal. Now on Sunday it costs two quetzals to remove the image at one o'clock. Anyone who wants a special visit must pay the *cofrades* so they can pay the priest.

When the image visits a house everyone kneels, the owners and maybe thirty or fifty visitors, and the image is passed over their heads starting with the owner and his family. The *alcalde* brings the image to their heads, and at each one the little bell is rung. The *cofrades* arrive and the neighbors also come over with presents. The image is placed on a table. The first and second *alcaldes,* the *deputado,* and the *mortomas* sit on the sides flanking the image. A little bell is rung for each visit. Foods are brought and these are taken by the *cofrades:* green corn [*elote*], squash [*huisquil*], chili, eggs. The *guaro* is separate.

When people have bad hearts, the image won't accept the drink. The key won't open the cabinet. The image takes on color from drinking. If the owner of the house so desires, the image is brought into the kitchen with the women and passed over the cooking pots. We *cofrades* are given *tamalitos* [maize dumplings], bread, drinks, broth, and boiled meat.

There was a man in Santa Ana who bought cases of *guaro* and beer and gave everyone who entered his house a drink. When the image came in he said, "You are going to pay for this."

He spent maybe as much as two hundred quetzals. After everyone received a drink they all began to dance, even the women and children, to violin music. The image went to all his houses, maybe six or eight, and at each a *bomba* [skyrocket] was fired. When we got back to town, we were like drunks from continual vigilance and excitement. We were given *octavos*, but we didn't get drunk. The *costumbres* performed for the image included the request that we be protected to serve the image.

When there is a house with a marimba we approach and the marimba stops. We enter the patio and *bombas* are fired, then the marimba starts up again. We *cofrades* dance first with the image on the patio. Then after dancing everyone goes inside and it is really delightful. The ceremonies last all night and include prayers, litanies, dancing, and merrymaking.

At midnight each night the *alcalde* of the *aldea* dances with the image. He [San Antonio] has a special tune on his violin which is also played when his clothes are changed. After one dance the music stops and the owner of the house gives everyone a drink. Then the music starts again and the owner and his wife begin the dance. After this men dance with men and women dance with women.

Once on a visit to Xequemaya, a house was nicely decorated: limes, lemons, and pomegranates were hung from the walls and ceiling. The owner told us that the fruit was for us to take in the morning. He also gave each of us two *octavos*.

Once in Los Cipreses, and who knows why, when the people were dancing a woman came in and some men started to beat her up. Someone threw a glass and it nearly hit the image. The culprit was jailed. No one bothers the *cofrades* at their table because everyone knows that their mission is very perilous. This incident may have occurred because the owner of the house had not completed his *costumbre*. Nothing happened to us because our *costumbre* was OK.[6]

The officials of the *aldeas* say that if an argument starts in the house during a visit, we should take the image and leave. This happened once, in fact, and the *alcalde* told us to go, to let the man and his wife fight alone. They followed us to the other house and presented a whole basketful of potatoes. They had to do this. The image likes happiness and correct behavior. People who ask for a visit should not be fighting. If there is no harmony, they should not ask for it. What kind of people are they who would do such a thing?

On the other hand, there are good people. One man is visited each year. He gives us baskets of bread and *aguardiente.* He has several nice houses and fine animals because of his faith. He gives a basket of bread for each of the houses he has made that year. He says the image pays for this, but here in the town center people are not like this.

In the hamlets people really mob the image, but here in the center nobody seems to care about it. It's right in the church nearby. The country people are more respectful. Once we were invited into a field, and the owner was picking roasting ears for us.

Someone, a visitor following us, asked, "Why is Tonio stealing the corn?"

It was intended as a joke, but the *alcalde* of the *aldea* scolded him for being disrespectful and told him if he didn't watch out his mouth would get him in jail.

The only thing that ever happened to me was that my feet became swollen from the cold because I didn't have shoes on the road to Pologua. Mud builds on our feet and collects pine needles from the floor, so that everyone seems to be wearing sandals made of pine needles. Sometimes we are given five or six rolls each. In Tunayac everyone gives bread, and we end up with a basketful each. Once, at four in the morning, we had maize dumplings [*tamalitos*], and then we thought nothing of them, but then it was nothing but bread for twelve hours until we arrived at a house construction site to bless it and had a meal of *tamalitos,* broth, and *aguardiente.* We were really sick of bread, but when there isn't any we want some. But there is nothing like *tamalitos* when you're really hungry. You never get tired of them; *tamalitos* and *aguardiente.* If the people at a house don't serve drinks they are reprimanded by the *alcalde.* We *cofrades* are cold and tired and must be given our drinks. Some people abuse us. They claim that we are only doing this for the food. But we don't ask for anything. People give us food if they want to, and we really suffer from the cold in August. Visits to private homes aren't so bad, but the fiesta trip is very hard.

There is a *r'awas* [sacred precinct or the rituals performed there] in Pasajoc. The new *cofrades* are shown this *r'awas* on the seventh of June before they enter the service on the eleventh and twelfth of June. When the day of the *r'awas* arrives, a certain day Ajmak, the image is brought to the *r'awas* for *costumbres.* There are *costumbres* of the *r'awas* all day, and that night a big fiesta in a house before the *r'awas*. Many people come to this house, up to a hundred, and bring wheat, potatoes, all sorts of good things. They put many candles before the image on this day Ajmak. The *r'awas* is in the house like an oven of adobe. The people burn [candles] on the floor below and the image is set on top. Eighteen large shards of crockery or roof tile [*tejas*] are removed from the *porobal* [hearth of the ovenlike altar] and placed in a line to the door, each with its little piece of copal.[7] [For the fiesta in Pasajoc the *cofrades* pass the image into the keeping of an unofficial *cofradía* from Pologua. The *cofrades,* who have been deprived of sleep during the days and nights of visiting and dancing, take advantage of the fiesta to catch up on their sleep. After the fiesta, they transport the Niño to Pologua.]

Now we spend three days in Pologua, but it used to be two days. Potatoes and peaches are given—really they are brought to the *cofradía,* nine bushels of them. They are not sold, they are given, and also packages of clothing and toys, pesos, and silver.

The biggest peaches are those blessed by San Antonio. People bring offerings from their fields and trees. When the image is in Pologua, people make pilgrimages from Totonicapán and San Francisco with peaches to lay them before the image.[8] There are so many people that they have a very brief turn, visiting [the image] for just a minute.

When we arrive in Pologua we all change our clothes, and we change the image's clothes also and fire off two *bombas*. The *alcalde* changes the image's clothes. People bring clothing as gifts and ask that these be put on the Niño. This is OK, but only the *cofrades* may be present for the actual changing. Clothes are changed and washed on the day Ajmak, and for the fiesta.

The C'amo Junab *(Changing of the* Cofradía*)*

On June 11 the *auxiliatura* officials go to the *armita* of the new *cofradía* with the outgoing and the incoming *cofrades*. Upon arriving and leaving, as each leans over and kisses the door of the Niño's cabinet, a little bell is rung. From nine in the morning until late afternoon they take an inventory of the Niño's possessions and supervise their transfer.[9] This is a tense time for the retiring *alcalde,* since he will be charged with replacing any missing items. A little cape with seed pearls and mirrors may cost over one hundred quetzals.

The inventory takes place on the patio of the house. The lists are kept and read in Spanish by the secretary. The outgoing *cofrades* rummage around through piles of kerchiefs, towels, cloaks, toys, and jewelry trying to find the correct items. Most of the bundles are not numbered or labeled. The *cofrades* do not understand the Spanish words, and items are located by trial and error. Late in the day, with smaller piles, things speed up.

The *c'amo junab* (new year) proper, is the time of ritualized change of personnel in the *cofradía*. An all-night dance in the *armita* by the new and old *cofrades* and by the *chuch axelab*, the women's *cofradía*, is followed by breakfast at the *armita* and a procession with the Niño to the church. There, "above the souls" before the main altar, the old and new *cofrades* kneel facing each other. The *pasados* place the crowns of flowers they are wearing on the heads of the *nuevos*. The *chuch axelab* then perform a similar ceremony with flower necklaces. After this the *nuevos* take the Niño back to their *armita* and continue the fiesta for the rest of the day.

The new *alcalde* is served the first drink, but he gives it to the *nima chichu*, the first lady among the *chuch axelab*. Then she is served a drink, which she gives to the *alcalde*. The dancing begins with the *cofradía* on one side and the *chuch axelab* on the other, facing each other in parallel rows. The *alcalde* and *nima chichu* dance out and meet, then return to their places. Following this the men and women change sides, then the *alcalde* and *nima chichu* dance out and meet again. This is followed by normal and less ritualized dancing of men with men and women with women.

This noteworthy ceremony duplicates the pattern in which a man and his wife start the dance when the Niño visits a private house. It involves a number of inversions of normal gender-role behavior: the highest ranking male deferring to a female, the sharing of drinks between unmarried adults of opposite sex, and the joint participation of men and women in a dance. This ceremony links the theme of fertility associated with the Niño complex to the theme of harmony between the sexes. "Bad" visits occur whenever there is intersexual discord before the image.

The Image Gives Signs
by Pablo Itzep

The image has something in its head like a knob or a stick. It is a dangerous saint [*itzel ri santo*]. The image used to leave town and go as far as Nagualá. It still goes to San Andrés Xecul and San Francisco, but now only with official permission. To get permission, the man requesting the visit must leave his land title with the *síndico segundo*. Once the *cofrades* were drunk in another town and the image disappeared. It was stolen. They cried and they searched for it all day. That night they found it back on the table again. It had come back by itself. Yes, great is the work of San Antonio!

It is seen to be miraculous, miraculous for the cow, the horse. The image is great for the animals. It is their saint, San Antonio. Sometimes people buy a nice fat piglet in the market. When they get it home it won't eat. It just gets skinny. Perhaps it was blessed by San Antonio at the house of the first owners, and it is ruined when it goes where they don't have this custom. Maybe it even dies. But if the image comes to the house the animal will get fat again.

Once, halfway through the mass at Pologua while the padre was praying, the big cabinet began to tip over and looked like it might fall, then it righted itself. This was a sign that later there would be a disagreement among the *cofrades* of Pasajoc. Everyone saw this, including the padre. The image is small, but it has its miracles. It gives signs and they always mean something. You should be prepared, then.

Once an *aldea* official was guarding the image, but he was ignorant of the consequences of doing so, and so he began to wish that he hadn't come. For this his stomach became swollen and he had to confess to the image with candles. No one had advised him. He was not prepared because no one had told him that he would have to stand guard. Since it was not his fault, when he confessed he got better. The *síndico* should have warned him about this but he didn't; thus the *síndico* had to take the blame.

Commentary on the Niño Complex

The Niño complex is organized around themes of sexual harmony and fertility and focuses on the household and smallest rural community, or *paraje.* The Niño is venerated in the rural hamlets rather than the *cabecera*. It is especially important in the highland ecological zone in the western part of Momostenango, where production is based on non-native factors: sheep, potatoes, and wheat, all introduced during the colonial period.

One of the Niño's main functions is the blessing of new houses and of households. The Niño is a lord of the domestic sphere, of the interior of the house, of the cooking pots in the kitchen. He controls culture-in-nature as represented by agriculture, arboriculture, and stock raising. He is the patron of the small isolated human communities in the wilderness that he visits. In a sense, he is patron of the country people themselves.

The face of the world is understood to be Juyup Takaj, which is translated as "Mountain-Plain" but for Momostecans also has the sense of "wilderness/cultivated land."[10] The Niño is a *santo del mundo* that appeared in a cave, its mountain or cave place (*ujuyubal*) a shrine much visited by pilgrims from Momostenango and other communities. Yet for the *cofrades* its most important, most powerful shrine is a massive adobe *porobal* located within a house in Pologua. There its most sacred, ritually prescribed observances take place. The Niño, though personifying natural fertility, is domesticated, brought within the house and within a specially prepared and ideally harmonious human community, to confer its blessings.

The Niño's fiestas at private houses re-create communities and renew them on a yearly basis at harvest time. The *alcalde* of the *aldea,* the sponsoring family, and the neighbors are brought together for a party celebrating amiability and social harmony. The greatest danger associated with the celebration is conflict between the sexes, especially between husband and wife. A *c'amal be* (lit., "guide on the road"; i.e., a marriage go-between) visits the image of the Niño with candles before going to ask for a girl in marriage for his client, thus reinforcing the image's connection to the domestic sphere, fertility, and idealized marital harmony.

PATRÓN SANTIAGO

Santiago's ritual complex is more complicated than the Niño's. It includes five dance teams, the official *cofradía,* and fiestas in two *cantones* in addition to the patronal fiesta in the *cabecera*. Two lineages whose ancestors were indigenous nobility—the Vicentes and the Herreras—claim to be the original and rightful owners of the image of Santiago. Santiago's visits to their *cantones* for fiestas acknowledges historical claims and reconstitutes colonial relationships, while reaffirming the authority of the administrators in the *cabecera*.[11]

The Vicentes' fiesta is in the *aldea* San Vicente Buenabaj in mid-November, and the Herreras' is in the *cantón* Pueblo Viejo, in the *aldea* Tunayac, in late November. The Patrón used to go to Pueblo Viejo during Lent, rather than November, and has only been visiting Pueblo Viejo for the fiesta of Santa Catarina since the 1920s. Santa Isabel has only been kept at Buenabaj since 1925. It is unknown whether or not Santiago used to visit María Concepción during her sojourn there in the seventeenth through nineteenth centuries. Neither can the antiquity of Santiago's visits to Pueblo Viejo during Lent now be established.

These visiting complexes annually reestablish contact among three images that were the patrons of three of the four *parcialidades* located around the town center during the colonial period. Santa Ana, the patron image of the fourth *parcialidad*, is not today involved with the Patrón. The folklore of Momostenango, which labels Isabel and Catarina as the Patrón's women, has nothing to say about Santa Ana, whose colonial image is still in the keeping of one of the prominent families in the *barrio* Santa Ana but lacks a communalistic cult institution.[12]

In the complex of the Patrón, these reminders—or maybe remainders—of colonial social structure can be separated from the fiesta in the *cabecera*. It has grown rapidly from a basic *cofradía* fiesta since the 1920s, concomitant with the centralization of authority and the increasing political power of the combined *cabecera* and nearby *aldeas* of Santa Ana, Xequemaya, and Los Cipreses, and with the withdrawal of the outlying *aldeas* from active involvement in Momostecan pueblo-level rituals. The change in emphasis from Holy Week to the patronal fiesta marks the social transformation of Momostenango from a loosely organized confederation of rather autonomous *cantones* ruled by locally prominent descent groups, vestiges of the older *parcialidad* system, into a Guatemalan pueblo administered by specialists in the town center.

In Momostecan folklore, the Patrón meets Momostecan blanket salesmen on lonely roads in distant places and protects them from thieves, and made an appearance on a battlefield in Totonicapán where victory was thus ensured for Momostenango. His *cofrades* and dancers acknowledge his protection of their health and prosperity during their service. Disaster follows lapses in his fiestas.

The Patrón is said to be a war chief, but has been converted from a conquistador (Santiago was the patron saint of the Spanish in their wars with the Moors and later was patron of the conquistadors) into an indigenous war captain, more in the tradition of Tecum. The social loci of importance in the Patrón complex are the *cantones* associated with the ancient native elite, as well as the *cabecera*. The Patrón is a symbol of sovereignty and unity with a strongly nativistic flavor.

The themes of the dances of the Patrón's fiesta in the *cabecera* construct and reinforce a context of appropriate meanings and associations for Santiago. Two of the dances, the Vaqueros and the Mexicans, represent the deaths of archaic hacienda-style Ladino patrons and subsequent family struggles over inheritance. Two others, the Conquest and the Moors, depict warfare with obvious relevance to Santiago in the Spanish tradition and as a war captain in Momos. It is interesting in light of this good fit to learn that the Conquest Dance was traditionally part of Holy Week, and was only moved to Santiago's fiesta in the 1920s. In the Monkeys Dance, an elderly indigenous couple mediates between Spaniards and the animal-owning lords of the four sacred mountains. The dancers erect an *axis mundi* reminiscent of Classic Maya iconography and mythology of kingship, as explained in chapter 4.

The Image of Santiago

The image of Santiago, called Patrón Santiago, Capitán Santiago, and Apóstol Santiago, is found in the nave of the church on the congregation's left side near the altar. It is a small image of a black-bearded, pale-faced man on horseback wearing a three-pointed crown, with a sword in his upraised right hand. Sometime subsequent to the original carving, crossed bandoliers were added. Santiago is patron saint and "captain of the army." His secretary, San Felipe, stands on his left and always accompanies Santiago in processions. It is said that as a war captain, Santiago cannot read and needs Felipe to keep records.[13] It is also sometimes said that the Patrón speaks only Quiché and so needs Felipe as a translator, and that Momostecans find Spanish difficult because their Patrón does not speak it. Santiago is also Venus as the Morning Star (Nima Ch'umil, "Great Star").

Travel to Fiestas in Cantones

The images of the Patrón and San Felipe are taken to visit San Vicente Buenabaj for the fiesta of Santa Isabel and to Pueblo Viejo in the *aldea* Tunayac for the fiesta of Santa Catarina. On the trip to Pueblo Viejo, they are accompanied by an image of Santa Catarina that belongs to a family in the *barrio* Santa Catarina of the town center.

For the fiesta of Santa Isabel, the images of Santiago and San Felipe are brought from the church to the *armita* of the Patrón in the town center on November 14. At two in the morning on November 15, they begin the trip to San Vicente, arriving there about twelve hours later. They spend the night in the *cofradía* house of Santa Isabel.[14] On the sixteenth the three images enter the chapel. On the eighteenth the Patrón, San Felipe, and Santa Isabel are carried in procession around the center of San Vicente and returned to the church. Masses are said on the eighteenth and nineteenth by a priest from Sija. The nineteenth is the day of the fiesta proper. On the twentieth, the images return to Momostenango.

The procession to and from the town center brings the Patrón and San Felipe through populated areas. It is controlled by the *cofrades* of the Patrón and the officials of the *aldeas* through which they pass, but the images are carried by representatives from San Vicente. This parallels the sharing of responsibilities between an official *cabecera cofradía* and a local *cantón*-based sodality in the San Antonio complex. Residents along the way lay pine needles by the roadside or on a trail into the patio, so that the images can stop. They feed the *cofrades* roasted corn on the cob (*elotes*) and give them mature ears of flour corn (*mazorcas*) to take away with them. When the images are in San Vicente, people also make gifts of *elotes, mazorcas,* and potatoes, which are later divided among the *cofrades*. A *chirimía* from Cabricán or Huitán accompanies the procession from the town center to San Vicente.

Signs at the Fiesta of Santa Isabel
by Florentino Ixbatz

The Patrón is dangerous [*itzel;* i.e., *delicado,* powerful and touchy]. We have a story of what happened to those of San Vicente last year. They came to the municipal building to get their licenses for the visit, but they wanted to transport the image by car. When the mayor heard this he tore up the license and the priest refused to give the mass if the Patrón wasn't there. He said he would be lonely without the image. So they went to Xela [Quetzaltenango] and got a priest, but they had to pay double because he wasn't theirs.

Right in the middle of the mass, when the priest was blessing the host, two skunks entered the chapel and let fly. Everybody ran out to escape the smell and the mass had to be completed under the trees. The Patrón's *costumbre* had not been performed because the image had not arrived. Also, when they went to see the Patrón's altar [*porobal*] after this, there were two snakes coiled up in it and this frightened them.[15] This year, they will be sure to bring the image. The Patrón is strong. He is a dangerous saint [*k'axlic santo;* lit., "a painful saint"].

The Fiesta of Santa Catarina

Up until about 1925, there was a fiesta each year in the *barrio* Santa Catarina for the image of Santa Catarina which is kept there in a private house belonging to an elder of the Chanchabac lineage.[16] The image used to have a title (*título*), a leather-bound manuscript written in Quiché, but this has not been seen since the 1920s. The fiesta was given on the twenty-fourth or twenty-fifth of November with a paid marimba. In those days the image made a trip to Pueblo Viejo before or after the *barrio* fiesta. Now there is no *barrio* fiesta.

At ten in the morning on November 23, Santa Catarina, Santiago, and San Felipe leave Momostenango for Pueblo Viejo in a procession with a band from San Francisco La Unión, accompanied by Mexicano dancers from Momostenango. This trip is through a largely uninhabited region of municipal forest. There are two resting places along the route, both marked by crosses, one at Pa Tzotzil and the other at Chitu Balam. The procession does not visit private houses along the way.

There are two chapels (*oratorios*) in Pueblo Viejo: a lower chapel belonging to the Herrera family, *caciques* who used to own the image of Santiago, and the older chapel, a *calvario* on a hill just above the cemetery. The images are brought to the lower chapel first, remain there over night, and are used in a Catholic Action mass in the morning. The Herreras were early and important converts to the Catholic Action movement. In the afternoon of the twenty-fourth, they go to the public *calvario* for a mass with all the residents of Pueblo Viejo. Thus the

Herreras continue to play the traditional role of the *cacique* lineage in a *parcialidad* sponsoring the fiesta for the entire community, but with their own separate private rituals. On November 25 there is a fiesta with a ball game (soccer) and dances (Grasejos, Mexicanos, and Vaqueros). While the images are in the two chapels, food offerings are brought, as at San Vicente. On November 26 the images return to the town center.

An Herrera elder in Pueblo Viejo reported that until about 1915, the Patrón was brought on the fourth Friday of Lent, but that this practice was discontinued because the pueblo was poor at that time of year and lacked enough food to have a good fiesta. August 15 was tried, but that was also too early for the harvest. It was therefore decided to celebrate the fiesta of the Patrón on the day of Santa Catarina. Until about 1925 Santa Catarina and Santa Isabel were both present at the fiesta, thus uniting the Patrón with "his two women." The people of San Vicente are not disposed to allow Santa Isabel out of their *aldea,* so this no longer occurs. Stories are told by *cofrades* and by dancers of what happens when something interferes with the Patrón's fiestas.

Problems at the Fiesta
by Juan Ixc'oy

The Mexicanos [a dance team] came from Pueblo Viejo to accompany the image, but the priest wouldn't let them dance in the patio of the church, so they waited in the hills. The priest didn't want them to accompany the image, and when he heard that they had he refused to say the mass in Pueblo Viejo. The next year the Patrón didn't go to Pueblo Viejo, but we *cofrades* went anyway to do the *costumbre* there. We said that we would go, so we had to go to do the *costumbre* at the two altars [*ujuyubal* and *ujal*]. We had to fulfill our obligation. It was not our fault that the image didn't go. We completed what we owed.

We were buying oranges in the market when an Herrera came up and spoke to me.

"What's up, brother-in-law? We are lost because the Patrón didn't come!"

"But that's not our fault!"

"My brother has died. He went to mass and was fine. A half hour later he was dead. He died in the church during mass."

When the Patrón doesn't go he will exact justice. This happened once before also. When the Patrón didn't come, there were two deaths in the fiesta. By all means he must come, because we have seen that he will have his justice!

This account and the similar one from Santa Isabel's fiesta suggest a genre-like category of stories about Santiago. In any case, during a time of change when the traditions were being challenged by Catholic Action, the *cofrades* were forced to mediate between factions in order to discharge their obligations and protect the pueblo, as noted in the account below.

The Fiesta in Pueblo Viejo
by Juan Ixc'oy

Costumbre is not done here [in the *cabecera*] when we go to Pueblo Viejo. It is done there on November 25. The image remains in the church but candles, copal, and incense are left at his feet the night before. We bring two dozen nodules of copal from here, four bunches of candles, and four ounces of incense.

The people there ask, "Why do you do this?"[17]

"Because since the beginning there has been Costumbre. When a *cofrade* leaves at the end of his year he must tell the new one the *costumbres* so they are not lost."

"Why don't you change this Costumbre?"

"We can't because it's not ours; it belongs to the pueblo."

They did this last time [at the last fiesta of Santa Catarina] and the municipal constables [*alguaciles*] came to my house to tell me to come to the *auxiliatura* next morning. I lived in my old house. They told me that the people in Pueblo Viejo wanted the shrine [*r'awas*] moved from its location behind the church. I said I couldn't do that. Its not mine. I would have to ask the *principales*. It just passes from one to another. It is not owned. If they don't like it there, they should see how many *varas* [unit of measure; nearly a meter] it occupies, three or four, and the pueblo should buy it from him [the owner] if he is of Catholic Action. The *principales* agreed to this. It shouldn't be moved. We *cofrades* would suffer. It's our responsibility. And what might happen to the pueblo?

They sent for the landowner and he said that he didn't mind its being there, but other people didn't like its position behind the church. The church and altar are of the Herreras. The church in the cemetery is of another family. The owner's father said it was from the time of the grandfathers and should not be moved.

"I will not let it be moved, and I will sign to that effect."

He signed and now the people have nothing to say. But later they raised another petition to try to have the spring-side altar of the shrine complex [*uja'l*] moved. They are of Catholic Action.

For both fiestas [Pueblo Viejo and San Vicente Buenabaj], we leave our houses for fifteen days.

He [Santiago] protects us well and gives us food. His *costumbre* is all the time, the ones, sixes, eights, nines, and elevens. Every fifteen days it goes. It doesn't fall over. It is well tied up [*ximitalic*]. If we forget even one, something will happen to us, so we must work hard, we cannot be lazy.

Fiestas in Other Aldeas

The image of Santiago, accompanied as always by San Felipe, is brought to the *aldeas* of Los Cipreses, Santa Ana, Tierra Colorado, and Xequemaya for fiestas without fixed dates. These are the four *aldeas* that, with the *cabecera*, now dominate the *cofradía* system. The *principales* of the *aldeas* decide on the appropriate day for the fiesta, with the general rule observed by all that it must be on a day Quiej, Ajmak, Noj, or Camé. The image visits each of these *aldeas* every two or three years. On the way to its fiesta, it visits houses along the route, as it does on the way to San Vicente for the fiesta of Santa Isabel. These visits are short, however, unlike the *visitas* made by the Niño San Antonio described above.

Santiago's Fiesta in the Cabecera

Santiago's festival, also known as *La Feria* and *La Fiesta Titular,* did not exist as such until the 1920s. During the first decades of the twentieth century, the image was kept in an *armita* belonging to the Herreras. There was an all-night party there with a marimba or fiddle on July 23. Santiago and San Felipe were carried around town. *Bombas* were fired to mark the stages of the celebration. A Moors Dance was given, and from time to time a Monkeys Dance was performed.

When the construction of the new church was completed in about

1915, Santiago was removed from the Herrera house—and from the Herrera family—and installed there, in the keeping of a *cofradía* with rotating fiesta sponsorship. The Conquest Dance was moved from Holy Week and made part of his fiesta. Within a decade or two, the Mexicanos and Vaqueros Dances were also added. Today the fiesta includes carnival rides and a huge market, food vendors and spectators from all over the highlands, and busloads of tourists. Ears of green corn roasted on charcoal braziers are served with lime wedges and coarse salt. Pickpockets and prostitutes work the huge crowds, and in the heat of the late afternoon bumblebees, drunk on spilled liquor, are unable to fly.

The *cofradía* role in the fiesta begins July 23 when Santiago and San Felipe go to the *armita,* where, on the twenty-fourth, the new *alcalde* is received. On the twenty-fifth there is a procession in the streets ending in church. On the thirtieth Santiago returns to the *armita,* where his clothes are changed at midnight and six *bombas* are fired. On the thirty-first, at six in the morning, riding on his specially decorated palanquin, he goes to the *calvario,* and then there is a big procession with marimba and dancers to the church, and another procession that night in the principal streets. On August 1, it ends with day and evening processions in the streets (see fig. 3.1).

Momostecans delight in discussing the fiesta and its major elements before and after it takes place, comparing them to those of fiestas in years gone by and in other towns. The processions and the dances enact the mythology of the Costumbristas. Tecum, Alvarado, and Aj Itz, the characters in the Conquest Dance, established the world order. The animal impersonators in the Monkeys Dance are possessed by animal spirits at a shrine before the performance. This renders them fearless when they do their tricks on the tightrope sixty feet above the pavement in the plaza.

The dancers of the four dances given each year—the Vaqueros (Cowboys), the Mexicanos, the Moros (Christians and Moors), and the Conquista (Conquest)—are called the four teams (*caj ch'ob*). Occasionally, every other year if the sponsor and his dancers are solvent, a Monkeys Dance is also given. On July 19 and 20 the costumes are brought into town by the dancers. On July 21 the teams enter town and present bouquets to the municipal *alcalde,* the *síndico segundo,* and the Catholic priest. They enter the church briefly after removing their masks and headdresses. There the priest accepts the flowers and exhorts them to

FIG. 3.1. Santiago and San Felipe in procession during the *fiesta patronal*, 1976. Note the decorated palanquin.

dance in memory of Santiago and not to drink too much. They proceed immediately to the little pole-and-pine-bough *ranchitos* in the plaza where the musicians are waiting. The Conquest Dance is unusual in having a "palace," a two-story scaffolding covered with pine boughs that has a thirty-foot watchtower on one end. The arrangement of the dance areas is shown in figure 3.2.

There is daily dancing through August 3, with each of the two teams that alternate in every dance performing seven times. On the two big days of July 21 and August 1, the Conquest Dance is given in full with the Spaniards riding into town on horses. On August 4 the dancers return to the church briefly for the farewell, and then go to the sponsors' houses to disrobe.

The Vaqueros and Mexicans Dances depict hacienda society and feature bullfights, the deaths of the hacienda owners, and concern over the division of property after death. The newer of these dances, the Mexicans Dance, was introduced in the 1940s and has become so popular that two performances are given simultaneously. The crowds love the colorful Mexican costumes, the lively *ranchería*-style music, the bullfights, and the clowning. The dancers shoot each other and visiting

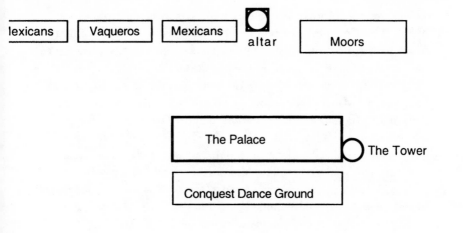

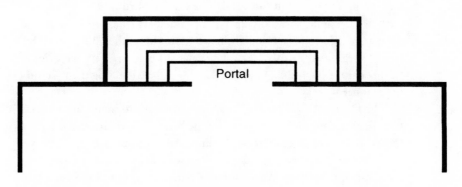

The Church

FIG. 3.2. The dance ground, Santiago's fiesta, 1976.

tourists with the little cap guns that come with their costumes. Many of the Mexicans also dance as Grasejos in Holy Week and are inspired comedians. The themes of the Mexicans and Vaqueros Dances, the deaths of patriarchs and conflicts over division of their estates, are of great interest to Momostecans. Here, where money is called "The Light of God" (U Sakil Tiox), the division of property eventually tests every family.

The Moors (Moros) Dance was imported from sixteenth-century Spain. The Conquest Dance was probably written by a Dominican priest with the help of natives in Guatemala about twenty years after the Conquest, and then used in the pacification of Vera Paz (Carmack 1973: 169). In Momostenango the Conquest and the Moors Dances are linked as "red dances" (*k'ak'atak xojoj*), that is, war dances. The Christians in the Moors Dance have become identified with the Quiché Maya in the Conquest Dance. Both Tecum, the Quiché war chief in the conquest, and the Christian king in the Moors, wear little stuffed quetzal birds in their headdresses. The Moors Dance takes two days to complete and does not attract large crowds. It is slow paced, with lengthy, incomprehensible Spanish monologues mumbled behind masks, and its traditional musical accompaniment by flute and drum lacks the "liveliness" of *ranchería* music. All the performers have long, stylized dance solos. The characters include a little Moor and a little Christian whose roles as jesters lighten the mood. The first dancers of both sides have to memorize seven hundred words, the second dancers five hundred, and the little jesters four hundred. The jesters, portrayed by prepubescent boys, mimic and ridicule the first dancers, the two kings. The Moors are said to have crossed the ocean to defeat the Christians who lived "here on this earth." The Christians, however, were victorious. In this dance, then, the Quiché are successful at defeating their would-be conquerors.

The Dance of the Conquest (La Conquista), the dramatization of the historical conquest of the Quiché by the Spaniards, is also called La'bal (War). Up until the time of the Ladino boss Teodoro Cifuentes in the first quarter of this century, the Conquest Dance was part of the fiesta for Capitagua in Holy Week and was danced in front of the cemetery where the Tzulab (Grasejos) dance today. In those days it had no connection with the Patrón, because the image of Santiago was in Pueblo Viejo Tunayac for the fiesta of the *parcialidad* Herrera during Holy Week. Momostecans are proud of their performance of this dance, which they claim is one of the most complete performances in Guatemala. Momostecan interpretations of the dance range from the largely mythical that sees Alvarado and Tecum as *mundos,* to the more or less historical among some more acculturated town dwellers. The Conquest Dance is discussed in detail in chapter four.

The Monkeys Dance, called Los Monos or C'oyab (Spider Monkeys), is ideally given every other year during the Patrón's fiesta. Its organization is described in chapter 2, and its symbolism and *costumbre* are described in chapter 4. It has elements of a deer dance—an old couple, four directions symbolism, and representation of a deer hunt (see Paret Limardo 1963)—which it combines with an acrobatic display by animal impersonators on a tightrope.

Santiago and the Rain and Winds

When the first big rains come shortly after Holy Week, the traditional people say, "Cape ri jap, cape ri Tiox" ("The rain comes, God comes"). While *Tiox* (*Dios*) means "God," it is frequently used in Momostenango to refer to a saint or to the saints as a group. The Dios Mundo is responsible for the maize, but the Dios Cielo—the God of Heaven (the saints and angels)—is responsible for sending the rain. When the rain is late or irregular, processions are made with Santiago, San Felipe, San Miguel, and San Francisco. In addition to processions with the saints, there are four masses for the rain (*misa jap* or *misas de agua*) paid for by the *auxiliatura* each year. These masses are on the days Noj, Ajmak, Quiej, and K'anil,[18] and are preceded by *costumbre* for Dios Mundo. When the rains come early or are on time, all four are not given. Masses are also given for the Patrón by private individuals to ask for protection of their milpas from wind and from hail. The latter practice is shared with Chichicastenango, where Santiago is called destroyer of the milpa and is believed to send hailstorms (Bunzel 1952: 58, 268).

The Santiago and San Felipe pair reflect the Quichean cultural pattern of dualistic authority described above, linking the chief element in the bipartite complex to rain, hail, and storm. This might be a Southern Maya pattern. For example, a chest called the Ordinance found in San Miguel Acatán northwest of the Quiché heartland (Siegel 1941) and the San Martín bundle in Santiago Atitlán (Mendelson 1965) are associated with rain and wind ceremonies, and each is also an element in a dualistic complex (Ordinance-Gaspar, San Martín-Yashper) functioning as a community protector and rain-wind deity.[19] The ancient Quiché combined an image (Tojil) and a sacred bundle (Pizom Gagal) in their corporate iconography, while in the colonial *parcialidades* saints and *títulos,* the latter often stored in chests, came to play these roles. It appears that sacred bundles and chests play a larger role in the community-integrating cults of the western and southern peripheries of the Quiché region, while saints dominate this corporate religious symbolism in the central Quichean area.

The Clothing of the Patrón

Clothing belonging to the images figures prominently in the complexes of the Patrón, the Niño San Antonio, Corpus, and San Simón. "Clothing" that may include blankets in the case of the Patrón, or little capes and handkerchiefs for the Niño San Antonio, is presented to the images by the faithful who hope to obtain protection from witches, good health, abundant harvests, or business success in return for their gifts. This clothing, together with other gifts like mirrors, toys, and old coins, is preserved by the *cofradía* in a series of chests and bundles. While such chests and bundles appear to be important power objects themselves in some other highland communities, as noted above, they seem to lack such significance in Momostenango. Midnight ceremonies at which the clothing of an image is changed by the *cofrades,* however, do figure prominently in the cults of the important Momostecan saints, are esoteric, and probably represent a residue of sacred bundle symbolism. Santiago's occurs on July 30. Only *cofrades* may be present for a changing.

Apparel for Santiago
by Juan Ixc'oy

When I came in the first year [about 1958], the Patrón did not have his apparel, but just one cape given by the pueblo. We, my companion Geraldo Peruch and I, went to report on this to the *síndico segundo.* We asked for support because the Patrón had only one costume and is an important image and so should have more.[20] The litter [*palanquín*] was in bad shape, and there was no chest to store his clothing. The *principales* were called to a meeting and they agreed, and we *cofrades* were sent to San Cristóbal with one hundred quetzals to buy clothes. Pedro Vásquez came and complained that he was not in agreement. He always walks behind the image, but he won't give any money.

The man who makes the clothes sent a sample. He wanted official agreement before he started work. We would have to agree on a date, the sixteenth of December, to go and get the clothes.

I know about these things because I was a dancer for fourteen years before I entered the *cofradía*. Once I danced in the Conquista. I was in the Moros twice. In other years I was a Vaquero. In my last year I danced as the plantation owner in the Vaqueros. Then I entered the *cofradía*. I've always danced and never had a financial failure, so I said, "Let's buy the clothes." [21]

I went to the Patrón's altar and asked him, "Why aren't your sons in agreement about your apparel? Do something to get your clothing!"

The people took up a collection, and Atonasio Pelicó was in charge of this money. I had thought of going to get the clothes alone. The people donated fifty quetzals and I was able to come up with seventy-five. We also had to pay for a fiesta with *bombas* and food at the *armita* to receive the *ropa*. The marimba came free, and also a *chirimía* and a violin. It was a very lively fiesta. When we came down to town, the people had bought twelve and a half dozen *bombas*. We had only one dozen. It was tremendous!

The apparel was bought for Santiago and Felipe because San Felipe is his secretary. He always goes because he is the scribe. The fiesta of San Felipe in May is sad; it's not celebrated. Felipe has no *cofrades,* so we do it.

Other men started giving clothing—Francisco Poroj, and a Señor Ixchop some days later—but I was working hard in the *costumbre*. [22] So when I left he had plenty of clothes: four pairs of clothes and one dozen feathers to wear on his head in processions. But for this we worked hard at *costumbre.*

I had to sell one dozen blankets at 3.60 quetzals each to get the money for his *ropa*. I went to Señor Gomez, and he wouldn't pay that much, but God was watching. I went to borrow the money from my uncle on Wednesday, 75 quetzals, and he agreed. On Friday I met a Chanchabac in the park, a customer of mine, and he agreed to pay 5 quetzals each. The Patrón, our father [Ka Tat], had helped, and so I earned 18 quetzals on the bunch. [23] I went to apologize to my uncle for the trouble. We had been sent to meet in the park!

Santiago Gives Signs

The Patrón communicates ambiguously with his *cofrades* and the pueblo by giving signs (*señas* or *retals*). Signs are noted when they happen, but their meaning is generally assessed after an event which they might have prognosticated has occurred. They usually warn of misfortune of some kind. The skunks invading the chapel and the snakes found in the altar (mentioned above), a color change in the image's face, an unexplained noise during a procession, or an appearance in a dream are examples of the kinds of signs given by the Patrón. Although other images also give signs, this complex seems to be especially pronounced in the case of the Patrón and the Niño San Antonio.

If a fiesta for the Patrón runs smoothly, this is a sign that the *costumbre* has been done properly and that the traditions have been followed faithfully. If anything unusual happens, it indicates sin or fault (*mak*) on the part of a *cofrade,* or the omission of an important *costumbre.* While the signs are generally said to be given by the Patrón, the omission or commission may actually have offended the dead *cofrades* or *primeros.* A fiesta is given for both the image and the *primeros,* and they are quick to punish their ignorant and inferior replacements. After a sign has been given, everyone waits nervously and uncertainly for the evil to fall. Examples were presented above in chapter 2 and in connection with the fiestas of Santa Isabel and Santa Catarina in this chapter, and another typical example is given in the second selection below. Sometimes signs are not prognosticative but directly punitive. A text from Florentino Ixbatz interprets problems with erecting the pole for the Monkeys Dance as a punitive communication from the Patrón.

Santiago Teaches a Lesson
by Florentino Ixbatz

Once the Patrón fixed us good. We missed one year [i.e., they didn't dance when they were supposed to] and the next year something happened. When we arrived in town on the twenty-second [of July], we had a really thick pole and we began to erect it, but we couldn't get it up. The *síndico segundo* and officials came and scolded us for being so slow.

"It's too heavy, and we're afraid if it falls it will crack the cement. The padre has scolded us about this."

"It's not the padre who is in charge here. That which commands you is tradition. You have to erect the pole."

We were hungry because it was after one o'clock. The *síndico* told us that we had to do it, so we whipped ourselves and then we managed to do it in thirty minutes.[24] We were being punished by the Patrón for lack of *costumbre* and for missing the previous year. The pole was eight *varas* [around seven meters or twenty feet], higher than the church and we had to cut it. We were really fooled by the pole. We had measured it, but it was too tall.[25]

The priest has said, "From now on only twenty-one *varas* [about fifty feet] and no more. You must value human life. These people are not dogs!"

As we had deceived the Patrón, the pole fooled us. The image is really something! If God and the Patrón give me life, I will bring the Monkeys out next year.

The Patrón Gives Signs
by Juan Ixc'oy

An example of a sign—when sickness came to an *alcalde*, to Miguel Hernandez. The procession was in the street in front of Tomás Ak'abal's when there was an explosion in the palanquin, so we stopped and set it down and we looked around to see if a rocket had fallen on it, but there was no evidence of that. I thought to myself, only God knows if the image is angry or if it is the *cofrades* [i.e., the souls of the dead *cofrades*]. Well I had arranged my road, done my *costumbre*. When time came for the fiesta in San Vicente, Miguel Hernández came to us. He was not well on that Wednesday, and that Friday he didn't know if he would be able to go on Saturday. His wife was worried. He had a fever. My blood gave a sign that there was something bad in the road. The *mortomas* also arrived there at the *alcalde*'s house.

The *alcalde* said, "A calamity is coming down on me; I am in a bad way."

He got sick on the way back from Pueblo Viejo. The representatives of San Vicente said they would send for a horse to carry him, but no, they were not responsible. I knew he would die, because the image and my blood had given signs. He was dying on the ridge above Momos. He asked the *mortoma* to bring him the emblem from the top of his official staff so that he could say good-bye. We arrived at the church at noon, and we had all said good-bye by two o'clock. At five o'clock he died.

His wife said that on Wednesday, after the purchases had been made, they had gone to the baths and he had slipped on a rock. The sickness came from this.[26] The sign was at the fiesta, and four months later this happened.

Another sign came when the *alcalde* Joaquín Gómez was leaving the service in the *armita*. This was the twenty-third of July. We were seated at the table with the image, and suddenly the table shook. That Joaquin Gomez! The next morning he would have left and a new one would have entered.

The *alcaldes* that I've known have died—Miguel Hernández, Joaquín Gómez, Jacinto Pérez, Adolfo Ajtún, Francisco García, Siquel Tzun—and here I am the same as always. I have done the *costumbre* well. This is my answer if I am asked why I am still alive and they are all dead. One has to please the *primeros* with candles, copal, and praise. That's why I'm alive.

If you go to burn [make offerings] but are not truthful you bring your death, but if you are truthful it's all right. They didn't do the *costumbre* right. It caused them pain to spend money to make *costumbre*.[27] I never refused to spend money on *costumbre*. I will even borrow money to pay for *costumbre*.

The image of the Patrón would speak to Diego Vicente in his dreams, and still speaks to some of his descendants in theirs. He also appears in the dreams of men who are in his service as dancers or as *cofrades* to encourage them to fulfill their obligations.

Patrón Santiago in Dreams
by Florentino Ixbatz and Son

[Don Florentino's son:] The first year I wanted to dance [in the Monkeys Dance]. I was to be one of the dogs, but on the twentieth when I awoke I was sick with fever. I decided not to dance the next day, but that night I dreamed that the Patrón came and grabbed me by the throat and said, "You [*at;* Quiché familiar form], are you going to work with me or not?" and threw me down; so I said yes, I would dance. He also said that if I would dance he would pay me thirty centavos. When I awoke in the morning, I was fine.

[Don Florentino continues:] The Patrón also fixed me because I couldn't get the dancers. He tested me. I dreamed that he came here to the house.

"How are you? Good day. How is the dance going?"

"Not well, sir, not well."

"I have completed my part. Why don't you come to me at the house?"[28]

So in the morning I got the second sponsor to go with me to try to complete it. We visited the dancers and asked them to please dance, and this time they all agreed. In fact, one of them had also dreamed of the Patrón. Now it was easy to get them. The Patrón had come to them too, and they knew that if they refused there would be trouble. This happens when *costumbre* is done well. When *costumbre* is lacking they beg off, saying that the Patrón has not advised them or saying that they lack the cash. The year that I didn't bring out the dance, the Patrón appeared to me in a dream and told me not to do it that year. I have seen that the image of Santiago is dangerous and will have his revenge.

It happened to me once that the Monkeys came and asked me to enter with them because I do *costumbre* [i.e., to be *chuch kajaw* for the dance]. I was ambitious for the *costumbre*, so I agreed. I thought better of it when they told me that I would have to feed all forty of them. The same night I dreamed of the Patrón. He came behind a big wall so I saw only his head, and at the same time a voice told me that when I did the rehearsal for the dance I would be burned by a *bomba*. Then a boy appeared and said, "They are firing the *bomba!*" So I hid under a tree. The *bomba* went up and up and it came down and hit my little toe.

The next day I came to burn [make offerings] in town, and I asked Don Benito [the retired *chuch kajaw* of the Monkeys] about the dream. He did his divination and said, "There is an obligation that is unfinished. It's something that happened in the last few days. If you don't do it, you will bury a son and be bedridden with sickness."

And I hadn't even gone before the Patrón with this or burned any candles! We just spoke of it in the house and still it had its effect. And I didn't believe it, but I was thinking about it.

I went to Xela [Quetzaltenango] and went to a spiritualist and explained it to him, including what the diviner had said. He laughed and said, "It's true what the diviner told you. Do you think you can fool with the Patrón? It's not any old image, it's captain of the army and has whip in hand. You had better comply!"

When I got back, I went to the *porobal* to arrange it. I went to Quilaja, Tamancu, Socop, Pipil, C'oy Abaj,[29] and I said I would put it on, but I would need help to afford it. I didn't want to die or lose my son. I called the forty names at the *porobal*,[30] and next day they came and asked me when we would organize the dance. They had been having signs in their dreams. The Patrón had been threatening them.

In two weeks I had another dream. I was going down a road and met the Patrón coming up. He got off his horse and took my hand. I asked him where he was going. He didn't answer but told me he had arranged for the dancers. He got on his horse and went on. When I awoke it was five-thirty in the morning, and I lay there wondering about the dream. Within a week we had the forty dancers without a problem.

Another dream came to me the next year. The Patrón came and said we would not do the dance, and, sure enough, I could not get the dancers. I came and prayed before him in church and said that it wasn't my fault, and I offered a mass instead, but there was no answer in my blood. So when the fiesta came, I met one of the dancers. They said they were all ready to dance, and why hadn't I brought out the dance. They were going to tell the *costumbre* it was my fault there was no dance, that they were ready. The *costumbre* would push me. I wondered if what they said were true.

Later in the day a Chiquimulteca asked me when I would bring out the Monkeys, and warned me that this is no game. In the afternoon I met another dancer who asked me when I would announce that I was bringing it out. He had dreamed of the Patrón the night before and had been told we would come out next year.

The next day I awoke early and went with my companion Daniel to ask about the dance. He too had dreamed we were in trouble. That night I dreamed that the Patrón came on his horse and said that he had taken care of twenty, and asked me what my problem was.

"But you told me not to bring it out!"

"This year that's true, but next year you'd better!" He was really angry when he rode away.

The images hear what one says and see what one does. This is the mystery [*secreto*] of the images. The Protestants say all of them in the church are but chunks of wood. Maybe it's true, but he who walked with Jesucristo in the first days was Santiago, and this image has power because it has the spirit of Santiago.

Santiago and Momostecan Mythology

The Patrón's relationships with the other images, described largely in terms of sexuality and kinship, were established when they walked the earth with Jesucristo in the liminal period before his death and resurrection as the sun of this world order.

The Patrón's Women
by Juan Ixc'oy

It is said that Santa Catarina and Santa Isabel are his women [*rixo-quib*]. He has a sister [*ranab*], Santa Bartola in San Bartolo.[31] There is another sister also, in Malacatancito I believe, named Munda.[32] Because the Patrón cannot speak Spanish, that's why he came here. The sister speaks Spanish, so she stayed there. This is the way we are today, because this is the way of our *santo*.

Santiago in the Liminal Period.   Juan Ixc'oy also reports that the Santiago of Momostenango is the youngest brother (*chi'p*) of some thirty images of Santiago brought from Spain. Another informant whose name I did not obtain related this distinctively different account:

There were two brothers in Pueblo Viejo. One of them went to San Cristóbal. The other came here to water his horse and he stayed here. His younger brother waits for him in San Cristóbal, but he stays here. The face of the Tiox in San Cristóbal is facing this way because he is waiting for his brother.

In the liminal period Jesucristo and the saints were opposed by Jews, devils, and a nature personifier and oversexed trickster called Yegua

Achi' who wanted to mate with the female saints and was eventually thrown from the roof of the cathedral of Esquipulas by the Cristo of Esquipulas and San Cristóbal.[33] In this story, since Santiago would not share his women (Santa Ana, Santa Catarina, Santa Isabel and María Concepción) with Yegua Achi', Yegua Achi' caused Momostenango to become infertile.

Santiago has another identity in the mythology of Momostenango, this one as a carved and painted image, a power object given to Momostenango in the post-sunrise world. The most elaborate of these accounts, maintained in the Vicente lineage, parallels and updates the Epigonal-Toltec myth in the *Popol Vuh*. Santiago's image is obtained by Don Diego, the Vicente ancestor, at a mountaintop altar at the source of civilization (now Spain rather than Tula). Santiago talks to him in his dreams and commands the founding of a new town. The sons of Don Diego, though, eventually help the Momostecans, aided by the spirit counterpart (*nagual*) of Santiago, to destroy their father's power, symbolized by his ownership of a man-eating *cabwel* (i.e., a *cabawil*). The Vicentes lose control of Santiago, who becomes patron of the pueblo.[34] The Herreras maintain a different account, more favorable to their interests, in which Santiago again appears as a power object bequeathed by elite ancestors to legitimize their descendants' rights.

The Patrón also figures in one widely told narrative concerning more recent times. The following version was provided by a raconteur whose name I did not obtain.

> *My grandfather told me that once there was a war in Totonicapán against the unionists. My grandfather was a lieutenant colonel. When they went to war the image was seen on the battlefield.*
>
> *There was a general, it is said, who passed through the battle, as in the old days the fighting was purely hand-to-hand. When the enemy saw this man passing on horseback in the thick of battle, they tried to capture him or to shoot him, but they couldn't do it.*
>
> *And what was this? The Patrón was helping us! And why? Because when we went forth, a bunch of candles like this [he shows a double handful] was placed before him that he help his people. So he went to the battlefield and the enemy saw him. Our people didn't see him. Our forces won this battle at the place called Chuwi' Utiuh. When a war is near, the Patrón's face turns livid.*

Social Functions and Cultural Meanings of Santiago

The material presented in this chapter serves to place the Santiago complex within a Momostecan system of meanings and within a social and political context. While the details of folk history remain suspect, the political context of recurring conflicts between descent groups, and between rural elites in the *cantones* and the urban "traditionalists" who dominate the *auxiliatura*, seems to be well established. Santiago always is found at the seat of local power and yet, since power never really comes to rest, appears to be almost constantly embroiled in conflict. The history of these conflicts is hinted at by both the competing claims in divergent origin myths and the ways in which his visits to *aldeas* recapitulate his historical associations with *parcialidades* and elite lineages. Most recently, as discussed in chapter 2, Costumbrista *cofrades,* some of whom were in the *cofradía* for many years, were viewed as becoming too independent by both the *auxiliatura* and the priest, and were replaced. The *cabildo* faction then founded a new *hermandad* of their own and built a permanent *armita.* Similar areas of conflict are associated with the municipality's increasing control, always mediated via the *auxiliatura,* over the economic activities of the *cofradía* of San Antonio.

The symbolism of the Santiago complex and its cultural meanings are at least partially revealed through a consideration of the Patrón's role in communalistic ritual and mythology, and of the personal relationships hinted at in accounts of dreams. The four dances, always performed at Santiago's fiesta, depict two themes. The Vaqueros and Mexicans Dances are both about the problems and tensions that accompany death and the transfer of property, and they illustrate this by depicting wealthy *hacendados,* one kind of *patrón* of critical importance in Quichean experience. Cosmogonic warfare also appears as a theme developed in two dances. In the Moors Dance, the forces of Tecum are victorious, while in the Conquest Dance, Tecum is overcome by the Spaniards under Alvarado. Since Santiago is a war captain, and since the politically powerful indigenous "militarist" faction rose to power through service to a local *caudillo,* these are also very appropriate presentations for his fiesta. The Momostecan Santiago is illiterate and speaks only Quiché. He has been transformed from his historical role as patron of the conquistadors into an indigenous war captain, a kind of Tecum.

It is in the expressive media of sign and dream interpretation that Patrón Santiago's personal meaning for and relationships with Momostecans becomes most clear. Here he is seen to be demanding, manipulative, and punitive. The signs that he gives are either prognostications of misfortune to come or indications of his displeasure. His role in dreams seems to be that of making demands for service and of threatening his servants. Yet those who truly serve him are protected and rewarded with good health, with safety on the road and in wars, and with prosperity in their business dealings. He is in fact an archetypal *patrón* as that role has developed in the colonial and neo-colonial phases of Guatemalan history.

REPLICATION IN MOMOSTECAN CULT INSTITUTIONS

The Niño seems in large measure to replicate the functions of the type of altar called the *winel.* Each *alaxik,* a localized clan or lineage segment, maintains a *winel* complex to ensure the productive and reproductive success of its married couples, as well as its milpas, orchards, and animals, through rituals performed by the *chuch kajaw* of the *alaxik.*

Santiago's functions of protecting individuals and families from danger, including witchcraft, are replicated at the local *alaxik* level by the *warabal ja* complex, mediated by the *chuch kajaw* of the *alaxik.* The same concerns are also handled, but for a more inclusive public, by the *mesa* altars and associated four-mountain complex, normally mediated by priest-shamans called *aj mesas.* Santiago's complex is directly linked to that of the Mam and the four mountains through the office of the *chuch kajaw re ri tinamit* (the priest-shaman of the town) who makes offerings on the four mountains and at the Patrón's hidden altar in the municipal palace to protect the municipal officials. The bipartite Santiago/San Felipe icon also mirrors the depiction of the yearbearer as an *alcalde* with a lesser mountain lord as his secretary. Accounts of the native altar complexes document their functional overlap with the cults of Santiago and the Niño.

The Origins of the Native Altars
by Florentino Ixbatz

Our ancestors made the *warabal ja* and the *winel* in the beginning. The *winel* is to protect the crops, to give thanks for the crops. One burns candles in the *winel* to call the earth to protect the crops. This has been left by the ancient ones.

The *warabal ja* is for spooks (*xibinel*). Suddenly one hears people outside and looks and there is no one there, or suddenly large rocks fall on the roof. This is *xibinel*. The *warabal ja* is to protect the house. It is a defense. The *chuch kajaw* burns [offerings] at the *warabla ja* to protect the house.

The *winel* is little, to guard the crop and talk to the earth, but the *warabal ja* is large: 4 E, 5 Aj, 6 Ix, thus it is said. This is for the traveling salesman, for his road, because in the old days they went on foot, to protect them from thieves and perils of the road. Two contents it has. It is also for the wild animals: to bind the coyote, the wildcat, the serpent, all the animals, that they not enter in the house. To protect the sheep, horses, cows, chickens.

They left the *winel* and the *warabal ja* planted for us. The *winel* is for the milpa and the *warabal ja* is to protect the house and the animals, large and small. This is what they left us. The bat comes to bite horses, pigs, and cows. The hawk comes and takes the chicks. We wonder, what can we do to protect our animals? So I arrange it at the *warabal ja,* and now the animals are fine. The *winel* is to protect the maize from *mu'uk*[35] and the worm called *leng* that eats the leaves of the bean plants, and for the *gallina ciega* ("blind hen," a June bug whose grubs damage the field crops). And finally, in the old days there was no good harvest and so the *winel* was invented, and since then there has been a harvest.

Origin of the Altars
by Domingo Castillo

The *winel* is for the milpa, because the milpa comes first. This is the *winel:* 7 Quiej, 8 K'anil. This is for the milpa, for the crop. Because in early times, they say, when they started to plant the milpa, in those days there was no president, only a king. Then the king provided all the seed for all the inhabitants, and there were lots of animals and all kinds of seeds, it is said.

Now when the milpa came up, it only rose to here [he shows a height of about two feet with his hand]. It gave no ears, there was no harvest. They planted a second time, and it happened again. Then there was a third planting. It came up, but there was nothing to harvest. The people then went to inquire of the king.

"Lord king, what are we doing when we plant, what are we doing with the maize? There are no tassels formed, there are no ears."

The king answered them. "Ask the Mundo, ask the ripening of the Mundo, and with this blessing your work will be good."

And so thus was begun the *costumbre* of the milpa, of the *winel*, 7 Quiej, 8 K'anil. This is the first.

Now for the second. Animals entered the milpa; 'possums and snakes, all the animals. Then, as now, this was awful. Among the people there were children. The animals also entered into the houses, and there was the problem of the little children.

"What are we going to do?" asked the mothers and the fathers. Now they already had the 7 Quiej and the 8 K'anil. Thus was begun the *costumbre* of 6 E, 7 Aj, and 8 Ix, the three. These three protect the children, the crops, and one's animals from the animals of the wilds.[36]

MAYA THEMES IN THE CULT OF THE SAINTS

The only two miraculous images in the church share some qualities. They were both *parcialidad* images during the colonial period. They both annually revisit the territorial units (the *cantones*) that have descended from the *parcialidades* in which they functioned originally. They perform the same functions on a general public level that are performed for lineages (*alaxiks*) by their specific *winel* and *warabal ja* altar complexes. In a classic case of what Vogt (1969) has referred to as structural replication, Momostecans have reproduced the same kinds of complexes at various levels of social integration in individualistic, shamanic, and communalistic cult institutions. These two Momostecan saints are integrated into, and seem to emerge from, a cultural pattern that has derived little inspiration from Spanish Catholicism.

The origin myths of Santiago and the Niño treat them as power objects. Within Momostecan Costumbrista culture there are no Catholic saints with official hagiography. Although Santiago figures in some liminal period stories as an active being confronting and overcoming an earth personifier called Yegua Achi', the origin mythology is essentially a post-conquest revision of the Epigonal-Toltec migration mythology telling how the image of Santiago was brought to Momostenango from

"Spain" (a mythical center of civilization) by an intrusive elite lineage. The Niño San Antonio is not a Catholic saint. It is a Baby Jesus removed from its position of sitting on the open Bible of a sixteenth-century statue of Saint Anthony. It is understood by Costumbristas to have appeared in a cave and to be a gift from Dios Mundo. Regardless of the historical origins of the physical images, the meanings of these images are intelligible in the Maya tradition of idolatry rather than the Hispanic or Catholic tradition.

The *cofradías* and dance teams that maintain and perform the cult institutions or complexes associated with Santiago, the Niño, and the two colonial period Cristos in the cemetery chapel also exhibit Maya cultural patterning. Dance sponsors, many dancers, and the leaders of the *cofradía* system—the *alcaldes* and *deputados* who take on multiple cargos and often remain in a position for many years—are motivated by fear of witches and see service as conferring protection. While so protected, and with the aid of their supernatural patrons, they may expand their businesses or purchase new lands without fearing witchcraft. There is a sickness vocation element in many accounts, as service is believed not only to confer protection against future attacks but also to bring an end to existing physical complaints that might interfere with adequate performance in the cult. Thus service is not only linked to legitimization of existing status positions, but is also seen as legitimizing entrepreneurial activities that can be undertaken during the period of service. The gains from such endeavors are rewards conferred by the supernatural patron on a loyal client.[37]

Sodality service, though, is an ordeal that combines sleep deprivation, sexual deprivation, ecstatic dance, and prolonged periods of drinking to intoxication. While successful service confers protection and economic benefits, a dancer or *cofrade* who is of two hearts, who questions the value of the service, frets over its costs, argues with a spouse, engages in adultery, or even has sexual relations with a spouse during a period of obligation will be severely punished. Even an unintentional lapse in *costumbre* can be punished with mental illness or death. Thus there is a trade-off of protection from one kind of supernatural danger for heightened risk of another.

The initial challenge in one of the important *cofradías* is to learn the altar locations and the days on which *costumbre* must be performed. Momostecans maintain this detailed knowledge by breaking it into segments owned by the part-time specialists who staff the sodalities. An incoming member must find out who has the knowledge he needs and make traditional payments of liquor and tobacco to have the knowledge revealed. Once the *costumbre* is known to them, and the period of service has begun, dancers and *cofrades* become obsessed with reading signs. There are two equally important categories of powers addressed by service. A sign or a punishment may originate either with the saint being served or with the *primeros,* the dead *cofrades* or dancers who oversee the work of their replacements.

Sodality service replicates on the supernatural/ritual plane the role of *auxiliatura* service in the political realm. The *alcalde* of an *aldea* mediates between the local community and the external authorities of the *cabildo* and the Ladino nation state. His work is overseen by the *pasados,* the *principales* who have themselves served as *alcaldes.* The *alcalde* of a *cofradía* or the sponsor of a dance mediates between the saints and the local community. His work, on the symbolic plane, is also overseen by *pasados,* but in this case they are deceased *primeros.* The community is represented by its ablest and most courageous members in forging alliances with, and interpreting the moods of, the powerful but often arbitrary and inscrutable external authorities. Through the sodalities, this system is projected into the supernatural by similarly able and courageous volunteers.

This symbolism of communalistic mediation has long made sense in Momostecan culture. The *caciques* largely played this role for their *parcialidades* during the colonial period and continue to play it in some rural *cantones.* It probably also existed in the older *chinamit* cults. These communities were represented by local elites who interacted with the powerful external forces and personalities of a colonialist power structure headed by the *aj pop* and *calel* of the regional *tinamit* and their patrons, lords in K'umarca'aj.[38]

Ethnographic and ethnohistorical data from Momostenango suggest that the earlier *parcialidad* and *guachibal* cults, like modern *cofradías* and dance teams, utilized a restricted membership to represent larger territorial units in the classic form of communalistic cult institutions. They were staffed from within relevant social categories (e.g., more localized internal territorial units like *parajes* or even lineages) that owned the positions,[39] by individuals who received a supernatural calling, often in the form of a sickness vocation. The knowledge of offerings, offering schedules, ritual symbols, and other sodality lore was owned by individuals and passed on to their replacements, in many cases their agnatic kinsmen, through initiatory instruction following traditional payments. In the older system, unlike the current *cofradías* in Momostenango, the leader of the cult would have been the head of the *cacique* lineage that led the *parcialidad,* a position called *calpul* in the sixteenth century and on through the colonial period, and still used to refer to *cofrades.*

Dance teams, like *cofradías,* function today, as they did in the past, as integrative multilineage sodalities within a territorial unit. This is exactly how the Monkeys Dance works in Xequemaya today. Dancers volunteer based on sickness and dreams. Dancing runs in families and the lore is retained in families. Dance scripts today are owned by individuals and passed on to their sons. Perhaps some codices were used and controlled similarly in prehispanic culture.

The modern Momostecan sodality tradition that crystallized early in this century lacks continuity of meaning with the Spanish Catholic tradition in those cases where the same icons are involved (e.g., Santiago and Jesucristo), and also represents icons that do not exist in the Catholic tradition (e.g., Niño San Antonio and San Simón, the latter discussed in chapter 5).

Although San Antonio lacks clear prehispanic iconographic prototypes in what is currently known of older Maya religion, the cult overlaps functionally with the *winel* altars. The modern sodality tradition demonstrates continuity with the Postclassic religious tradition in maintaining two major communalistic cult institutions, one focusing on a corporate patron god with rain, storm, war, and planet Venus associations (Santiago and Tojil), while another, to be described below in chapter 5, focuses on a bipartite complex of celestial deities linked to the overcoming of liminal beings hostile to the human world, to the sun, and to the regeneration of maize.

In the chapters that follow, the focus shifts to expressive culture itself, to the stories that are told rather than the institutionalization of the telling. In chapters 4 and 5, the expressive culture of the Conquest Dance, the Monkeys Dance, and Holy Week are presented with native exegesis to explicate their meanings and to explore their ideological significance.

PART 2. THE RITUAL SYMBOLS AND THEIR MEANINGS

4. Cosmogonic Tree Raisings and Sunrises

At least three distinctive cosmogonies are enacted in the communalistic rituals of the sodalities. Two are presented in this chapter. In one, featured in the Monkeys Dance, a central tree is raised and a four-cornered world is laid out around it. In another, the world is transformed by conflict between liminal beings of an earlier creation and an emerging sun. This chapter explores the sunrise cosmogony enacted in the Conquest Dance. A different manifestation of the sunrise cosmogony, expressed in the Jesucristo mythos, is presented in chapter 5. The third cosmogony, also part of the Jesucristo mythos, ritually depicts the life cycles and intergenerational succession of sun and maize personifiers in major rites of renewal. It is presented in chapter 5. The world tree also appears in the symbolism of this cosmogony, where its flowering and burning are as important as its erection.

WORLD TREES AND MOMOSTECAN COSMOGONY

On Good Friday in 1976, the *cofrades* of Santa Bárbara showed me that San Simón was a flowering cross. I wondered if the Momostecan Holy Week might offer a key to the interpretation of the iconography of Palenque with its foliated cross icon and its depiction of God L as a cigar-smoking old man, almost as if the artists at Palenque had seen San Simón (Cook 1981: 602). Recently, epigraphy and archaeoastronomy have opened up the meaning of the Palenque complex and its flowering crosses.[1] The central panel in the temple of the cross at the northern apex of the group of the cross at Palenque depicts the world tree. From the temple's south-facing portal, the dazzling Milky Way can be observed when, shortly after the solstices, it crosses the center of the sky from south to north. Then it embodies the Wakan-Chah arrangement, the Classic Maya celestial manifestation of the world tree, its base on the southern horizon rising from the constellation Scorpio, and its apex reaching to the eight-partitioned "house of the north," the celestial dome. In Classic iconography this "tree" stood for first father, and for the Maya kings, whose chests were crossed by a double-headed serpent bar. In the celestial prototype, this was the ecliptic crossing the Milky Way. Creation at Palenque was understood to involve the raising of this *axis mundi*, the primordial Wakan-Chah, to separate the earth and sky, and the "seating" of three stones. The *axis mundi* remains an important Mayan icon. For example, in Santiago Atitlán a world tree figures in creation mythology and one is carved in the altarpiece (Carlsen and Prechtel 1991: 33–35, Christenson 1998: 99–103).

In highland Maya village cultures, the ritual of constructing a house — of erecting the vertical posts and establishing the three-stoned hearth — is a sacred undertaking and embodies a humble version of the symbolism of the Palenque creation account, which is possibly itself derived from Formative or proto-Classic house-raising rituals. The prominent place of tree-climbing motifs in Momostecan myths,[2] the erection and climbing of a greased pole by the Tzulab dancers at noon on Good Friday, and the "foliating" of the large cross in the cemetery during Lent represent living cosmic tree symbolism in Momostecan expressive culture.

The Tree in the Monkeys Dance

The most impressive Momostecan *axis mundi* is a twenty-meter-tall pine tree trunk. Trimmed and stripped of bark, it is erected in the plaza just outside the church doorway in a ceremony that takes place every other year during Santiago's fiesta as a central element in the Monkeys Dance (C'oyab; lit., "Spider Monkeys"). The dance begins with an old couple enacting a deer hunt. At the conclusion of the successful hunt, jaguar, lion, and monkey impersonators, possessed by spirits of animals that have been called from the Mundo (Holy World) through a sacred boulder, cross a tightrope from east to west from the roof of the church to the pole and then descend to the west along a slanted guy line onto the dance ground on the plaza.

Santiago's festival comes during the *canícula*, a hot and dry period when the green corn ripens at the very end of July. Freidel, Schele, and

Parker (1993: 116) note that the Chorti call the Milky Way the road of Santiago, and that on July 25 the Milky Way is in its north-south alignment, making the cross with the ecliptic that they refer to as the Wakan-Chah arrangement.[3] The correlation of the Wakan Chah and the Monkeys Dance with its tree-raising symbolism is provocative, and the standing tree trunk, crossed by the east to west rope down which the primordial animal spirits descend from the celestial realm—the roof of the god's house—into the primordial world, is striking Maya imagery.

During the fiesta in the year before a Monkeys performance, the sponsor visits Santiago and promises the dance. A practice pole is set up at his house in January, and six practice sessions are completed there, one each month. On July 17 the dancers go to get their costumes in Totonicapán, and on July 18 there is a vigil with violin and marimba at the sponsor's house. On July 19 and 20 the dancers do their tricks on the dance pole at the *autor*'s (sponsor's) house, and each dancer brings a twelve-arm's-breadth's length of rope which, combined with two such lengths provided by the sponsor, are twined to make the cable used in the dance.

On July 21 the dancers go to town and present themselves to Santiago at the *cofradía* house and begin dancing, but they only do the deer-hunting part of their performance. That afternoon they change into street clothes and go to the cemetery to select a tree. Before sunrise on July 22, they go and cut the tree down, burning copal nodules around its base on nine earthenware roof tiles before felling it. The pole is then erected at noon in front of the church, set in a hole in which thirteen wax candles have been placed as an offering.

During the course of the dance, its official *chuch kajaw* performs daily *costumbre* with the dancers at a huge cliff-edge boulder called C'oy Abaj at 5:00 A.M., to call the animal spirits into them. He burns nine copal nodules at the base of the pole after it has been erected, and burns additional copal at the end of the cable fastened to the pavement where he sits straddling it. This *costumbre* of the pole and cable is to protect the dancers. If the dancers are not also ritually pure, however, this *costumbre* will not suffice, and they may become afraid or be badly burned and cut by the rope or maybe even fall.

There are two groups of dancers: those who act out the deer hunt skit and those who do tricks on the rope. The first group is composed of an old man, Pedro Boston, and his wife, Catarina, also called Xinula (Ladina).[4] They have two dogs, and there are two pairs of deer, large and small. Four Spaniards called *segales* (probably derived from *seglares* [seculars]) ask Pedro to perform *costumbre* for a successful hunt. He visits the four corners of the plaza and performs a deer-hunting skit.

A Jaguar (*balam*), a Lion (*coj*), and two Monkeys (*c'oy*) who are said to be male and female do the tricks on the rope. The dancers are possessed by animal spirits the *chuch kajaw* has called from the Mundo at C'oy Abaj. This part of the dance constitutes a test (*prueba*), viewed in part as a test of skill and athletic prowess, since each dancer works out a unique routine, but it is also a test of the dancer's personal supernatural power. The texts below present a description and exegesis of the Monkeys Dance by Florentino Ixbatz, an initiated priest-shaman of *aj mesa* rank who has served as *chuch kajaw* of the dance and as dance team sponsor. One of his sons, a performer in the dance, also contributed to the texts.

The Story of the Monkeys Dance
by Florentino Ixbatz

There is a man with a book on the story of the Monkeys.[5] He knows the names of the dancers. There are ten dancers with rattles in addition to the ten animals.[6] If I live, next year we will bring out the Monkeys [Dance].

The basis for the story [of the dance] is a hunt. Pedro Boston [or "Botones"; see Paret Limardo 1963: 15] went to hunt at Socop.[7] The animals have an owner.[8] Pedro and Catalina went to arrange a snare to ask for the deer, the lion, the jaguar, monkeys, and doves. The trap is copal incense and candles. The mountains are demanding, so we use copal, candles, and *estoraco* [a tree whose bark is cut into pieces and used as incense].

Anhelo is the first dancer, Vigilancia is the second of the ten. Each dancer has a special marimba tune. The first Deer has his marimba. The first Deer is male, the second is female, but there are two big ones. The first little male Deer has his tune and also the female. The first *segal,* second, third *segal,* also have a tune each. Then Pedro Boston has a tune. Then the Jaguars and Monkeys have their marimbas. Agustín Itzep had a book, but he has died. Pablo Ajtun is called to teach the dancers. It costs forty quetzals, eight practices for each of the forty dancers. Each has received his part on a page at a cost of twenty-five centavos.

The eight Anhelos line up, four on each side. They cross over to circle each other and then return, starting the dance. Then they all go before the marimba to recite their lines, with the two Deer together in between their two lines. Some of the shorter parts cost only ten centavos. I don't know if the man [i.e., Señor Ajtun] is going to come or not. My son can play the marimba. Maybe he won't want to come. Maybe he won't want me to get his book.

When Pedro and Catalina begin to dance, the burning begins with nine pieces of [roof] tile. This is when the rope comes.[9]

The deceased Agustín Itzep had a son and he taught him the *costumbre,* also the names of the marimba tunes, but he forgot it all. Bernardo Vicente taught me about the *costumbre.* I have been *chuch kajaw* for twelve years, and have done the Monkeys *costumbre* six times, once every other year.

When the dance begins, Pedro is seated and the ten dancers come to ask him a favor.

"Jesús, why do all these people come, why not come one at a time?"

"No, Don Pedro, don't be afraid. We only have business with you."

"OK, what do you want?"

"We are going to hunt."

"OK, Spanish gentlemen, son of my *compadre,* son of my *comadre,* why not? There is a trap for the deer. Forests and mountain peaks are possessive so there is a snare. Copal, candles, incense for deer, jaguars, monkeys, and doves. They will all fall."

Because thus it is on the face of this earth, on this prairie, on this plain, on this mountain, because it is all owned.[10]

After this the first male begins to dance, and then the large female Deer and then small male and small female Deer. When they are dancing, the grandfather arrives. The name of this dance is Gather All Together [*mulaj*]. Then they all begin to dance, including Pedro and Catalina. Then Pedro Boston dances alone with Catalina and gives his lines. He tells his story in front of the marimba after dancing. Meanwhile the *chuch kajaw* has gone and begun his *costumbre* under the dance pole.

Then the old man stops in the middle of a ring of dancers and his dogs begin barking because they are hungry. The *segales* meanwhile have gone out to hunt. Then the old woman arrives, and Pedro scolds her for coming so late when he is dying of hunger, grabs her ear, and slaps her twice in the face.

She says, "Can't you see I was lost in the bush?" She gives him a plate with *tamalitos,* but very brusquely, with disrespect. She puts them on the ground, not in his hand. He gets mad. She whistles and gives the *tamalitos* to the dogs.

Then they go to the corners, and Pedro sings that he is going to get his deer: "I am going to place it in my bag." He goes to the four corners and does this, singing in Spanish. Then Catalina asks him to do a favor, but he refuses and she gets mad again.

At this point the rope is attached to the pole, but hanging down to the ground.[11] Then Pedro comes carrying a deer. He has gone to the bush, selected the largest of the four deer standing there, shot it with his pistol and carried it back. Actually he just carries it four times around the square and drops it in front of the marimba.

Then he says, "I am tired from carrying the deer."

Before he kills the deer, he asks Catalina if he should kill the oldest or the youngest. She is with him. She says, "The oldest; the meat is better even though it's tough." Actually Pedro carries a deer home, and another follows Catalina.

Dance Ritualists and *Costumbre*
by Florentino Ixbatz

Ten years ago I was asked to serve as *chuch kajaw* for the Monkeys. Two people came to ask me. There are two books, one with a Señor Itzep, but the better work is with Don Pedro Ajtun. These books have the story, but I know the *costumbre.*

The *costumbre* of the ancestors is to go to the four mountains[12] to ask that the spirit powers of the animals be given to the dancers, and to protect them from evil eye, from bad spirits. In 1940 a circus performer, a clown, witnessed the tests [*pruebas*] in front of the church.[13] He prayed to himself that the Jaguar would fall. To protect ourselves, we burn [offerings] at the base of the pole before the tests. The Jaguar was dancing on the rope when he felt a pain in his rib, and he asked the *chuch kajaw* what was going on. If it wasn't for the *costumbre* he would have fallen!

Then I begin to burn at the base of the pole. This is for evil eye, for bad people, to protect the dancers. The dancers are people, not animals, but they feel nothing when they test themselves on the rope.

[Don Florentino's son (a dancer) adds:] When we are up there and look down and see the crowds looking up, we feel nothing, we are calm. But we feel it when we come down.

[Don Florentino continues:] Yes, this is because of the *costumbre*. The rope is very *delicado* and so is the *costumbre*. There is *costumbre* at the four mountains and Paklom, and from Paklom we go to C'oyabaj.[14] Here it is asked that any outstanding debts of the dancers, problems with the *warabal ja* and with our grandmothers, our grandfathers[15] be put aside. On July 17 we begin the *costumbre* for [protection against] evil eye and everything. First we go to the four mountains to ask for the power. The *porobal* [altar for burning] at the base of the dance pole is for protection against bad people. When there is a lack of *costumbre*, the rope swings violently and increases the chance of falling. The *costumbre* is of God and is also of the Mundo.

[Don Florentino's son interrupts:] At the first *costumbre*, the Jaguar and his companion [i.e., the two Jaguars, one from each team] go with the *chuch kajaw* to Quilaja[16] carrying the copal, candles, and incense to request spiritual power for the Jaguar, and for the others too. The two Lions go to Tamancu.[17] This is their service, but it is for all. The male Monkeys go to Socop.[18] The female Monkeys go to Pipil.[19] Now it is nearly time for the fiesta."[20]

[Don Florentino continues:] The dancers practice in costume for two days. On the third day [July 21] they go to the town center [as opposed to practicing at the dance sponsor's house]. One year they had to have their practices before all the *costumbre* was finished. In this year it was very difficult to erect the dance pole, and the dancers did not get along well. There was trouble. Long ago all the *costumbre* was done six months in advance, in January, and so there were no problems.

This [1976] is a year of *costumbre*. We advise Patrón Santiago of our intention to dance on the twenty-third [of July]. The *chuch kajaw* visits the Patrón at the *armita*. The Patrón has been removed from the church to the *cofradía* house. He says, "*Tat* [father], we are going to bring out the Monkeys this coming year. We ask your help."

And the same is done again on the thirty-first [at the end of the fiesta]. After this, on the twenty days numbered one and the twenty days numbered six, *costumbre* is performed all year, to ask that all the dancers stick with their promises to dance. After this is done, then we erect the practice pole at the [sponsor's] house in January. Then we have a meeting there. And when we practice there, we do the same *costumbre* as at the church [during the fiesta].[21]

To be a Jaguar, a Lion, a Monkey, you have to observe sixty days [of sexual abstinence and *costumbre*]. This runs from the third of June to the third of August. From the third of June they are bound and must burn a candle each day.

A Jaguar now deceased, Antonio Sebastián, had his own personal *costumbre* starting the first of July and running for nine days. He did tricks on the rope that were terrific; [he was] the only one who could do them. He would lie on the rope with his arms out to the sides holding the rope between his ankles.

Those who are false with *costumbre,* the strands of the rope open and bite them, they come down injured, their pants get torn and they are cut on the thigh. To protect against this, they burn their candles and there is a *chuch kajaw.* The *costumbre* of the old-timers was forty days before the fiesta without drinking *guaro,* [liquor] and also no sleeping with women during these forty days. Thus they avoided discord and remained content. The rope bites us [*cutijo ri colop*] if we don't complete the *costumbre.*

Calling the Animals from the Stone
by Florentino Ixbatz

It is said that long ago the people received the dance costumes at C'oyabaj [a place name that means Spider Monkey Stone].[22] Bernardo Vicente told me when I began the *costumbre,* "I have a presentiment if the *costumbre* is going well, but don't forget the dogs are going to be barking in the stone [of C'oyabaj]. You are a good *chuch kajaw* for the Monkeys if you can hear the dogs," said Don Bernardo, "but if you can't call the dogs, then you can't do anything."

And it's true. I heard them howling inside the stone, but only once. Also at that time the spider monkeys came out. The people saw them while I was doing the *costumbre.* All the animals are inside. This is why it is called C'oyabaj.

The butcher, Martín Perez, says his wife went to bathe and saw the lions, jaguars, and monkeys and a man performing *costumbre,* but this was before the time of the *costumbre.* He asked if it wasn't us. I told him, "No, we haven't gone yet." He wondered what it was.

"Maybe my wife will die for this. She is frightened."

What happened? His wife is a Protestant. Maybe she doubted and was shown this to end her doubt. She saw this at two in the afternoon, not at night.

A Señor Pedro Ajanel asked one year, "Are you going to bring out the Monkeys this year?"

"Yes."

"Ah, I found a monkey drowned in the pool, so I thought this was the year." [23]

Diego Ixc'oy was working there, gathering stones, and he wanted to dump over [destroy] the *porobal,* but a strange animal came to his house and scared him, so he didn't go back. He found skeletons of deer among the stones. He wanted to take all the stones because he is of Catholic Action, but he was badly frightened. The animal came to his door. It had four eyes. If he had disturbed the *porobal,* who knows what would have happened. In the bottom of the canyon is the figure of a jaguar. There you have to do *costumbre.*

Erecting the Tree
by Florentino Ixbatz

The Patrón fixed us good one year. We missed a year. The next year something happened. When we arrived at the town center on the twenty-second of July, we had a very thick heavy pole. We began to erect the pole but couldn't get it up. The *síndico [segundo]* and the officials came and asked, "Why haven't you got it up?"

"It's too heavy, and we're afraid if it falls it will crack the cement, and the padre has scolded us about this."

"It's not the padre who is in charge here. That which commands here is our tradition. You have to erect the pole."

We were hungry because it was after one in the afternoon. The *síndico* told us we had to do it, and then we did it in thirty minutes. We were being punished by the Patrón for lack of *costumbre* and for missing the year before. The pole was eight *varas* [that is about eight meters] higher than the church and we had to cut it. We were really fooled by the pole. The priest has said, "From now on, only twenty-one *varas* and no more. You must value human life. These people are not dogs."

The pole was swaying during the first tricks and so Antonio Sebastián said, "In the future, only twenty-one *varas*." He knew a lot. He died during a year of service as a dancer. The Jaguars had wanted a taller pole.

As we had deceived the Patrón [saying we would do the dance and then postponing it], the pole fooled us. It is a tremendous image. So if God and the Patrón give me life, I will say a *novena* [nine days of prayer] to bring out the Monkeys again this year.

There are nine shards of pottery or roof-tile at the foot of the practice pole and dance pole, but those at the dance pole must be new, not used. On the twenty-first of July at eleven in the morning they dance, but no longer in the patio of the sponsor's house, [i.e., the dancers have now moved their performance to the plaza in front of the church] and at three in the afternoon they go to bring the costumes to their lodgings[24] and change into street clothes and all go to the cemetery to look for a tree—the municipality issues a permit—and select one.

The next day at four in the morning they go to the tree with nine tiles and place them around the base of the tree and burn copal, and the Jaguars, Lions, and Monkeys dance around the tree to the marimba in both directions. After this they begin to cut the tree, and when it's down they peel the bark. When the tree is ready, they lay the nine tiles along the trunk and dance around it again.

Also at five in the morning on the twenty-first of July, the *chuch kajaw* is doing *costumbre* at C'oyabaj, waiting for the marimba. The Jaguars and Monkeys get dressed there in the ravine, and then they climb the rock acting like animals. The *costumbre* is performed there daily from the twenty-first of July through the fourth of August.

After the fiesta, the nine pieces of tile are brought and left at the water of the altar of Patrón Santiago [*puja'l* Santiago].[25] The pole, even though it is green, is easily carried by twenty men. It is light because of *costumbre*.

From the twenty-first of July, *costumbre* is done twice daily: in the morning at C'oyabaj and, second, beneath the dance pole. There are fifteen days of *costumbre* twice a day. Also, they drop thirteen unburned candles into the hole before they erect the pole [*cuculeaj ri che';* the word used for "pole" is "tree," i.e., *che'*] in it. So the pole is seated atop the candles.[26] This dance is not done annually because of the large amount of *costumbre*. It is expensive and very *delicado*. The candles are left buried in the earth. I don't know the *secreto* [esoteric or magical significance], but since the beginning of the dance it has been done like this.[27] We find the candles from other years when we open the hole. Wax does not decompose in the earth.

Raising a tree and crossing it with a rope running from east to west at about the time of the Wakan-Chah arrangement of the Milky Way and ecliptic might document survival from the Classic Period of an iconographic complex. The Chorti and the Spanish call the Milky Way the Road of Santiago (Schele 1992: 149), and it seems likely that this is a conscious association in Quiché country. I do not know, though, if any Momostecans relate the dance pole to the Milky Way, or the rope to the ecliptic.

The explication of the Monkey Dance by this village expert calls attention to the difficulties inherent in understanding the significance of the survival of formal elements in the communalistic cult institutions of contemporary part-time ritual specialists. Don Florentino never made even a passing reference to the night sky, nor to any stories of a world tree. I was not aware of the potential significance of celestial counterparts for ritual symbols in 1976 and so didn't ask about them. I certainly cannot state that such identifications are not made by some. I do believe that if this lore existed in the form of conscious models or rationales for Don Tino, it would have been called up as he attempted to make the ritual intelligible to us. Like other Momostecans, he views their communalistic rituals as fraught with *secretos,* esoteric knowledge that perhaps someone else knows, and that was known at one time but has been forgotten. The formal elements in the ritual are still of paramount significance and derive from an ancient tradition. It is living ritual, but the living myth that supports it is the myth of the *primeros* rather than surviving intellectual constructions from Classic aboriginal cosmology.[28]

Don Florentino Ixbatz knows that wax candles must be buried in the hole where the world tree is seated, and sees this as a *secreto* known to the *primeros,* but he doesn't know why and probably no one else does either. Saler (1960) characterized the ritualists of El Palmar as explicit practitioners but vague theologians, a phrasing that seems apt for their Momostecan counterparts. Traditionalists maintain their position in the community by performing its *costumbre* on the grounds that it was established by the *primeros* and has descended from them in a chain that cannot be broken. This rationale, combined with fear of the *primeros* and the desire to retain power and prestige, may be sufficient motivation to retain outward forms for a long period. The survival of formal elements, though, does not guarantee intellectual continuity within a theological or cosmological tradition.

THE CONQUEST AND THE SPANISH SUNRISE

The trauma of the conquest, like the sunrise in the *Popol Vuh,* transforms the world order drastically and all at once, but then is followed in the cosmogony by a creative process of successive differentiation (Radin 1956). Lacking access to detailed records of the past, and lacking a cultural imperative to develop critical historiography, Momostecans are satisfied with telling and reenacting the stories that account for the origins of their institutions.

According to Don Domingo Castillo, the religion called Costumbre—also known as Poronel (burning)—goes back to a time "before the Spaniards came and built the churches." Yet many key ritual symbols in the public enactments of Costumbre are understood to date from the conquest or its aftermath. They are said to be for foreign saints. In one important myth text, Santiago and San Felipe are given to Momos in a post-conquest world by the spirits of Tecum and the other indigenous characters portrayed in the Conquest Dance.[29] These supernaturals, lumped together in Momos as a group called the Principales del Mundo, correspond to the Compañía del Mundo in Atitlán (Mendelson 1959, 1965) and include the K'ak'ic'oxol, the red dwarf who acts as a mediator and patron for shamanic divinitory practice. The origins of the miraculous saints are portrayed as post-conquest but nevertheless autochthonous, a very interesting take on syncretism.[30]

The Conquest Dance embodies another version of the sunrise cosmogony enacted at Easter, and used to be performed during Holy Week. An elderly Momostecan in one of the wealthiest acculturated families from the town center owns the book where the script for the dance is found, and his father owned it before him. This same book is also used to teach the dancers in the neighboring town of Santa María Chiquimula their parts. The Conquest Dance text, probably written originally by Dominican priests and their Quichean counterparts in the mid-sixteenth century, exists today only in Spanish versions with nineteenth- and twentieth-century provenance (Carmack 1973: 168–170, Bode 1961: 216–219). The dance depicts a struggle between the forces of Pedro de Alvarado, whom the Quiché identified as Tonatiuh, the Mexican sun god, and those of Tecum, a personifier of pre-sunrise liminality but also a culture hero deified after death. One Momostecan analogy holds that Tecum would not accept that his time had come and resisted the cosmic process that would elevate Alvarado, just as modern Guatemalan dictators often refuse to leave office when their time has come and must be forced out by the military. According to the *Popol Vuh*, the Xibalbans and the Wucub Caquix (Seven Macaw) lineage similarly resisted the Hero Twins in their roles as the transformative agents of the Heart of Heaven.

Nevertheless, the Spanish conqueror of the Quiché, Pedro de Alvarado, and the enemy of Jesucristo, San Simón, are sometimes identified with each other as a supernatural called Don Pedro, making a one-to-one correspondence between Alvarado and Jesucristo as suns somewhat problematic within the Quichean tradition. Costumbrista thinking about the conquest is ambivalent. This ambivalence is reflected in exegetical comments on the dance myth, in the roles played by conquest characters in parallel texts, and in the anomalous feature of the morphology of the conquest myth that Pedro Alvarado, in the role of the sun, is not killed and reborn.

Interpretations of the conquest range along a nativistic/accommodative continuum. One elder explains that Aj Itz made consistent errors in his divinations during the dance and so misled Tecum, causing the Quiché defeat, while another interprets Aj Itz' gestures to signify death and defeat for the Quiché, a defeat blamed on their leaders for not heeding this warning. There is obviously tension rather than relief in the crowd when, in the most dramatic moment, Tecum is killed. Yet a Costumbrista informant from a family of dancers whose father was Tecum for eighteen years explained that Alvarado wanted peace and the battle was Tecum's fault. All that Alvarado wanted to do was bring civilization and religion. The Spaniards perform *costumbre* at the Ventana Mundo (World Window) altar before riding into town. In this widely held interpretation, shared by many Catholics and Costumbristas, the prehispanic period is a Xibalba and Alvarado is a culture hero, a civilizer.[31]

Yet a prominent Costumbrista leader explains that in the Conquest Dance, though the Principales del Mundo—the Quiché characters led by Tecum—are invited to the yearbearer's fiesta, this invitation does not include Alvarado, the Spaniard, the enemy, for it should be a purely native fiesta. Interpretations of the dance and evaluations of its characters within the Costumbrista community are varied and complex. In the larger community, ideological differences flavor the interpretation of Aj Itz, who is a witch and deceiver for the Catholics and a culture hero and deity for the Costumbristas. Aj Itz' performance is enjoyed by everyone, though, since regardless of what he represents he is funny and since some interpretations and sentiments are also related to issues of ethnic pride that crosscut factional lines based on religious affiliation.

Aj Itz is the focus of Momostecan attention. The only moment in the entire performance that rivals his divination with the *vara* as a moment of excitement in the crowd is the placing of the dead Tecum in his coffin. In both cases, the crowd rushes in close and is so thick that observation becomes difficult.

Characters in the Conquest Dance

There are seven adult Indians and seven Spaniards in the dance who have lines to learn, as well as Malinches — prepubescent girls who dance in front of the palace — and Aj Itz Chiquito and the little Rey Quiché, whose parts are played by boys. The seven Quichés are the Rey Quiché, Tecum (the war captain), Tzunum (the captain who succeeds Tecum), Chávez, Ix Cut, Saquimux, and Aj Itz. The Spaniards are Don Pedro Alvarado (the captain), Carrillo and Cardona (his two ambassadors), Porta Carrera, Calderón, Crijol, and a seventh whose name may be Moreno. Alvarado, reciting 2,200 words, has the most demanding part in this or any dance.

Tecum is distinctive because of his brown face and the quetzal in his headdress. Aj Itz, also called Tzitzimite, is distinctive because his costume and mask are red, like San Simón in Holy Week, identifying him as the K'ak'ic'oxol. The Rey Quiché has a pink face with a white beard. The other Indians have bright pink faces but lack beards, although they all have golden mustaches. All of the Spaniards are pink-complexioned and all have golden beards.

The Action of the Conquest Dance

The plot of the drama may be summarized in ten steps. The description is based on the performance of July 21, 1976.

1. The Quiché people are at peace in their homeland. They are dancing in front of the palace, a counterclockwise round, occasionally breaking up into pairs dancing around each other. The music of the *chirimía* and drum is accompanied by tambourines held by all the dancers except the children: Aj Itz Chiquito, the little Rey, and the three Malinches. The Rey Quiché carries the Guatemalan flag in his right hand and the tambourine in his left. The little girls dance mostly in place; they form a line in front of the palace and hold a handkerchief in each hand. The little Rey and Aj Itz Chiquito occupy the ends of the line. Aj Itz dances with a gold chain and little Aj Itz doll in his left hand and a red hatchet in his right hand. He is dressed in red and has a red face. Aj Itz Chiquito is the same only he does not hold a doll.

This "act" lasts from midmorning until the Spaniards arrive in the early afternoon, but, except for the Aj Itz pair, all continue dancing until war is declared. Sometime before the arrival of the Spanish ambassadors, the Rey Quiché goes up into the palace with a few retainers, and the Guatemalan flag is placed on the right side near the watchtower.

At about noon, Aj Itz climbs the tower and through mime warns that the Spanish are coming and all will die. This is for the benefit of the spectators, but the dancers ignore it. He points to the west and makes a hacking gesture at his legs and chest followed by a hand-flicking gesture. A little bit later the Spaniards come down from their position at Ventana Mundo on the western ridge on the road to Pueblo Viejo. When they reach the edge of town, a *bomba* is fired, and at this signal Aj Itz leaves the palace with his censor and goes to meet them.

2. It is an impressive sight when the Spaniards ride into town, sitting high on their prancing horses. Light glitters on sword hilts and epaulettes, and their golden beards shine like the sun. They are met by Aj Itz on the corner before the bridge west of town on the road to Santa Isabel (see fig. 4.1). Alvarado remains there alone while his companions, accompanied by Aj Itz on foot, ride into town. While one Spanish soldier stands guard with the Spanish flag on the Paklom corner, the others make the rounds to the *alcalde, síndico,* and padre asking permission for Alvarado to enter. Alvarado rides up to the Paklom corner where they await him and delivers a Spanish-language oration to his cohorts, muffled by his wooden mask and the noise of the crowd. Then they all ride around the park four times with Aj Itz running wildly in front, swinging his censor of smouldering chili powder for all he is worth while martial music is played on a bugle. Then the Spaniards group at the Paklom corner again and sit waiting.

3. Aj Itz returns to the palace, and after dancing for a little while he

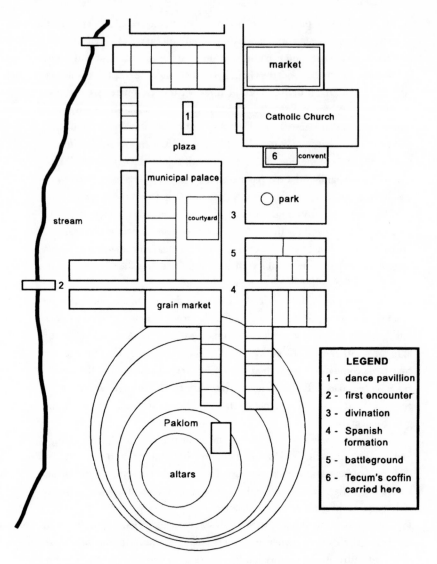

FIG. 4.1. Schematic map of central Momostenango for the Conquest Dance, 1976.

returns with his table, two chairs, and Aj Itz Chiquito. The table is set up in the street between the municipal building and the park and covered with a purple cloth. The crowd surges up close and it becomes difficult to see what is happening. Aj Itz is seated facing the Spaniards on Paklom, and Aj Itz Chiquito has his back to them. Aj Itz dumps out his little cloth bag containing a handful of scarlet seeds and four small rock crystals. It appears to be an actual *vara,* the divining kit kept by initiated daykeepers.

He holds a crystal up before his face, then pushes aside part of the pile and begins rummaging in the rest, selecting beans and appearing to converse with them, miming all the while to indicate that his blood is speaking in various parts of his body. This performance, a parody on the real divining procedure, amuses the crowd immensely.

At this time two Spaniards with unsheathed swords at rest on their right shoulders come down from the corner, the crowd is pushed back, and the soldiers begin walking around Aj Itz counterclockwise and two abreast. In a little while one of them raps the table with his sword, and Aj Itz looks around confused, as if he cannot see them. This is repeated several times until Aj Itz himself is struck, stands, and sees the Spaniards. They begin haranguing each other, brandishing weapons. Then the Spaniards chase him around for awhile.

After another harangue, the two Aj Itzes go to the palace and the Spaniards take their seats and play with the beans which have been left behind. They take turns cleaning each other's shoes with the bag that the beans were in. Later, when the Spaniards are chained, Aj Itz turns the tables, cleaning his shoes and those of the Quiché group with the Spanish swords.

4. Aj Itz reports to Tecum, who has a long unintelligible soliloquy, mumbling sixteenth-century Spanish behind a thick wooden mask while brandishing a blue and white banner with a quetzal emblem on it, the Guatemalan flag.

5. Aj Itz returns to the Spanish ambassadors and, with lots of wrestling and clowning, blindfolds them. Wrapping his long chain lightly around their wrists, he leads them to the palace (a two-story scaffolding structure in the plaza), where they are harangued by Tecum. Tecum tells them in essence that he and not Don Pedro Alvarado is the authority. The Rey Quiché remains alone in his palace while Tecum harangues and finally tells them that there will be war.

6. Aj Itz then returns them to the divining place, from which they return to Don Pedro. He harangues his men and tells them there will be a battle, the strategy of which is outlined in some detail.

7. Tecum and his men are near the convent at the northern end of the street that runs between the municipal palace and the park, while the Spaniards are to their south at the Paklom end of the street. The Spaniards dismount and advance to the drumroll and bugle while Tecum's men advance to the *chirimía* and wooden drum (*tambor*) until the two advancing lines are about seventy feet apart. The music stops and they face each other, the Span-

iards with drawn swords and the Quiché with little stylized one-piece bow and arrows (except for Aj Itz, who still holds his little hatchet). They advance on each other, the Spaniards with a skipping step meant to suggest that they are on horseback. They meet, but there is no real clash of weapons. The combat is stylized and abstract without contact. They surge back and forth a few times, then change sides and do it again and again. During one of the skirmishes, Tecum's bow knocks Alvarado's sword from his hand, an accident that provokes laughter from the crowd. Finally Alvarado and Tecum exchange their weapons for lancelike sticks with their respective flags attached. After a short skirmish, Tecum receives the mortal "blow"—actually he is not touched—and begins staggering to show he is dying, and the fighting stops. His men surround him and walk around with him several times, while the Spaniards form up at the church end of the street and prepare to march to the palace.

While Tecum is staggering around, his coffin is brought. Some cloths are laid in the street and he lies on them while his headdress is removed. Then he is placed in the coffin, quite ceremoniously, while a thick crowd of spectators surrounds the action closely. While this is happening, the Spaniards are marching to the palace.

8. The Spaniards, carrying their flag, march to the palace, then counterclockwise around the dance area several times, and up the stairs and down again while they await the coffin.

9. Tecum's men bring the coffin from the park to the dance area in front of the palace and carry it around counterclockwise. Tzitzimite follows it around weeping and lays the little doll on it, and then follows it off to the courtyard of the convent next to the church.

10. The final scene is a farewell (*despedida*). The Rey Quiché and Alvarado are in the middle of a single line of dancers, with the Spaniards on the south and the Quiché on the north facing the church to the east across the plaza. The line dances forward and backward (east to west) several times. The Spanish and Quiché embrace each other in pairs, and then form the line again and dance briefly, finally kneeling facing the church. The performance ends at about 5:30 P.M. in a plaza packed with spectators but by then emptied of other dancers. Although the action of the dance does not make this clear and the words of the actors are largely unintelligible, the crowd understands that at this time the Rey Quiché and Alvarado agree to have the Quiché people baptized and to become "like godparents" for the orphans of the war.

Additional elements that are not explicit in the performance are read into the performance by knowledgeable observers. Thus, for example,

FIG. 4.2. The musicians' stand represents Utatlán (K'umarca'aj). Note the watchtower pole by the basketball backboard on the right.

it is common knowledge that Tecum only dies when his spirit alter ego or *nagual*, the quetzal bird, is slain, while the Indians slay Alvarado's horse because they believe that he and the horse are one being (see figs. 4.1–4.15).

I obtained a fairly complete explanation of the dance from one of the two Alvarados of 1976 (there are two teams) about a week after the fiesta. Don Miguel had just completed a *novena*, nine years of dancing as Alvarado, and for the eighteen years before that he danced as Aj Itz, first as the *chiquito* and later as the *grande*. His father danced the role of Tecum for twenty-six years, and once hired a band to accompany Tecum's coffin "to make it like a real funeral."

The Story of the Conquest Dance
by Miguel Castillo

Momos and Chiquimula present the complete story using the same book. San Francisco does a shorter, inferior version.

The Rey Quiché is Oxlajuj [13] C'at, while Tecum is Belejeb [9]

FIG. 4.3. Tzitzimite (Aj Itz) climbs the watch-tower. He signals that his blood is warning that destruction is coming.

FIG. 4.4. Aj Itz meets Pedro de Alvarado on the western entrance to town and attempts to drive him away by burning chilis in a censer.

FIG. 4.5. Undissuaded by the acrid chili smoke, Alvarado rides into town carrying his battle flag.

Jun Ajpu. Tecum, Tzunum, Chavez, Ixcut, Saquimax, Aj Itz [and the Rey Quiché], there are seven on the side of Tecum and seven on Alvarado's side.

The Spaniards are Pedro Alvarado, Carrillo, Cardona, Porta Carrera, Calderón, Crijol. All seven [32] have their lines to say. Alvarado is a captain, the others are officials. They come from Mexico. Alvarado conquered Mexico first, then they entered in Xe Quiquel. The Rey Quiché was king of all the Indians, but Tecum did not want to accept the peace. Alvarado sent his two officials, Carrillo and Cardona, to consult with Tecum. Alvarado wanted to make peace, he didn't want war, but Tecum would not accept it.

So here in Momos we tie Carrillo and Cardona; the two soldiers are tied by Tzitzimite with the chain. This is in the story, because Aj Itz was the secretary of Tecum. [33] Then, it just happens that when the soldiers come to have a consultation with Tzitzimite, he is doing his *costumbre*. He has his way, he has his pact, what do you call it—

FIG. 4.6. The battle flag, emblazoned by a little peace or victory sign cut out of a U.S. flag, and the legend "Capitán Alvarado en C.A."

FIG. 4.7. Aj Itz and his younger brother, Aj Itz Chiquito, conduct a divination in front of the municipal palace.

FIG. 4.8. Disturbed by Alvarado's emissaries, Aj Itz stands and looks for them. Note the "lightning hatchet" in his right hand.

a wizard. He does like so [touches his calf], his blood, when something happens his blood jumps, he knows that something is going to happen.

On that day he was sitting raising his questions [i.e., sorting his red beans in a divination] when they came after him. So what he did was, he told them to wait and he went to consult with his lord, Tecum, to see if the Spaniards could enter, because Alvarado did not want war. So Tecum had Tzitzimite bind them like prisoners and bring them before him. Tecum would not accept what Alvarado wanted, so he declared war.

FIG. 4.9. The Spanish army in formation at the base of the Paklom hill faces north down the cobblestone street in front of the municipal palace.

FIG. 4.10. As the two armies clash, Alvarado and Tecum duel with swords.

FIG. 4.11. The swords are replaced by the Spanish and Guatemalan flags. Tecum is about to receive a mortal wound.

He sent Tzunum and Tzitzimite to the Rey Quiché, because before he declared war he sent them. The Rey Quiché said as he was an old man he would leave Tecum in charge. The Rey Quiché had dreamed that something grave would happen. When he dreamed this, Tecum was sleeping, so he sent his two princes.

The story says, "Tecum, Tecum, as you are not vigilant your enemies have assembled. At your doors they have arrived."

This is what the princes say. Then Tecum wakes up and talks to the king and asks for the flag, and the king gives it to him, gives him power. So once Tecum had the flag he was disposed to declare war. He did not want peace. Alvarado came on his horses and sent his ambassadors to ask for peace, but as Tecum did not want this he declared war. Alvarado goes on to say he is more powerful and has better weapons. He doesn't want more than to have peace, to bring religion, but if war begins he will be a cruel enemy.

So when they come back, they tell of their mistreatment and Tecum's declaration of war. Alvarado has another long speech, mostly about how to dispose his troops on the field of battle. He mentions his use of Tlaxcaltecos and the important role of a Spaniard called Moreno. He knew that he would win the war. Now in a place called Pachaj, in San Cristóbal Totonicapán, is where the prin-

FIG. 4.12. The wounded Tecum is supported by his captains. Note his dark face and the quetzal that frames his forehead.

FIG. 4.13. The triumphant Spaniards enter Utatlán.

ces thought to kill Alvarado by shooting his horse. They thought it was one single body. So they killed his horse, and then they entered into war.

But later the Spaniards saw their chance, because the *nagual* [spirit alter ego] of Tecum was the quetzal. Then Alvarado gave a stroke to the little quetzal, as this is not a strong animal and is easily killed. This was the *nagual* of Tecum, and when it was struck then Tecum fell. That which is done in the dance is a symbol, no more

FIG. 4.14. Tecum, in his coffin, is carried around the plaza while the Spaniards and the Rey Quiché make peace at Utatlán.

FIG. 4.15. The coffin is carried into the convent yard to represent the burial of Tecum in a hidden "flowery place."

than that, of Alvarado striking Tecum. But this is not correct. Alvarado struck the quetzal.

After this Alvarado won. This is why the place is called Xe Quiquel [Under Blood], because of the death of so many Mayas and Spaniards, so that blood ran in the streets like water, like a river. In Pa Chaj, in San Cristóbal, is where Tecum fell.

So Alvarado won and put everything in order. The body of Tecum was brought before the Rey Quiché and he sent the two princes. After the battle, Alvarado names Carrillo and Cardona to be ambassadors, or sentinels. He put sentinels immediately at all the points [indicates four with his hand].

So the Rey Quiché sent the two princes to Alvarado and they met Crijol, a general, the last soldier. This Crijol was a sentinel when they arrived. He told them to remain there and he would consult with his chief. Alvarado accepted their embassy and they came to make peace with him.

Tzunum is the one who takes Tecum's place and the flag, and so he wants to continue the war. This is why Alvarado put out sentinels, according to the story. Francisco Carrilas and Juan de León y Cárdenas are in charge of the sentinels.

But the two princes came to say the Rey Quiché does not want war, he wants to become godparents with Alvarado for the little ones, the orphans, male and female. So this is what we do. The princes arrive after the battle and we make a triumphal march in a circle, and the princes bring Alvarado to the palace with the Rey Quiché.

In a speech to the princes, Alvarado treats them with consideration and asks them to be seated, as he is a cultured man and no fool. He blames the war on Tecum. He goes and talks to the Rey Quiché, and they become like godfathers. Baptism came from this. In that time they weren't baptized, so when Alvarado came he had to baptize everybody.

He says, "On Sunday all will be baptized." The Rey Quiché and all were baptized by him, and he became as godfather of the orphans.

So now there is peace. After the war Alvarado has to go with the Rey Quiché and make peace, and after this all get together, the Spaniards on one side, the Indians on the other side; they make two turns behind like this, then they all kneel and say:

Jesús, María Santísima,
[Jesus, Holy Mary]
Jesús Sacramentado,
[Blessed Jesus]
Viva, Reina de los Indios que murió [murieron],
[Live, Queen of the Indians that died,]
Dios Animas.
[God (or "Holy") Souls.]

This is what the Spaniards say when Tecum dies. If Tzunum had been raised up, there would have been another war. When Tecum died and the Rey Quiché received the flag and crown, he ordered that Tecum be buried in a flowery place. Tzunum was in charge of this and did it, but he did not agree with the Rey Quiché on peace and wanted to start a war.

The father of Don Napo had the script [*historia*], and this same script is used by Napo to train the dancers in Chiquimula. Many have told us that they want us to go to Guatemala City with this *historia,* but we haven't. I don't know why. There are 2,200 words in the part of Alvarado, and all must be memorized, but because of the masks and noise these words are often not heard.

Aj Itz
by Miguel Castillo

Aj Itz is the secretary of Tecum. He is not a witch [*brujo*]. He comes to know things through jumps in his blood and using his *vara* [divining bag]. He has faith in the *vara.* If his blood jumps, if he feels something, he asks questions. He plays his game with the beans and learns why.

Aj Itz is the bodyguard of Tecum, he is the medium [*control*]. He channels well. This Aj Itz means many things in our language because he represents many things, and he who sees him sometimes dies.

[Question:] The K'ak'ic'oxol?

[Don Miguel answers:] Yes, he who sees him, it is his fate—it is a bad sign. And the K'ak'ic'oxol is only in the places where there are *riscos, tierras coloradas* [*riscos* are stalagmite-like erosional features;

coloradas are where the topsoil has eroded down to underlying red clays or volcanic tuffs], hidden places he likes.

There are many here who have seen him, and then they die. They are frightened. They are in the bush when suddenly they see him. They stop. They see him in the rocks, or maybe they see the Chiquito [the little Aj Itz]. They get a fever and they die.

Aj Itz has a pact with the evil one, the Devil. So in his story he says he goes to consult with him. This is his only vice, like his sport, his game. But he was secretary to Tecum, and when his blood moved he had a presentiment that the Spaniards would enter and that something grave would occur.

The little doll that he carries is his little brother, a baby, and the Chiquito is also a brother to Aj Itz. Tecum is their father. This is why when Tecum dies he is the only one to cry, because he is the youngest of all the brothers. The three of them remain, a big one and two little ones.[34]

The baby is placed on the coffin to guard it, to protect it and make sure that the Spaniards do not touch the body of Tecum until it is time for Tecum to be buried. Then he [Aj Itz] takes it back in his hand. The chain is because Aj Itz is like a constable, a policeman. The chain is like the handcuffs of a policeman.

The Meaning of the Conquest
by Miguel Castillo

So if Tecum had accepted the peace he wouldn't have died, and neither would so many people. This still happens today when there is a government that doesn't want to make peace or avoid war. Then another [presidential aspirant] declares. As when Castillo Armas entered through Esquipulas and took Chiquimula and Zacapa, and President Arbenz didn't do anything. It was the same as what Alvarado did. It happens that if a president doesn't want to leave his office that another wants to enter, he rules badly and won't leave. This has been explained to me by my father and other elders who know of old times. Maybe he won't give up his office, so a war begins. This is like what happened with Alvarado.

Some presidents are good; they deliver their place without problems. There is an election and a new one comes in. But in the old days the presidents would not give up their places, so war would begin. Tecum wanted to rule only by himself, but it didn't work that way because Christopher Columbus discovered America, and after him the Spaniards came. This was the origin of the Conquest.

There is an altar called Ventana Mundo in the mountains to the west where the Spaniards do *costumbre* before entering town. This is because the Spaniards came with faith in God and prayed to God that there would be peace. He did not want to kill, so he did his *costumbre* with his whole company. But as it was he had to stain his hands.

Who knows how many years old this story is now? From the *caciques* [colonial indigenous chieftains], the Cakchiqueles [a Quichean people who opposed the Quiché proper from the fortified center of Iximche], this story came at first. One died, another remained, so. Now I have nine years of doing Alvarado. At each fiesta I spend 200 quetzals. This is lost money. I lose my work for fifteen or twenty days, and this is out of my pocket. Our *costumbre* costs 125 quetzals. If there were no dances, there would be no fiesta. It is for the dances that people come in from the *aldeas,* from Guatemala, Sacatepéquez, the coast, Quiché. They come to see the history of the conquest.

The Vaqueros Dance is nothing but a bullfight. The Mexicanos is the same as the Vaqueros. The Conquest is the same in Chiquimala. In San Francisco is the second [version]. In Totonicapán is the third. It's not the same. In Quiché also it is different. There is a man from Mazatenango who comes each year, and he says that here in Momostenango is the best history that he has seen.

The Conquest Cosmogony

Don Miguel's account calls attention to an esoteric level of interpretation. The Rey Quiché is identified with the day 13 C'at, and Tecum with the day 9 Jun Ajpu. In Momostecan calendric lore, C'at is the day of the *mesa* altar. C'at is also one of the secretaries of the Holy World in the yearbearer complex, associated in Momostenango with the south or southwest at Joyam.[35] Thirteen is known to Maya scholarship as a number with celestial associations, while nine has underworld associations (see Thompson 1970: 280–282). Jun Ajpu is the principal day of the dead; 9 Jun Ajpu is the day, with its companion 8 Cawek, on which the *chuch kajaw rech tinamit* (the priest-shaman for the town) performs *costumbre* in the *calvario* for the *auxiliatura*. These two mythic personages are, then, personifiers of days having considerable cosmological and ritual significance and representing a symmetry in the way that Momostecans portray the ancient authority structure: The king with celestial and quadripartite directional associations, like the yearbearers, and his war captain a lord of the dead, like Jesucristo and the original Jun Ajpu. Maybe the oral tradition has retained the Postclassic calendric names of these two historic figures (see Colby 1976), but the symmetry of the names seems too coincidental, suggesting a cosmological rather than a historical product.

It was Aj Itz who most interested Don Miguel. Aj Itz is the secretary of Tecum. Aj Itz is his bodyguard and his defense. Aj Itz is the *control* (medium) of Tecum, and also his son.[36] During the fiesta, Aj Itz constantly harasses other dancers. Once he was threatening some Mexicans with his little hatchet and using abusive language. They caught him and gave him a beating that left him staggering. During Alvarado's speeches, Aj Itz strikes poses like the Spanish leader, makes similar flourishes, and otherwise mimics him. He suddenly rushes off the dance ground into the crowd to threaten a tourist with his hatchet. I received several light blows myself one afternoon. He approaches Ladinas and female tourists and holds his little doll near their breasts to be suckled. If someone tries to take his picture, he bends over and shows his posterior, although without dropping his pants.

Aj Itz has many meanings in Momostecan culture. He is a symbol for the mediator between autochthonous (Tecum) and foreign (Alvarado) powers, a mythical cognate of the *auxiliatura* in the political realm and the sodalities in the ritual realm. He also represents the mediator between the dead or spirit Tecum (and by implication the *mundos* for whom Tecum has come to represent the preeminent model), and the living community.[37] In this guise he represents the role of the priest-shaman in an obvious way, as was undoubtedly intended by the original ecclesiastical authors of the drama. In this guise he is defended by the Costumbristas as a diviner who they rightly point out does not practice witchcraft or sorcery in the performance. Nevertheless, in the light of his name, Aj Itz, which has come to mean "witch" in Quiché, and by virtue of the fact that they for the most part no longer accept a distinction between good and evil magic, he is seen as a witch by Catholics and Protestants.

He is a supernatural, the son of a powerful *mundo* who has survived a world transformation. In a widely told story, as the K'ak'ic'oxol he is an assistant to the lord of the mountain who brings a mortal into the lord's presence and then returns him to the world with a magical dance costume. At the same time, though, some informants identify the K'ak'ic'oxol with the Mam (yearbearer),[38] a major mountain lord in his aspect as an *alcalde* of the Holy World who has his abode on one of the four sacred mountains.

The most emotionally and politically relevant aspect of the meaning of Aj Itz in the Conquest Dance is related to nativism. He ridicules the Spaniards. He weeps for his father, Tecum, while the rest of the Quiché nation rejoice in the new peace and their new *patrón*. With his little brother, Aj Itz Chiquito, he embarrasses foreign women, and with his hatchet he enacts the repressed urge of many Momostecans to openly attack the weird, wealthy, threatening outsiders who show up at the fiesta in charter buses and limousines, wearing glasses and hung with cameras with which they will increase their wealth by recording the fiesta to sell in their strange homelands. These foreigners, while opposed by Aj Itz, are linked to San Simón, who wears glasses and an ascot and is said in Momostenango to be a gringo or an Englishman. San Simón and Aj Itz, both dressed in red and playing corresponding roles in world transformation myths, seem to represent inverted or even opposed aspects of the same kind of being.

The Conquest Dance is given a nativistic gloss in which Aj Itz resists the personifier of the new order, in its narrative guise as Tonatiuh/ Alvarado the new sun, and in its contextual guise as the visiting foreigner in the audience, an element in the crowd that he identifies as the Alvarado of an ongoing conquest. Sewed onto the Spanish flag in the 1976 performance, and accompanied by the caption "Captain Alvarado in Central America," was a red, white, and blue cutout in the form of a hand, with the forefinger and middle finger raised in a V-sign, for victory or peace, identifying the United States as the Spain of an ongoing or recurring conquest.

As the K'ak'ic'oxol opposes Alvarado/Tonatiuh, but nevertheless survives the Spanish sunrise that overcomes Tecum, so Simón is an adversary of Jesucristo, and yet is not entirely overcome by the Cristo sunrise which otherwise erases Jews, Devils, and Xibalba. The traditional etymology of "Maximon" (the San Simón of Atitlán) as derived from "Mam xmon" (the bound Mam who is freed to preside over the five unlucky days between solar years) supports this bundled complex of overlapping identities. San Simón, Maximon, and the K'ak'ic'oxol all represent variations of the theme of the underground survival of powers from earlier, superseded epochs.

This leads to consideration of the problematic identification of San Simón with Don Pedro Alvarado, as, for example, in the lore of Santiago Atitlán (O'Brien 1975) and especially at the shrine to Don Pedro at San Jorge La Laguna. There, a glass case in the *armita* of Don Pedro displays a conquistador's plumed felt hat, as well as the cigars and glasses of San Simón. In the light of these substitutions and overlaps, the Alvarado sunrise may also be conceptualized as the rise of San Simón, a return to power of forces that Jesucristo was not able to vanquish completely. Every world-transforming sunrise in the Quichean tradition leaves a remnant of the preceding world order intact, potentially ready to return to power, expressing the Maya millenarian myth.[39] San Simón and Aj Itz or the K'ak'ic'oxol seem to play a similar role as mediators between human beings and the surviving beings of earlier world orders that have gone underground in the mountains. Thus the equation of Xibalba the underworld with Xibalba an ancient and defeated people is a central Quichean concept.

Perhaps Momostecan ambivalence about the conquest cosmogony is given ultimate expression through a morphological anomaly. The Conquest Dance narrative structure does not reproduce the Maya millenarian myth in its complete form, with Alvarado as the transformative sun. In the core or basic type myth given varied expressions in many tales, the sun is killed (Jesucristo by the Jews, the Twins by Xibalba) and then reborn to effect the world transformation. For all of Alvarado's sun imagery, and his sunlike defeat of Tecum, it is Tecum who is killed and buried. This may be interpreted within the Quichean tradition as Tecum playing the role of a false sun, like Wucub Caquix (Seven Macaw) in the *Popol Vuh*, the interpretation favored by Don Miguel and his father, who see Tecum as someone who tried to remain in power after his replacement was on the scene and he had lost his legitimacy. Yet in a plausible nativistic interpretation the rebirth of Tecum is implied as the as yet unrealized transformative sunrise, with Don Pedro, or Alvarado-Simón, playing the role of a temporarily ascendant One Death cognate.

This chapter has considered two cosmogonic models given expression in Santiago's fiesta: the primordial erection of an *axis mundi* in the Monkeys Dance and the millennialistic sunrise myth in the Conquest

Dance. There is a third major cosmogonic model embodied in the cultural performances of the sodalities, one that combines what Mendelson (1965) identifies as the Mesoamerican rain-god cycle with what Carlsen and Prechtel (1991) define as the Maya myth of vegetative regeneration. All three cosmogonies are in fact combined in Holy Week's rich symbolism, where Jesucristo both personifies the maize and arises from his grave as a new sun, the huge old cross in the cemetery bursts into flowers, San Simón is a flowering cross seated at a table in the plaza, and the Tzulab dancers, depicting the young rain gods, erect and try to climb a greased pole. An exploration of the themes and meanings of this ritual complex are presented in chapter 5.

5. Secrets and Ordeals of Holy Week

The Costumbrista celebration of Holy Week takes place against a colorful backdrop of factional displays. There are little services in the Protestant churches, huge masses and processions with hundreds of participants organized by Catholic Action, and crepe-draped and floodlit evening processions by Ladino and acculturated Maya *hermandades* accompanied by rattling portable generators and brass bands playing funeral dirges. The Costumbristas' unobtrusive performances are staged by *cofradías* and dance teams in the cemetery and its chapel, at the cemetery gate, in several *cofradía* houses, and in the plaza in front of the church. *Cofrades* carry images of Jesús Nazareno and Cristo Crucificado in procession, largely ignored by the larger community (see fig. 5.1). They also make pilgrimages that link the saints and the jungles of El Palmar, once a Momostecan colony, to the flowering of the crosses and altars in Momostenango.

Costumbrista Holy Week embodies two interpenetrating cosmogonies. The first depicts Jesucristo as the sun in an enacted version of the Quichean millenarian myth, which has been considered in some detail in chapter 4. The second is a complex expression of regenerative symbolism related to the flowering of the cross and the brief ascendancy of San Simón or Maximon.[1] Two variants of this cyclical model have been explored in interpretive literature on the ethnographic Maya, both times from the perspective of Santiago Atitlán.

The wider relevance of a rain god cycle, reported initially from the Huasteca by Guy Stresser-Pean, emerged in Mendelson's interpretation of the Maximon and Martín complexes in Santiago Atitlán (Mendelson 1958: 6, 1959: 59, 1967). The solar year is interpreted as an expression of the personified life cycle of the rain deities; young "orgiastic" *mams*

FIG. 5.1. Cristo Crucificado procession from the church to the *calvario* during Lent in 1976.

bring the rain and fall with it, fertilizing the earth, later to become bringers of sickness and to end the year as old sterile *mams,* the prototypes for Maximon. More recently Carlsen and Prechtel (1991: 26–27) have described an Atitecan cultural complex embodied in language as *k'ex,* the transmission of life and identity from grandparents to grandchildren, and in myth as Flowering Mountain Earth, the *axis mundi* manifested as a tree or maize plant which is the source of the world, generating the forms of existence as its fruit. They argue that a central Maya concept that Atitecans call *Jaloj-K'exoj* links human generational succession to agricultural metaphors, especially to the life cycle of plants. Momostecan Holy Week symbolism functions as a vehicle for the expression of these related themes, confirming that they are indeed keys to understanding the underlying meaning of a wider Maya tradition (see fig. 5.2).

Sunrise symbolism is enacted at dawn on Easter. The period from the decoration of the cross at the southern entrance into town with flowers at 4:00 A.M. on Tuesday in Holy Week through sunrise on Easter Sunday takes place in the pre-sunrise liminal world. Within this five-day period of liminality, there is an intense crisis period from dawn

FIG. 5.2. Jesús Nazareno procession. Jesús carries a flowering cross from the *calvario* to the church during Lent in 1976. Note the dead cornstalks from last year's harvest awaiting burial with the coming of the first rains.

Wednesday through dawn Saturday, when Jesucristo (Corpus) is dead, his altars are closed, and the Tzulab dance at the cemetery gate. A master chronology of events—helpful in following the complex story that is told in bits and pieces throughout the rest of this chapter and throughout Holy Week—is presented in table 3.

In chapter 6 I will argue that Holy Week has descended from a poorly understood and little-documented rite of renewal of the ancient Quiché, observed and described briefly by Las Casas in sixteenth-century Vera Paz, where he called it an Indian Lent. This tradition, continuing in Costumbrista culture, includes at its heart an ordeal that re-creates a journey to and from Xibalba as the mechanism for renewing the world. Costumbrista Holy Week is a Quichean rite of renewal that makes only passing reference to the Christian tradition.

The *cofradías* organize and oversee visitation with, and adoration of, the two colonial images of Jesucristo called Capitagua and Señor Sepultado (or Corpus), which are kept in the cemetery chapel (*calvario*).

They are also responsible for the temporary erection of the image of San Simón in front of the church, as well as several sacred journeys to the coast to collect greenery and flowers to decorate village crosses, the *calvario,* and the main altar in the church. They carry Jesucristo from the cemetery to the church in the darkness before dawn on Easter Sunday, arriving at the plaza with the first rays of the rising sun. In a communalistic cult institution separate from the *cofradía* system, the Grasejos (Spanish, "fools") or Tzulab (Quiché, "contraries") dance during Holy Week at the cemetery gate and in the main plaza.[2]

All of this together represents a coherent embodiment of Costumbrista cultural themes. Each element is, however, described separately below. Then they are assembled into an overall interpretation of the central meanings of Holy Week. The four main elements in Costumbrista Holy Week—San Simón, the Jesucristos of the cemetery, the sacred journey to the coast and subsequent flowering of the cross, and the dance of the Tzulab—are treated as multivocalic and highly condensed ritual symbols (Turner 1977) which need to be explicated in order to understand Holy Week. This explication leads to an interpretation of Holy Week as the paramount expression of the Quichean religious tradition carried out by the sodalities. Two intercalated stories—one about the rising or returning sun initiating a new world, another about fertility and regeneration in the life cycle of anthropomorphized nature—are embodied in these communalistic cult institutions. Their enactments renew the world.

SAN SIMÓN

In Guatemalan towns and cities, a straw image of Judas is constructed during Holy Week and usually hanged and burned. In the highland Maya towns the image, called San Simón or Maximon, combines attributes of a mountain lord (*dueño*), a Catholic saint, the Maya old Mam or outgoing yearbearer, and Pedro de Alvarado, the conquistador.[3] In Momostenango, San Simón is a central ritual symbol in the Costumbrista Holy Week. Maximon is also a miraculous image, with year-round visitation at shrine centers along the southern edge of the traditional Quiché world. This Maximon has become a supernatural patron for many Guatemalans, both Ladino and Maya, representing all social classes, and has an increasing international following (see Chicas Rendón and Gaitán A. 1995).

Table 3. The Holy Week Chronology

	Flowering Cross	San Simón	Corpus or Jesucristo	Tzulab	Candles and Miscellaneous
Saturday	Cofrades leave Momos.	Bunchgrass is collected at cumbre by alcalde of Santa Bárbara.	Warabal ja is opened for Corpus fiesta.		
Palm Sunday	Cofrades collect flowers at El Palmar.		Warabal ja is opened. Corpus fiesta.		
Monday	Cofrades return to Momos.		Warabal ja is opened. Corpus fiesta.		
Tuesday	Cofrades decorate cross at south entrance. Night: present flowers to mask of Simón and cofradía saint. Flowers viewed by thirteen teams.	Night: mask greets flowers at foot of cofradía saint.	Warabal ja is opened. Corpus fiesta.		A.M.: candles come from Antigua.

		Crisis Period Starts		
Wednesday	Cofrades decorate cemetery cross. Replace Corpus crown with flowers.	Warabal ja is closed. Dead Corpus placed on table. Crown replaced by flowers.	Dance at cemetery.	
Holy Thursday	Body made. Night: mask on body. Viewed by thirteen teams. All-night vigil. Simón seated in plaza. All-night vigil at *armita*.	Dead Corpus on table.	Dance at cemetery.	P.M.: *varas* and *cofradía* emblems replaced by candles. Night: mini-*carnaval*.
Good Friday	Simón seated in plaza, burned at noon.	Dead Corpus on table. Until 1950s Corpus was crucified.	Dance at cemetery. Climb greased pole in afternoon.	
		Crisis Period Ends		
Saturday		*Warabal ja* is opened.	Dance in plaza, with snake if they have one.	
Easter		*Warabal ja* is opened. Dawn procession of Señor Resurrección.	Dance in plaza.	At mass, emblems and *varas* returned.

The Atitecan Maximon image, the most important Maximon for Mayanist scholarship, is a wooden puppet that lacks arms, has jointed legs and a jointed neck, and has a gourd or wooden blank for its head. It is wrapped in corn husks and rags and is then dressed in several layers of clothes. The face is a mask made to replace one stolen by zealous priests in 1950. An older mask, made by a native prophet named Francisco Sojuel, is kept hidden (Mendelson 1959: 57). In the 1950s Maximon was kept disassembled in the attic of the *cofradía* of Santa Cruz, and assembled and displayed between Tuesday night and Friday afternoon of Holy Week and on the fiestas of San Miguel (September 29) and San Andrés (November 30). Today the image remains constructed year around, and is visited by pilgrims at the *cofradía* house of Santa Cruz. It has also come to have its main fiesta on October 28, like other shrine center Maximons.

Atitecan folk history accounts for the origin of Maximon as being when the important turn-of-the-century prophet Francisco Sojuel felt that the straw San Simón of Holy Week should be made of wood like other saints (Mendelson 1959: 58). There is also an origin myth that it was constructed by several powerful diviners to prevent the seduction of village wives while their husbands were away on business. They carved a talking tree into a puppet. Dressed in Atitecan clothing, the puppet was set to guard the village, but it became a seducer of men and women itself and had to be rendered harmless (Mendelson 1965: 131–133). In a more complex variant of this myth (Tarn and Prechtel 1986: 177–78), Maximon is carved from the *tzité* tree as part of the original creation in order to control the sexuality of a sterile witch named María Magdalena, whose seductions drive men mad and destroy fatherhood. Maximon overcomes María, but becomes a bisexual seducer himself and so must be taken to pieces. To control him, a wife named María Castellana is made from part of his own body. This Maximon has two wives, an old indigenous sorceress named Francisca Batzbal and the flirtatious young Ladina María Castellana.

Ruth Bunzel (1952: 223) noted strong anti-Ladino symbolism in the Judas ritual of Chichicastenango and Momostenango, where Father Rossbach had stopped it because it was sadistic. Informants reported that the image had to be burned so it would not walk around frightening people (1952: 414). Eric Thompson (1950: 133) had discovered that the Kekchi Maya in Alta Verapaz had transferred the symbolism of the burial of the old Mam, their yearbearer, to five days during Holy Week, but he had not linked this to the Maximon figure. Then, following his careful study of the Santiago Atitlán Maximon complex during field-work in 1952 and 1953, Mendelson argued convincingly that the transitional five-day *uayeb* of the ancient Maya had been inserted into Holy Week, with Maximon as the old yearbearer or Ocel (Mendelson 1958: 6–7, 1959: 59, 1967: 406–408), an argument that has gained general acceptance (Thompson 1970: 299). More recently, Dennis Tedlock (1993) has argued that the syncretized Maximon, which he calls Grand-father Judas, originated in April 1773 when the Maya yearbearer's new year festival came during Holy Week and immediately afterward Antigua was destroyed by an earthquake.[4] The Quichean Maya then transferred the symbolism of the five unlucky days at the end of their year to Holy Week, linking their Ocel, the old Mam bound in the earth, to the Hispanic Judas Iscariot figure, creating a composite icon, Mam-Simón, or Maximon (Tedlock 1993: 221–222).[5]

In Atitecan thought, Maximon is the old Mam and little angels associated with San Martín are young fertile *mams* embodying the core Mesoamerican rain god cycle in which orgiastic rain godlings annually age into old sterile bringers of sickness (Mendelson 1967). In an early interpretation, the Atitecan conflict between Maya worldview, represented by San Martín, and Christian worldview, represented by Jesu-cristo, was seen as mediated by Maximon who, as Judas the traitor and also as *dueño* of the daykeepers, represented the uneasily syncretized Costumbrista tradition (1958: 5).[6]

The dramatis personae in the Holy Week presentation in Momos-tenango correspond precisely to the three-part symbolism of Atitlán. Maximon is San Simón, the Martíns (or young *mams*) are the Tzulab dancers, and Jesucristo is embodied as Corpus. These seem to represent three separate kinds of beings portrayed in the drama of renewal. Yet Momostecan mythology links the Mam as Pastor del Mundo with Jesucristo and depicts the Mam as a shepherd with his whip over his shoulder, the image of a Tzulab dancer. Thus all three beings overlap. They represent variants on a single idea, perhaps aspects of a deity or, more probably, considering the aged attributes of Simón and the uncontrolled sexuality of the tricksterlike Tzulab, the Stresser-Paean type stages in the life cycle of some generic and multifaceted rain god/maize god/fertility deity.

The Maximon of the shrines may be a late-nineteenth-century development, while the linkage of the Holy Week Judas with the Ocel probably dates back to the eighteenth century or earlier. A search for the meaning of San Simón to the Quiché may legitimately focus on the more widespread, and probably earlier, venue of San Simón in Holy Week. The setting for this inquiry is Momostenango in the 1970s.

The San Simón of Momostenango

In Momostenango, the term "San Simón" is used far more commonly than "Maximon," and the Momostecan representation of this deity, constructed during Holy Week, is denoted as "San Simón rech waral" (San Simón of here) to distinguish it from the images at the southern shrines.

The mask and clothing for San Simón are kept in the *cofradía* house of Señor Resurrección (Corpus). Each year the *cofrades* of Santa Bárbara, San Miguel, Santa Ana, and San Pedro Galuna are responsible for making the body for the image, dressing it in its clothes and mask, and setting it up in the plaza in front of the church. Then it is seated at a table in the shade of a large willow branch or cut sapling. Bunchgrass for the body is collected near Joyam, a major altar in the highland zone (*cumbre*) south of Momostenango on the road to San Francisco El Alto. The deep scarlet pants and jacket are made of Momostecan wool died with cochineal. The other clothes and appurtenances, such as glasses and handkerchiefs, are given to the image by the faithful. The mask appears to be the only element with inherent power, but the bunchgrass cross that forms the body is assembled under ritualized conditions, and the whole image, once assembled, is treated with simultaneous respect and disdain.

The *alcalde* of Santa Bárbara bears responsibility for making and caring for the image and is the *alcalde* of San Simón, but the thirteen teams are all present in the *armita* of Corpus when the mask is placed on the completed image on Wednesday night of Holy Week. The sixteen men of the four *cofradías* have maintained a minimum of nine days of sexual continence and *costumbre,* and the *cofrades* of Santa Bárbara have kept twenty days, having just returned from a ritualized journey to El Palmar, which is described below. The public display begins at dawn on Holy Thursday. On Wednesday and Thursday nights the four *cofradías* keep watch over the image at the *armita* of Corpus.

At noon on Good Friday the image is taken into a walled yard near the plaza, undressed, and pulled apart, and the heaped straw is burned along with the willow "tree" that shaded the image. The burning of the "two companions"—*ts'oloj che'* (*sauco;* a willow) and *iquim* (bunch-grass)—is noted as an important symbol by informants, but it is not ritualized.[7] No shaman is present, and the *cofrades* ignore the burning, which is carried out by an assistant, while they count and divide up the money offerings that were left at Simón's table.

In 1974 Simón was first publicly presented at 5:00 A.M. on Holy Thursday. He was seated all day on a wooden chair with a table before him in the scant shade of a large willow branch in the cement-paved plaza opposite the church near the Costumbristas' altar but facing the church doors. The image wore a red woolen jacket cut like a suit jacket, red pants, and black shoes. Cigarettes and a pair of glasses with one cracked lens were tucked into the jacket's breast pocket. A paisley ascot was around its neck and a red bandanna was around its head. The face was a red enameled wooden mask with black hair and a black mustache. A straw hat was on its head, and four more straw hats were in the branches of the willow.

On each end of the table were shallow enamelware pans containing dried maguey leaves, which were said to be fish (*car*). A pair of dice, several balls of copal incense, and a little metal cup containing chili sauce and a spoon occupied the center of the table, while a row of bills of foreign Central American currency was arranged immediately in front of the image. A tied bundle of dried thorny branches of the sort that are sometimes used to inflict a very painful whipping were under the table. The image's drinking glass and his ashtray were placed on the side of the table nearest the younger men who served him his drinks and smokes.

The image was flanked by two benches. On the bench at its left hand sat four hatless older men, the *alcaldes* of the four *cofradías,* with Santa Bárbara nearest the image. On the bench to its right, four younger men were seated wearing white straw hats. One of them would rise periodically to gently tap the ash from the cigarette burning in Simón's mouth[8] or to put it out and light a fresh one by holding the end in a match flame until it ignited without putting his own lips to it. From time to time Simón was served a drink. *Aguardiente* or wine would first be poured into a water glass; then, while one of the young men tipped the chair back, another would pour the drink carefully into the mouth of the mask. Drinks were served all around, starting with the *alcalde* on Simón's immediate left. Simón was served last.[9]

When I approached the table there were only five or six spectators because nothing was happening. My presence quickly attracted a crowd of twenty or so men, women, and children aware of the opportunity I represented for the *cofrades* to make jokes. In 1974 the joking was low-keyed and friendly, the *cofrades* claiming that Simón was my brother, that he spoke English, and that we were both gringos. The glasses in his pocket were a sign of his gringo identity, and they would not believe that I did not own any glasses. The *alcalde*, a very polite and dignified elder somewhat more serious than the others, explained that they were *cofrades,* that they were in charge of the saints from foreign lands, and that Judas was English.

I also visited the image during Holy Week in 1976. On that occasion the jokes were a bit more outlandish, had a strong sexual component, and the general feeling seemed to be rather more tense than in 1974. The *alcalde* in 1976 was a different man than in 1974, and was very drunk at 7:30 A.M. on Holy Thursday when I went to see the image. He began by saying in Quiché that the image was my father. He made some remarks about *tziquin,* the Quiché word for bird that in Momostenango also means penis, while pointing to the image's groin.[10] He requested that I donate my organ to the image, pointing to the image's genital area and then holding his cupped hands under my own and gesturing towards the image as though transplanting a seedling. The spectators found this quite amusing.

I was asked to sit on the bench with the younger men. When I did so they all got up in unison, which again resulted in laughter. The *alcalde* then began asking me whether I kissed or maybe ate girls or penises (*catij la ali* or *catij la tziquin*). Another joke was to ask me whether one of the young men present was my son or my father. The joking was interspersed with requests that I buy some of their fish at ten centavos a pound, or that I give Simón some glasses or a hat. I was repeatedly asked whether Simón was pretty (*jelic*) and good (*utz*). No one laughed during this part of the performance. The crowd of spectators was small, about fifteen people. The Quiché, mostly men and boys, found it very funny, but an elderly Ladino visitor who was rooming in the *pensión* frowned in clear distaste and disapproval. In 1974 the remarks seemed primarily to concern the gringo identity I shared with San Simón; in 1976 they focused on our shared sexual irregularities.[11]

The more hospitable *cofrades* in 1974 invited me into the closed courtyard to watch the burning of the image on the afternoon of Good

Friday. Simón in his chair, the willow "tree," and a bundle of faggots from under the table were carried to the door in a high wall northwest of the plaza at noon. The *cofrades* went in and, to my surprise, invited me to enter with them. No one else was allowed to enter. Considering what I took to be their desire for privacy, I expected to see something ritualized and esoteric that would reveal the meaning of Simón. I was disappointed when they unceremoniously stripped the mask and clothes from the bunchgrass cross that formed the body, calling my attention to the fact that it was a cross, laid the liquor-soaked clothes in the sun to dry, hung the mask in the branches of a tree, cut the vines that held the bunchgrass together, heaped it up with the faggots and the *ts'oloj che'* (willow) cut into two-foot lengths, and started it burning. No incense was burned. No one chanted or prayed. In fact, the *cofrades* ignored the burning altogether while they divided up the 1.50 quetzals or so that people had left on Simón's table.

They left a young man tending the smoldering hay and staggered out into the street. Shortly afterward I also left. I was later told that the ashes of the willow and grass, along with the preserved ashes of all of Simón's cigarettes, are buried in a small cave near the site where the bunchgrass is burned. I was also told that the grass from his body is very efficacious for making protective crosses, but I saw nobody attempting to save any. The *cofrades* said they would sell me the grass for seventy-six quetzals, an offer that I declined. While the final disposal of the body seems to be a very mundane affair, its initial preparation and handling up until noon on Good Friday are ritualized and fraught with signs and dangers.

San Simón
by Juan Ixc'oy

The origin of San Simón here in Semana Santa [Holy Week] is by the *cofrades* of Galuna, Santa Ana, San Miguel, and Santa Bárbara. These four images have to take care of San Simón. This Simón is of bunchgrass, nothing more, but it is very *delicado*. When the eight *mortomas* go to get it they only select the bunches in briar patches or in ravines where no people have been.[12] The *mortoma* must go with his machete and his brush hook [*os*]. If they bring this good grass the image is straight like a man, but if they bring soiled grass it droops and sags. Santa Bárbara is in charge of this.

There are nine days of *costumbre* before Holy Wednesday. The sixteen men [four *cofrades* from each *cofradía*] have to observe continence during this time, and when this *costumbre* is well done by Santa Bárbara the image looks real straight. On Holy Wednesday the thirteen teams [*oxlaju chop'*] come to see how the image looks. If it looks bad, then Santa Bárbara is in trouble.

The clothing is in the *cofradía* of Aj Señor because it has great significance [*nim u bantajic;* "great its making"]. Thus it is that I have seen the San Simón of Momostenango. He has his power. We got his new clothes for him, and he protects us. My companion in making the outfit was Anselmo Itzep. Because we saw that his clothing was old and patched, Anselmo asked me where we would get the material.

"We'll weave it ourselves and dye it with cochineal." This is just what we did, and it came out fine. A *cofrade* of San Miguel bought him new shoes.

Now once I went to Sam Pras [the neighboring town of San Francisco El Alto] and left a bundle in a food booth while I went and had a drink. When I opened it later there was a new shirt in it that I hadn't put there, so I decided to give it to San Simón. A man had told me earlier that if we made him clothing it would be nothing compared to what he would give, and it was true. I went to Xela and a man offered me a tie for sixty centavos and I got it for twenty centavos. It was cheap because of the power of Simón.

After this I went to the *porobal* [altar] to thank him for these things. I asked Simón to take care of the man who had left the shirt, to bless both of us, and also that nothing happen to me. The man might have left the shirt by mistake, and when he came back it was gone. He might have lit a candle against me.

A *cofrade* of San Miguel got new boots. They had belonged to a man who died of alcohol intoxication [*goma;* a hangover]. They were worth 8 quetzals and he got them for 1.50 quetzals. So we have seen that he has his miracles. We got everything cheap. So we got his clothing and hardly felt it in our pockets. He always protects our business dealings.

Now, about his *porobal.* Nine days before Holy Wednesday it is opened, and it is closed on Monday after Easter.[13] This *porobal* is on the Paklom, and Santa Bárbara is responsible for this.

This year Simón was fat but floppy, so the sixteen *cofrades* responsible for this were called by the thirteen teams, and then they called the *alcalde* of Santa Bárbara and said it was his fault. His *costumbre* was lacking. Only bunchgrass in flower should be used.

When he [Simón] is seated[14] he is given his drink, because this is the custom. Sam Simón is made in the *armita* of Aj Señor,[15] and when he is seated the thirteen teams come to see. The sixteen *cofrades* have a double expense. They have to give an *octavo* [an "eighth" of *aguardiente*] to all the *cofrades* of the thirteen teams, two *octavos* to San Simón, and four packs of cigarettes. Every little while he is given a drink, and in between he has his cigarettes, and the cigarettes do not go out. Now, if we light a cigarette and do not smoke it, it will go out![16] There is an ashtray for the ashes.

He is brought to the property of Narciso Cifuentes [a Ladino] to be burned, and there is a little cave where his ashes and the ashes of his cigarettes are buried. Before this we give Don Narciso a dozen eggs for the use of his property. All the straw spilled at the *armita* is burned at this time also. The place where he is burned has not been changed. Who knows how old it is? The owner always gives permission, and when one dies the new one will do the same.[17]

On Holy Thursday he is kept in the *armita* all night, and there is a vigil there by the sixteen with his candle lit. Four pounds of candles are needed for the two nights, and the *cofrades* sleep with him. There are two nights of vigil, Wednesday night and Thursday night. On Monday his *porobal* is closed. The content of this is that it is done at the same time the saints are returned to their cabinets in the church, because Simón walked at the time of Jesus, and was his enemy.

The *alcalde* of Santa Bárbara directs all this. The other three have little to do. Santa Bárbara arranges the *costumbre*, the other three contribute. The *alcalde* of Santa Bárbara has to drink as much as is given to San Simón, two *octavos* each, and when the thirteen teams come they bring four bottles of wine and each has a cup. What is left, about half a bottle, must be finished by Santa Bárbara.

The mask of Simón is with Aj Señor [i.e., Señor Sepultado or Corpus]. When the *alcalde* of [the *cofradía*] Aj Señor sees that the mask is dirty, he reports to the thirteen teams and they say, "Go ahead, it's your duty."[18] So he has to put candles before the mask for nine days before he goes to the mask maker in San Cristóbal. The painter there does not charge to repaint the mask because it's of San Simón.

He says, "We always pay masses for San Simón, and so we *moreros* [dance mask makers; from *moros*] always have the force of Simón with us."

Last year it had been seven years since it was painted, and so Aj Señor took it to be retouched. This has to be done on good days: Aj, Ajmak, Quiej, or Ak'abal.

When flowers are brought from the coast on Tuesdays during Lent, the *cofrades* sleep at the cross in Los Cipreses, and then on Wednesday morning that cross and the one at Two Heads are adorned and rockets are fired.[19] Then the flowers are brought to the *armita* of the *cofradía* that made the journey, and with violin music they are presented to the mask of San Simón that is there to receive them.[20] It goes out six times each year for this. It is put with the image if there is one there. On Tuesday the image is removed from the church and Aj Señor brings the mask to the *armita* and it is placed below the image facing forward.[21] This takes place during the forty days that Simón walked with Jesucristo.[22] Then on Wednesday the mask is placed on the body.

Momostecans visit Maximon in other towns as pilgrims. Juan Ixc'oy notes that there are ten Maximon shrines, but he only knows of seven: Zunil, San Andrés Xecul, Cantel, Noguero (Sololá), San Jorge (near Panajachel), Santiago Atitlán, and San Andrés Itzapa. With the exception of San Andrés Itzapa, these are all in the departments of Quetzaltenango or Sololá. Three out of the seven are directly associated with Lake Atitlán, and all lie along the southern margin of the Quiché region.

Visits to Maximons in Other Towns
by Juan Ixc'oy

A *chuch kajaw* went with us as our guide because we didn't know the way, where the altars were. We went on this pilgrimage because our parents [*ri kanan katat*] had bought a field in Cho k'inom, but the neighbors there didn't like it and bewitched my father [*xquiban itzibal*], so we went to ask a favor because of the witchcraft that had befallen us. We were six brothers and now only two of us are left because of this evil. We are still alive, but at what a price. My brother now is blind from the evil [*rumal ri itzibal*], but his woman is a go-getter, a hard worker, and he takes care of himself. I am all right because I have fought with the *costumbre*. My brother spins, but because he is blind even this is difficult. They have no children. All because of the witchcraft directed against our father. So for this reason I went to my *chuch kajaw,* and we went to San Jorge to ask for help. My last brother who died, we buried him on February sec-ond before the earthquake. If we had died in our house, who would have buried us?

There, in San Jorge, there is a San Simón.²³ The sacristan there is a good man who let us use his pots to cook, and gave us firewood, and prepared the censer for us. The sacristan asked if we wanted to go directly with Simón. We said no. For this we would have to ask permission. Our license was with San Jorge. The *chuch kajaw* had not told me that Simón was there. Without license he would not have listened to us.

The sacristan agreed that this was true. He related a story:

"Here at the end of November is the fiesta of San Andrés.²⁴ Two men came from the shores of the lake. Believe it or not, one was crying. He went to San Simón, and I followed to see what was happening. He was crying and shaking Simón by the shoulders and saying, 'If you really have power you will do what I ask.' Then he left.

"Later during the fiesta, this man's pants fell down to his feet in the plaza in front of everyone and he didn't even notice, he didn't feel anything. So later he came back crying with shame and asked me what he should do about San Simón, because he had thought that he had no power, but now he knew better. This is something incredible, but I have seen it!"

I have seen a Simón that is in Zunil. He is given a whole *octavo* to drink, and who knows where it goes. Once I brought candles for some others, but I warned them that they would have to observe the four days because Simón is *delicado.* I went to Zunil and arrived at the *ujuyubal* of Simón that is in a cave, and I began to burn [offer-ings]. When the fire was burning, I poured in an *octavo* and I drank one myself, and I began to burn incense and candles. Five minutes after I started burning, the *guaro* [liquor] came up again and I nearly drowned.

Maybe this was because the people had not observed the four days? I got a sign from my blood. Something had happened in the house! I suspected that it was a man from Patalup who had given me candles.

When I returned, I was at Simón's altar at Paklom at seven in the morning giving thanks. You have to ask permission there before you go to visit. The man from Patalup was supposed to meet me, but he didn't show up. In a few hours his brother arrived.

"Today we are burying my brother. We went to cut firewood and a tree fell on him."

I told him how I had a sign of this in Zunil. So I saw that San Simón is very *delicado*. When the tree fell on him, his woman went to him and pulled him out. Maybe he had gone with her, or maybe with another woman and so had fallen in the trap. The woman said that she had observed the days, so maybe it was with another woman.

There is also a Simón in San Andrés Xecul. All are the same, and they are all *delicado*. I visited the one in San Andrés. There were lots of people in the room. They brought liquor by the gallon and gave a cup to Simón, and then one to everyone in the room. I didn't feel well and didn't want to drink. The man said it was OK, and so I continued with my *costumbre*. The result came later.

A friend came by to visit and offered me a drink, and I drank 1½ *octavos* and I found that I was shaking with cold. He said I should have another to warm myself, so I did but I only got worse. This must have been because I refused to drink with San Simón. I went to the *porobal* and asked his forgiveness and permission to visit again. The second time I drank with him, and this hasn't happened since.

San Simón and the Mesa

One of the hidden meanings (*secretos*) of San Simón in his public presentation during Holy Week is that he is a cross. It follows from this, as another *secreto,* that the little tableau in which his image is displayed is a representation of the *mesa* altar, a tablelike slab of stone set across supports of stone with a cross behind it. San Simón is a cross seated behind a table. The *mesa* is the altar associated with witchcraft and defense against it. The altars on the four sacred mountains where the yearbearers are seated are *mesa* altars. Only initiated priest-shamans with the rank of *aj mesa* may burn offerings at *mesa* altars, for which a day C'at is preferred. Its cross is decorated with pine branches, that is, it is "flowered." Like San Simón in the plaza, it becomes a flowering cross at a table.

The Rey Quiché in the Conquest Dance, the old king who authorizes the war fought by Tecum and later makes peace with Alvarado, is linked to the day C'at, as noted in the explication of the Conquest Dance in chapter 4 above. The day C'at, its *costumbre,* and the mesa altar itself have strong associations with aged authority figures. This *secreto* links San Simón to the yearbearers, strengthening his identification as the personification of a *mam,* the old Mam, the Ocel or patron of the five "unlucky" days. It also provides a model for a Quichean visualization of the *mesa* altar on a sacred mountain. The yearbearer, the lord of the mountain, stands behind it as a flowering cross. San Simón is a flowering cross dressed in human clothes, as the talking crosses of Yucatán are dressed in *huipiles* (loose-fitting blouses).

CORPUS AND SANTA CRUZ

The image of Señor Sepultado, more commonly referred to as Corpus, is a small colonial image of the reclining post-Crucifixion Jesus. It is kept in a glass case in a "cave" excavated into the wall and floor at the east end of the *calvario,* a whitewashed adobe building whose doors open to the west. The *cofradía* of Santa Cruz is responsible for washing the clothes and caring for the image under the supervision of the *cofradía* of Aj Señor (Señor Resurrección), the chief of the *cofradías* and the actual custodian of the image.[25]

On All Souls' Day and on various days Ajpu, the Momostecan days of liberty for the souls of the dead, Corpus is placed on a table located at the foot of Capitagua, a large Crucified Christ standing in front of the screen that blocks access to the cave. Then, in its main role in Momostenango as lord or owner (*dueño*) of the souls of the dead, it is visited by petitioners.[26] Petitioners may also visit on 8 Aj and 8 Ajmak when the image's clothes are washed and changed. It is also laid out on the table during Holy Week when, from Wednesday through Friday, it is dead and without power. Visitation is not appropriate until Saturday. Then Jesucristo has returned from Xibalba but has not yet ascended as the sun.

Prior to the 1950s Corpus was crucified in the church on Good Friday, but on alternate years to allow the Ladinos to crucify their Señor Sepultado kept in the church. Following an altercation when both groups crucified their images in the same year, the outraged priest forbade any further crucifixions. The large cross was moved from the church to the cemetery where it is decorated with jungle greenery on Wednesdays during Lent and Holy Week by its two owners, the *cofradías* of Santa Cruz and María Concepción.

The *alcalde* of Santa Cruz offered the following statement on the dynamics and the meaning of service to this powerful *imagen delicado*.[27]

The Service of Corpus
by Pedro Contreras

Ujunubal [His ones], *waquibal* [sixes], *wajxaquibal* [eights]; these three days only within each thirteen days have *costumbre*. But from one to one is thirteen days, and six to six and eight to eight, all thirteen. In the *junubal* I go to burn at Pa Cho [Water of the Image],[28] at the altar there. *Waquibal* I go to Paklom and Wak Chob'.[29] *Wajxaquibal* I go to Chutisabal.[30]

In *ujunubal* there are one dozen *copales* at Pa Cho and four bunches of candles, or two bunches if I have no money. It is the same on six and eight.[31]

When I have money I also burn incense on these days. But if we put two bunches at *junubal*, we must do two on six and eight. When I have money I also have a singer of responses to please those who came before, all the dead since the origin of the image. I pay for the responses, the litanies. A major litany is fifteen centavos, responses are two centavos each. A litany for all of the saints is twenty-five centavos. The *cofrades* have to pay. It is not from the alms of the image, although some private donors help out. If not, I have to pay because it will fall on me. The image protects me. I am eating fine, so I have no trouble paying.

In the *ujunubal* I go to church after Pa Cho, offering two bunches at Pa Cho and two at the church where I go above the holy souls,[32] but I burn the candles at the Well of the Sacrament and the Well of Santiago, two altars in the same place: Uja'l Sacramento and Uja'l Santiago. As one's blood directs, one burns [offerings] at one or the other. There is also a third, but I don't know it. There is a spring there, behind a wall, which never dries up. It used to be one just went from Pa Cho and burned in church, but I have to make the loop. If not, the souls of the dead will get me.

The *secreto* of Santa Cruz is to buy six two-cent candles, present these before the image, and then go to his altar [*ujuyubal;* lit., "his mountain place"]. And also one ten-cent candle is left standing and burning before him. This was done by our ancestors; they planted this and thus they left it for us.

The altar behind the *calvario* is for burning copal. It can't be burned in the *calvario,* so the ancestors left this for us. There are three: one behind the *calvario,* one in the cornfield in front of the *calvario,* the water of the altar [*uja'l*], and the third on the other side of Ch'uti Sabal in a field. This is for *costumbre* of the image and nothing else. The field's owners have known about this and allowed it from the time of my grandfathers, my great grandfathers. But he [the present owner] ignorantly moved it, and his son nearly died because of this. He should have gotten permission of the owners [i.e., the souls of the *cofradía* and the image of Corpus], but he made *costumbre* and his son recovered. The *costumbre* of Santa Cruz is a bit difficult.

On 8 Aj and 8 Ajmak, Señor Sepultado's clothing is washed and he is put out on the table. At eight in the morning we come to the cemetery with fiddle music, we four *cofrades*—the *alcalde,* the *deputado* and two *mortomas*—and one *capitana* and her two assistants. We come to his cave and remove the case [the glass case within which Corpus is kept reclining as a corpse] and bring it in front of Capitagua [the colonial period crucified Christ which stands over a table in front of the cave]. There is a special drape used to remove the image from the cave. The image cannot touch one's clothes. So I bring it from the cave in the drape and place it on the table before Capitagua on Aj, Ajmak, Holy Week, and All Saints' Day. I get the key from my pocket and open the box, and we present the four ten-cent candles and light them and they last all day. In Holy Week he needs two pounds of candles, four half-pound candles. They last all day on Good Friday. This is why I was afraid when I began. The image is heavy. This is my lot in life [*ri nu pinibal;* lit., "this is my cup"].

On 8 Aj a *bomba* is fired in front of the cemetery when all is arranged. And a *bomba* is also fired when the clothing is washed at the *armita*. And another *bomba* is fired when he is returned to his box. Also, at five in the morning four pots are brought to Pa Cho to bring water. But now it has been filled with earth, so we think we will go to Uja'l Sacramento for the water. Four men go to do this, and I swing a censer while they fill the pots with a dipper. When the pots are full, we put red and white flower petals in them.

We arrive at the *armita* and bring the chest of clothes and pick out the dirty stuff while burning incense, and when the clothing is removed we fire another *bomba*. Still with incense burning, we wash the clothes. We fire a *bomba*. We use six *bombas* in the day.

The day before, we go to the church and get the image of Santa Elena, which is brought to the *armita* and set on the table. Behind the table is a big hole, and a candle is burned there. When the candle is gone, the water from washing is dumped in the hole. Another *secreto:* I just came from the cemetery where the women are washing the glass case in which Santa Cruz [again this is Señor Sepultado] is kept. After this the women come and pour the water on the altar behind the *calvario*.

I didn't know what to do when I entered. The *pasados* showed me. I got sick with a headache and fever from fear when I entered. There was all his clothing, and there was a disagreement about it which made me afraid. There are two whole chests of clothes and an inventory which is registered.[33] But now it's all in my head. I know what to do and I am not worried.

We have to guard the cemetery in our turn and arrest anyone found there late at night. The mayor tells us we must follow the *costumbre,* as he must in his office. We have to be in the cemetery. Also on 8 Batz and 8 Quiej we have to do *costumbre* all night. Once I was burning at the *calvario* at five in the morning when the custodian came and said, "All right, you can burn here, but if I find a private citizen here I must arrest him."

To perform *costumbre* here at five in the morning, a *cofrade* from Xequemaya would have to arise at two o'clock! It's good that we have the service [*patan*] while we still are potent. Even so I get tired. An old man could not do it.

All the *cofrades* have been given orders to arrest and jail any private citizens found burning at the altar behind the *calvario*. If a private person burns there and gives offense, it can injure a *cofrade*. He doesn't know what's been done there. The altar is kept closed. It's like the *vara* [divining kit]. It cannot be given to others to use. It must be guarded. My grandfather served thirty years with this image because there weren't enough people, unlike today, when we only serve one year.[34]

Now the big cross in the cemetery used to be in the church. This [Corpus] is the image that was crucified. But when the Señor Sepultado Grande came, the cross was moved to the cemetery.[35]

Now for the *costumbre* in Holy Week. Forty days are observed without sex. For 8 Aj and 8 Ajmak there are twenty days. The women [*capitanas* and *axeles*] also do this. It is a very dangerous image. A *mortoma* had no respect. He got sick and can't be cured because he disobeyed the *costumbre*. We put our food on a table to eat, but if the food is dirty, even though it's on the table, we don't eat it. It's the same with *costumbre*.

Twenty days before the washing, I call them all together to warn that there are twenty days of *costumbre,* and they must be careful. Also, *costumbre* begins with the beginning of Lent, forty days of *costumbre* because it is an image of great antiquity. Thus I was instructed by those who left it to me, and if I leave I have to instruct the new one. It is a continuous chain. The service of Santa Cruz is a massive undertaking [*sibalaj nim u bantajic*]!

First go to the *uja'l* near the house of Domingo Pérez on the road to the *riscos* [scenic area with deeply eroded clays and tuffs]. Then go to the image's *warabal ja.* This is in Pa Tura's above the *riscos* where there are many altars. After this to Monte Cristo [Ujuyubal Katat; lit., "Our Father's Mountain Place"] above and east of the cemetery.[36] There are many altars in the milpas there where his altar is called Cruz Pasión. From there to Pu Ja'al next to the stream by the cemetery, and finally to Pu Chac'et behind the *calvario*. After this, if one has time, one goes to another *uja'l* near Pasabal, but if not we simply bring those candles to an *uja'l* near the cemetery. Then one brings candles to Santa Cruz [Corpus] and burns them before him, and goes above the souls of the dead in the *calvario* and tells them it has been done.

"I am sorry if it is not what you did, but it is done."

A *mortoma* went with his woman, and she criticized him for spending money in the *cofradía*. After this she had a chill, and then a high fever. He came to me. My blood moved and I knew she had done something. So I sent him with a candle to have her confess to the candle, then we put it before the image and asked his forgiveness. She was well the next day. The image is very sensitive. One or two incorrect words and we are punished. His *costumbre* is very perilous.

In Holy Week his *warabal jas* are opened for four days. One is in Pa Turas and another in Monte Cristo. Now there are three, another in Uja'l. They are opened from the Saturday before Palm Sunday through Tuesday for his fiesta. They are closed on Wednesday. They are closed Thursday and Friday when he is stretched out in the cemetery.[37] The *warabal ja* is also opened when they go to bring the flowers. All are open till they return.[38]

The Calvario *Complex*

The cave in the eastern end of the *calvario* represents not only the tomb for Corpus but also an entry to the underworld inhabited both by the human dead and liminal beings like Xibalba and the Jews who were defeated and erased from the world in world-transforming sunrises. Corpus is the lord of the dead. When he is removed from the cave and from his little box and laid out on his table, at the feet of Capitaugua, it is possible for the living to visit their deceased relatives in the *calvario* and cemetery.[39] On the Day of the Dead, the dead may leave the cemetery and revisit their homes for a festive meal. At other times, the dead are said to be in purgatory, either in their tombs or below the floor of the *calvario* and the church. Thus the removal of Corpus from the cave operates much like the removal of the "door" of a lineage or sodality *warabal ja,* giving the dead a period of liberty and even calling them out to oversee human affairs. The *calvario* thus serves as a kind of *warabal ja* for the entire community.

Additionally it is a gateway to Xibalba, the underworld inhabited by liminal beings from earlier world orders. During Holy Week the *cofradías* with responsibilities in the cemetery, especially the combination of Corpus and Santa Cruz, act on behalf of the community and the cosmos in a role similar to that of the priest-shaman acting on behalf of his lineage. Mediating in the calling up of the *primeros,* they open and close the passage connecting the two worlds.

There is, however, an exception when the removal of Corpus from the cave does not set the holy souls free to visit the world. During Holy Week, from Wednesday morning through Saturday morning, Corpus is on his table but he is said to be dead. His *warabal ja* is closed. During these three days all the *warabal jas* are closed. The Holy World (Dios Mundo) is also dead or asleep. San Simón is in power and the Tzulab contraries dance. By opening the passage to the underworld but closing the *warabal jas*, thus enclosing the souls of the *primeros*, the *cofrades* release the liminal beings from past creations into the world.

Following Mendelson's lead, this complex within Holy Week is here understood to be a syncretized version of the yearbearer cult.[40] This highly heuristic hypothesis helps to enlarge on the meaning of the Corpus complex. In the Kanhobal-speaking area north of Momostenango, for example, in Santa Eulalia (La Farge 1947: 123) a cave in a nearby mountain, called Yalam Na' (Under the House), is said to extend under the church. Twenty days before the five-day intercalary period (the *uayeb*) that precedes the installation of the new yearbearer, the souls of all the children retreat to the cave. Five days before the beginning of the intercalary period, all of the adult souls retreat to the cave. On the first day of the *uayeb*, they all return together and are received by the people at their church. A similar custom involving the same cave is also reported for the people of San Miguel Acatán (Siegel 1941: 73). The entire population "dies" and is "reborn" with the sun in each new year.

While this complex has not been reported for a Quichean town, there is indirect evidence for something like it. A cave extends under the ruins of K'umarca'aj to a position approximately beneath the temple of Tojil. It plays a very important role in rebirth symbolism during pilgrimage-based rites of passage for Momostecans today. In addition to the *calvario* cave, catacombs are also said to exist under the church in Momostenango. The world-renewing role played by the *calvario* cave in the Momostecan Holy Week version of the new year ceremony, then, is related to a prototypical highland Maya pattern expressed variously in renewal rites linking the cyclical rebirth of the Sun Christ with human rebirth.

The period from Wednesday through Friday in Momos is an inversion. The Sun Christ in his aspect as lord of the dead and the holy souls visits Xibalba, while the ancient liminal beings defeated when the Jesuscristo (or Jun Ajpu) sun first rose are spewed up onto the surface of the earth. Thus a mythical temporal return to primordial chaos is at the same time symbolized as a sort of spatial inversion in which coastal jungle vegetation festoons the town crosses, linking Momos symbolically to a place of alien Ladino power and tropical diseases that lies below—the modern Xibalba.[41]

SERPENTINE FLOWERS FROM THE COAST

In a three-day trek to the Pacific Coast, junior members of the civil religious hierarchy in Santiago Atitlán obtain fruit, present it to Maximon, and then use it to decorate the main altar for Easter (Mendelson 1958: 2). The theme of vegetative regeneration in Atitlán that underlies this practice is a major theme of Holy Week (Carlsen and Prechtel 1991). Journeys are central to the narrative structure in Maya mythology[42]—for example, the visits to Xibalba of the Hero Twins in the *Popol Vuh,* the migration sagas of epigonal Toltec epics, and the life of Jesucristo, who is portrayed as wandering around and finishing an unfinished world while pursued by the Jews. Journeys are central to Maya ritual, for example, in visits to sacred mountains, caves, and shrines, and in taking saints not only in procession to ceremonial centers but also on longer journeys to visit neighboring communities.

Sacred journeys in Momostenango include visits to sacred mountains on behalf of clients by priest-shamans; traditional pilgrimages (*romerías*) by a company, with Chiantla, San Jorge, and Esquipulas being common destinations; the *cantón* and private fiesta visits of Patrón Santiago and Niño San Antonio (chap. 3); and a series of journeys to El Palmar during Lent and Holy Week to gather greenery and flowers to decorate the town crosses, the main altar in the church, and the *calvario.*[43] This three-day journey clearly corresponds to the three-day trek of the Maximon/Holy Week complex in Santiago Atitlán. As in the Atitecan case, the Momostecan complex is directly related to San Simón. His mask greets the returning pilgrims with their offerings of greenery at the *armita.* The three-day duration of the journey is the length of time that Corpus is dead and the world is inverted. The journey to and from the coast, though, takes place while the culture hero–transformer Jesucristo is still alive and while he and the other saints shared by both Momostenango and El Palmar are present, with their *warabal jas* open in both places.

The "flowers" are actually mostly leaves called *canti'* (the Momostecan version of *cantil,* a Central American term for the fer-de-lance [*Trigonocephalous specialis*], a dangerous pit viper). Each week during Lent and during Holy Week, different *cofradías* are responsible for this trip. These are the *cofradías* of images found in both Momostenango and El Palmar. As is true of most *cofradía* undertakings, this trip is an ordeal that tests the ritual purity of the participants and the power of their protective *costumbre*.

The trip for flowers, like the construction of San Simón, is under the control of the thirteen teams, overseen and directed specifically by the *alcalde* of Señor Resurrección (Aj Corpus), the keeper of Simón's mask, and is a ritualized undertaking requiring sexual abstinence and *costumbre*. As in the case of San Simón, the appearance of the product of the *cofrades'* labors is judged by the thirteen teams, and if it is found wanting the *cofrades* involved are severely reprimanded by the thirteen teams. The trip tests their commitment, their ritual purity, and the strength of their *costumbre*. It is frightening and stressful and requires cooperation from all involved. The *cofrades* are accompanied by a *chuch kajaw* if none of them is competent to perform the *costumbre* along the way and in El Palmar. They are also accompanied by the *nima chichu,* the "great lady" of the women in service to the same image.

An account of the trip to the coast was provided by a former *cofrade* of San Francisco and Santa Cruz, two *cofradías* that make the trip to El Palmar each year.

The Coastal Pilgrimage
by Pedro Contreras

The *costumbre* of Santa Cruz is a great undertaking. One needs two pounds of candles just for Holy Week. Three twenty-five-cent candles are left here and three are brought to El Palmar. There is an image there where we go to get the flowers [*cotsi'j'*].[44] These candles are for the flowers. We bring twenty quetzals in cash to buy the flowers. First the *cofradía* of Aj Señor [Señor Resurrección or Corpus] goes, then Aj Santa Cruz, third Santiago, and then Aj María, Aj Sam Pras [San Francisco], and finally Santa Bárbara, and all must bring twenty quetzals.[45] When a *cofrade* is weak, he regrets the expense.

The three candles are brought to the image of Santa Cruz in El Palmar, or to Santiago. That is, all the *cofrades* who go to bring the flowers find their images there also. It is a pilgrimage for them. Palmar used to belong to Momostenango.[46]

The *warabal ja* [of the saint] is also opened when we go to bring the flowers. Now there are actually three, and all are opened until we return. It used to be that all the *cofrades* went by foot and the *alcalde* had to go with them to Chula Joyam in the *cumbre* [ridgetop bunchgrass meadows between Momostenango and San Francisco El Alto]. He was prepared with candles, copal, and incense, and he had to do *costumbre* in the *cumbre*. Then the travelers went on to the coast and the *alcalde* returned home.[47] The altar has been ruined, though [when the road was put through], and now it does not exist, so this is not done.

Those who go for the flowers also do *costumbre* there on the coast. There in El Palmar, above the church, is a great altar [*tanibal*] where candles and copal are burned. If this is not done the flowers [*k'ancaj;* "yellow sky," an arboreal blossom] and branches will dry, and the leaves [*canti'*] will turn into snakes.[48] It is *delicado* because the *warabal ja* here is opened, and because permission was formally asked at Paklom. It is just like going before a justice here in this earth. One must have a license.

The assistants who go with the *cofrades* to get the flowers must also observe twenty days without women. A helper ignored this once. The landowner climbed a tree to cut branches, and he saw a huge snake in the tree and was afraid to move. When he came down the assistant admitted that he had been with his wife one week ago, and we all scolded him. He had to arrange it with a candle. When we returned the snake was gone, but we had to pay the fine before an *alcalde*. When one is put in jail, one pays a fine and is released. It's the same before the [Dios] Mundo.

We pay the man who climbs to cut the branches with a six-*octavo* bottle of *aguardiente* and fifty centavos worth of sweetened bread [*xekas*]. If we do not give this, how will we find the flowers? We need to get eight hundred flowers of *canti'*, and if it is not complete the *alcalde* is scolded by the thirteen teams.

The *capitanas* come with us. When the flowers finally arrive, the *alcalde* must give two six-*octavo* bottles to each of the men and one bottle to each woman. This takes place on Wednesday. The drinks are served and the *alcalde* is told to bring the flowers to decorate the cross in the cemetery the next day. After this decoration there used to be a *bomba*.

Well, after the *cofrades* give the landowner the bread and his bottle, he goes to cut the flowers. He also gets three hundred *ta-*

malito wrappers [*maxanes*] to wrap the bundle. He gives with his whole heart. He knows his land like we know our milpas.

The flowers are *delicado*. We all have to observe forty days. The flowers smell like perfume, the branches are so green. But if the *costumbre* is bad they wither and we are reprimanded. This *costumbre* for the flowers was left us by the ancestors. They had to figure it out, how to protect the flowers. Now we don't have to think about it. Sometimes I wake up in the night at two or three in the morning on the ones, sixes, and eights and think about the *costumbre* and get up to do it.[49] The image enters into my mind.

It used to be that the flowers were brought through Xela [Quetzaltenango], and the police there would take the flowers because we had no license. They wanted a bribe, but with *costumbre* the police don't worry about this. They are made to think about other things. We used to have to get a document from the mayor's office to show it was for the image and not on business. With this the police would leave us alone, but only with *costumbre*. This happened when we went on foot, but now it is much easier. Even so the bundled branches must be hung on the side of the bus in plain sight, and sometimes at the booth they still ask to see the license.

When we arrive at the owner's house we all sit down. We give him the bread and a glass of the liquor which is called *jorón* [cold drink]. Then we give him the bottle. Then he says, "Early tomorrow I will go to see your flowers."

In the morning we bring a ladder to get the branches from the *c'oyol* tree.[50] The branches have long spines. The owner cuts them, and his assistants collect them and wrap them in bundles tied with the *maxanes* or cordage that we have brought.

Monday morning we leave the coast and arrive at the big curve at the cross in Los Cipreses in the afternoon, and sleep there. At four in the morning on Tuesday, the cross is decorated with *canti'* and we fire a *bomba* so the people will know that the flowers have arrived. We also adorn the cross at Two Heads, firing another *bomba*, and the people know it again. Then they are waiting for us in the *armita* and there is another *bomba*. There is less fuss when the image is a female.

In the *armita* we are greeted with four *octavos*, one-half an *octavo* each to remove our exhaustion. Then there is a meal. After we have eaten, a *mortoma* goes to get the thirteen teams who are waiting after the mass. After viewing the flowers the thirteen teams are seated, and each is given a cigarette and a drink. Then they remind us that tomorrow we will have to go and decorate the cemetery. We all bring the flowers to the cemetery, where the cross is decorated by its two owners, Santa Cruz and María Concepción.[51] This takes eighty leaves of *canti'*. Each week the old decoration is removed and replaced with fresh flowers.

Also, little crowns of the flowers called *k'ancaj* are made for Señor Sepultado in the *calvario*. This is done by the *cofrades* of Santiago, Corpus, and Maria, but Santa Cruz places the crown on the image. The old crown is brought to the *armita* of Corpus when the new one is made. The *esplendor* [silver crown] is removed at this time [during Lent and Holy Week when the flower crowns are substituted for it] and brought to the house of the *alcalde* of Santa Cruz. But this year it was brought to the house of a petitioner, someone from Quetzaltenango, for nine days, so he could burn candles before it. There is a license for this through the *auxiliatura*. It can only be done during Lent, because then the crown of flowers takes its place. For this the *cofrades* of Santa Cruz have to guard forty days, because each week they attend the image. So there is much work for the image. It is all in our heads. It doesn't all fit. I didn't know what to do when I first entered. The *pasados* showed me all of it, and I got sick and suffered a headache from fear. Now it's all in my head and I know what to do, so I am not frightened.

Corpus and Liminality

The three days of the journey to the coast is the liminal period of a rite of passage for the men and women who make the five journeys. Tuesday is a day of rest, when aggregation is marked by decorating (flowering) the cross at the entrance to town from the south and by presenting the flowers to the mask of San Simón, which stares forward from a position at the feet of the *cofradías* patron saint at the saint's *armita*.

When Santa Bárbara makes the final trip in Holy Week, another three-day crisis period of liminality ensues after the transitional Tuesday and runs from dawn Wednesday until dawn on Saturday. This liminal period affects all of Momostenango, whose central plaza is temporarily converted into the hacienda of San Simón while the contrary Tzulab perform at the cemetery gate to the east. The power of San

Simón is exhausted by noon on Friday. The image is taken apart, and the body, a flowery but now wilted cross, is burned.

Saturday marks another transitional day. Corpus has returned to power as lord of the souls, and there is a great celebration of visiting with the spirits of dead relatives in the *calvario*. The Tzulab Dance now moves west from the cemetery to the central plaza abandoned by San Simón, where they may dance with a snake in the afternoon, preparing the way for the final return of Jesucristo. Jesucristo, as Corpus, continues to lie down and gather strength. He has returned to the world from Xibalba and liberated the souls, but has yet to rise as a sun on the renewed world. On Sunday, now in the guise of the little image of Señor Resurrección, Jesucristo finally leaves the cemetery. In the darkness just before dawn he travels west to the town center with his *cofrades,* while the angel Michael races back and forth between him and María Concepción, who awaits him at the foot of the Paklom, the sacred center of the cosmos. They meet there and travel together north from the foot of the Paklom to the central plaza, arriving at the church portal on the eastern side of the plaza at dawn just as the sun's rays first touch the plaza's western edge. The Jesucristo sun has risen on the renewed world and stands within the portals of his celestial house, the house of God (*rochoch Tiox*), the house of the saints, that will now bring the spring rains. The Tzulab perform one last dance all day long in the central plaza before this house of rain bringers and the new sun. A description of the Tzulab completes the Costumbrista Holy Week complex.

THE TZULAB

The dance that is called Grasejos (Fools), La Culebra (The Serpent), Tzulab, and occasionally Patzcar in Momostenango is performed for the dual aspects of the lord of the souls, Capitagua (the crucified Christ) and Señor Sepultado (the entombed Christ) during Lent and Holy Week, and for the fertility deity called Niño San Antonio during his visits to rural houses at harvest time (see chap. 3). *Tzulab* is said by Momostecans to mean foul-mouthed tricksters, fools, or contrary persons.[52] Though Mace (1970: 20) finds that *patzcar* means dressed in rags in Rabinal, where a very similar dance called by that name is performed, Momostecan informants offered no definition for the term except that it was an archaic term for the dance.[53] The dancers in Momos use braided leather whips and sometimes dance with live snakes, hence

"La Culebra," while in Rabinal, as well as near Lemoa in Santa Cruz, they dance with staffs carved to look like snakes. The dance called Baile de Maner in Chichicastenango (Bunzel 1952: 426) and the Patzcar Dance of Rabinal (Mace 1970: 24) share a charter myth that in ancient times a holy image, Santo Tomás, the patron of Chichicastenango, and the Divino, the monstrance in Rabinal, could not be moved. It was the secret of these respective dances that the dancers were able to move the objects into the church or the *cofradía* (Mace 1970: 24). In Momostenango the Tzulab perform resurrections and precede Jesucristo on his journey from the eastern cemetery threshold to the sacred center, opening the way for him, as rain prepares the earth for planting and opens the germinating seed.

Observations of the Tzulab in Momostenango

The Tzulab dance in front of the cemetery on the Fridays of Lent, and on Wednesday, Thursday, and Friday of Easter week, and then in the main plaza in front of the church on Saturday and again on Sunday. San Simón, who occupies the plaza on Thursday and Friday morning, has been removed by noon Friday. The Tzulab then come in and take his place. On Friday at noon, before they move to the plaza, a greased pole is erected and climbed by the Tzulab at the dance ground in front of the cemetery for a prize of five quetzals. On Saturday the Tzulab are supposed to dance with serpents if serpents are found in the cemetery by the *chuch kajaw* of the dance.

I first witnessed the dance on the last Friday of Lent in 1974. The dancers, accompanied by a tiny one-man marimba, were at the cemetery gate (fig. 5.3). A couple of dozen vendors were set up under white awnings along the sides of the road leading to the dance ground selling fruits, soft drinks, sweet rolls, and hard cookies. Sixteen dancers were present, including one female impersonator and two children.[54] The "woman" had a bandanna over her face and wore a hat in the manner of shepherd women in the highland bunchgrass–prairie zone, but otherwise was dressed as a typical Momostecan woman, even wearing a woman's sandals. She had a braided whip over her shoulder and a rattle in her right hand. The children wore light-brown flat and featureless masks. The thirteen remaining dancers wore variously colored horsehair fright wigs with bits of leather and bright cloth tied into some of them. Under the wigs their heads were swathed in strips of cloth that

FIG. 5.3. The Tzulab Dance in front of the cemetery during Holy Week, 1974.

held the masks in place so that they could be lifted enough to drink, but not enough to expose the dancer's face. They wore typical Momostecan trousers, many bright blue in color, with several layers of old torn shirts or patched and ragged suit jackets (fig. 5.4).

They wore layers of shirts, or had them partially stuffed with rags, in order to absorb some of the force of the whipping. The masks were varied. Some were brightly painted Conquest-style masks, with pink faces and golden hair and mustaches, while others were crudely carved with little or no painting (fig. 5.5). They all carried or wore braided rawhide whips, and one of them had a stuffed weasel tied onto his back.[55]

The woman kept time to the marimba with her rattle. The dancers kept up a constant hubbub of shouts and mumbled comments. There was frequent laughter on their part and in the crowd of spectators. In a repeated performance all day long they took turns singly, or in groups of two or three, dancing with the woman, while her guardian pulled

FIG. 5.4. Seven Tzulab stand in a line. Note the variety of masks and costumes of these contrary vagabonds.

them away one at a time (fig. 5.6). When he had pulled a man away they faced each other, and the one who had been dancing raised his left arm and was whipped once or twice on the side, back, or buttocks, giving a loud cry (fig. 5.7). He would then rush back, sometimes reaching the woman's side before the man who had struck him. Sometimes a dancer would be pulled away by his arm, by the whip worn over his shoulder, or by the sleeve of his coat or shirt. Later in the day, when all were quite intoxicated, they would be pulled by the scrotum, to the delight of the crowd. The woman's guardian would occasionally dance with her, and during these interludes he would lift his whip up under her skirt to about knee height. The other dancers did not make such overt sexual advances but would sometimes try to carry her away on their backs.

In 1976, on Saturday of Glory in the plaza before the church, even more ribald behavior occurred. The dancers stroked the woman's genital area with their whips and then sniffed the ends. One dancer had some yellowish-brown material between his second and third fingers which looked rather like overripe cheese or crusty mashed bananas. He held this under the nose of another dancer who staggered around shaking his head before coming back for some more. One dancer carried a stuffed cat and another a stuffed weasel, which were brought together ventrally and jiggled up and down.

The dancers kept up a running commentary of lewd remarks, insults, and general profanity. Bad language was directed at the sponsor of the dance, who should merit respect, and was also directed at images of the saints as well as the onlookers and other dancers. On that Friday afternoon in 1974, about four hundred spectators stood in a ring five or six deep around the thirty-foot-diameter dance ground. The images of Jesús Nazareno and Virgen Dolores were being carried by *cofrades* from the church to the *calvario* and had to pass among the dancers at the cemetery gate. The spectators gave way and the marimba stopped playing. The dancers, however, only reluctantly moved aside. They continued shouting and joking, gesturing at the crowd and directing insults and lewd remarks toward the two saints.[56]

The performance of 1974 included an element linking the Tzulab

FIG. 5.5. In the heat of the day, the Tzulab remove their jackets. Note the fright wigs and variety of masks. Nabe Mu's (at center) carries a whip over his shoulder.

FIG. 5.6. Xinula dances with suitors.

and San Simón. A little straw-filled dummy sat in front of the marimba on a child's wooden chair, as though watching the dance. It wore a green plastic pail on its head for a hat and had a cardboard mask for a face, with a cigar in its mouth. A paper sign with the legend Traveling Agent (Agente Viajero) was pinned to its shirt. It was obviously San Simón; the Simón in the plaza in 1976 had an Agente Viajero sign pinned to its red jacket. Late in the day, after the images of Jesús and Dolores had passed through the dancers, as the shadows lengthened and the air grew cold, the Tzulab took turns carrying one another and the little Simón on their backs, looking for all the world like yearbearers from a codex.

On Easter Sunday 1976, at the end of their five days of dancing, the Tzulab put on a skit just before dusk. An afternoon's intermittent drizzle had wet the streets, but the dry season dust had simply turned to greasy mud which made the cobbles slippery and collected in depressions in brown puddles. The afternoon was overcast but warm. They had stopped dancing in the plaza and were wandering up the street between the park and the municipal building. It was nearly supper time and the afternoon crowd had thinned to about a hundred people, mostly women and children from the dancers' families.

As they walked along joking with each other, one of them suddenly fell and lay motionless on his back. The others then in turn jumped or rolled over him from his left to his right, and back the other way. One dancer pretended to attempt ventral to ventral copulation, humping vigorously for perhaps ten seconds, which caused some laughter in the crowd. Another placed a stuffed cat between the fallen man's legs with its nose on his genitals. They all stood around for a few minutes commenting in Quiché, bringing sporadic laughter from the crowd.

One called out, "He is dead!" in a loud, clear voice three times. Then they began a ceremony to revive him, initially without success. A dancer squatted at his feet and pretended to play the violin, using the butt of his whip as the instrument and the lash as a bow but without any sound. This had no effect. When this failed the dancers grasped his arms and legs and partly carried and partly dragged him about thirty feet, while one of them made very good imitations of the sound of a

FIG. 5.7. Nabe Mu's whips a Tzul, while others dance with Xinula in the background.

violin. He was then revived, and the group continued on without further ceremony.

The violin is played in a number of ritual contexts in Momostenango. Its main associations are with the Niño San Antonio, the *calvario* Christs, and the Mam, whose new year in March is celebrated at the houses of *aj mesas* by fiestas with violin music. Like the Tzulab, the Niño is a fertility deity, and they dance at his festival in Pologua. Like a Tzul, the Mam is pictured as a shepherd boy with a whip, and the violin celebrates and perhaps helps to effect the return of the Mam to power in a never-ending cycle of annual succession. The Tzulab Dance plays a role in telling this story of cyclical rebirth which is the essence of a Quichean conception of deity.

Snake handling is ideally a part of the dance performance. The sponsor of the Easter season dance observes sexual continence and performs *costumbre* for the forty days from "first flowers" (i.e., the first week of Lent when flowers are first brought to Momos) to Easter Sunday. Before Wednesday of Holy Week, he or a *chuch kajaw* in his employ goes out into a wild area or to a certain place in the cemetery with his rattle (*sis sis*) and calls a snake. If *costumbre* is done perfectly, the snake will come. It is kept in a gourd under the marimba during the first three days of the dance. On Saturday, when the dance has moved to the main plaza, the snake is removed and each dancer in turn takes it once around the circle. This has the character of an ordeal, since the snake will bite anyone whose *costumbre* is imperfect, especially if they have had sex during the dance period.

The Tzulab
by Juan Ixc'oy

Sometimes there are forty, but if not there are twenty, ten on a side making twenty.[57] First they make the wheel. The Nabe Mu's [First Ladino] is in charge of starting the dance. He makes turns around the twenty on the other side, then the twenty on his side. *Sicoj* in Quiché, or *pepinar* in Spanish is the name for this step. After this is finished he makes a circle. All hold hands and make four counterclockwise circles, then four the other way, but running. Then the *pepinar* is done again by the "husband" [Nabe Mu's].[58]

When the two lines are formed again, all run their hands through their hair as though trying to tug it out by the roots. Then they stick out their elbows at right angles and begin poking each other. Then with hands folded behind they hit shoulders together. After this they begin dancing with the woman, and each has a turn as her guardian. When all have had their turn, a bull comes out. They fight it and one of them is killed.

After this killing they come out to dance two by two. They dance out from the sides, back to back, passing in the middle, while the others dance in place. Then they dance down the line and cross diagonally. The *pepinar* takes place again on the part of the Nabe Mu's. After this one of them drops dead. The Nabe Mu's is advised that one of them has died, and he tells the others to search for the dead one. In turn each dances around both lines, but they can't find him. The Nabe Mu's repeats that they must find him, and so they begin to scurry around like ants. All this time he is thrown down in their very midst and they can't find him! Then four are sent out and they fall over him and return and report this. They are sent to fetch him, and carry him back on their shoulders like a tree trunk. The Nabe Mu's orders that he be brushed free of earth, so they brush him. Then the Nabe Mu's observes that he has not been struck, so he must have died of drink. When this skit is over, they dance with the woman again.

Following this there is a *pepinar,* a wheel, only this time with whips as nooses around their chests rather than hand in hand. Then they begin somersaults in turn [called *pitzcay* or *p'olaj*], then the leapfrog during which each in turn leaps the whole line of his fellows. Anyone who falls is given a whipping by the Nabe Mu's who watches from the side. He says, "Think" [*chatnawok,* using the familiar form] as he strikes. Anyone who raises his head while someone is jumping over gets hit too. Anyone who falls must start over. After the leapfrog they do somersaults again, each in turn somersaulting over the prone bodies of his companions, then they go back the other way.

Finally there is the farewell. The woman dances with each in turn, doing diagonal crossings between the lines. The story is so long that the performance is never completed in one day. It could be done in twelve hours, but it is always started too late.

There is a separate *r'awas* [sacred place for burning offerings] for the Tzulab. Thirteen roof tiles are brought and laid in a row, and the dancers do a [slalom type] dance down the row and back in turn with copal burning.[59] They must pass each other coming and going, and if a tile is kicked and broken the *chuch kajaw* scolds them for not keeping the *costumbre,* for sinning.

He says, "It will fall on me. I brought the thirteen, and what will I do now with this broken one?"

The whole team is scolded, and the *chuch kajaw* must replace the broken one.

Commentary on the Tzulab

The Tzulab is a syncretized performance combining traditional Maya motifs and themes with elements from a sixteenth-century Spanish dance called Los Matachines (The Clowns).[60] Los Matachines descends from a genre of late medieval sword dances, including both the Spanish Moors (Moros) dance and the English morris dance, introduced to aid in converting the Indians within New Spain (Campa 1979: 231). In Mexico City it is performed in honor of the Virgen, but in other places on the Day of the Holy Cross. Campa reports an "undocumented" thesis that the dance was performed by newly appointed Indian bishops in Mexico and was introduced to take the place of Aztec fertility goddess dances celebrated on the hill of Tepeyac. Speaking of the female character identified with La Malinche in the Mexican dance, he reports:

> . . . *she is a young bride, whose purity is indicated by her white veil. The horned Torito, representing worldly lust, tries to abduct her, but Abuelo, or grandfather, holds him back with his long whip, as the Matachines gather around to prevent her abduction.*
>
> (Campa 1979: 231)

The dance is also performed by the Yaquis of the southwestern United States and northern Mexico on the Day of the Holy Cross, but in a version that utilizes their traditional circle dancing and ceremonial drinking. These two features are also prevalent in Momostenango. The Momostecan version of the dance retains a bullfight and the idea of protecting a young woman from sexual abduction. However, in Momos her husband, not her grandfather, is protective, and in the interests of furthering his own sexual designs rather than protecting the woman's virtue. Meanwhile the Matachines have become Tzulab who try to abduct the woman rather than protect her. The dance is about exaggerated and virtually uncontrollable male sexuality, and female inconstancy. The males are phallic, playing suggestively with the butts of their whips and allowing a snake to crawl through their pants. In their contrariness they are unnatural; by Quiché standards their behavior is crazy (*mo'x*). Their appearance as shepherds and their use of the whip links them to the Mam.[61] It is a Maya fertility dance representing oversexed, contrary supernaturals whose main attributes are that they are dressed in rags, carry whips or snakes, and are disrespectful, with "no one over them when their day comes." Additional features that are not part of the Matachines but are found in Momostenango are a resurrection episode and the erection of a greased pole at noon on Good Friday at the precise moment when San Simón is disassembled, as well as the occasional dancing with serpents on Saturday.

Matachine motifs are present at the core of the Tzulab, but they may represent an accretion that offers, or once offered, safe cover for a dance that is really about something else. An additional key to its meaning can be found in the condensed version of a creation myth from Santiago Atitlán.

> . . . *María Magdalena. She is a very powerful witch who has
> destroyed all the females of the previous creation, the number one
> "lust woman" (*chojtal ixok*), the one they call Mrs. Vagina, the one-
> seeded girl who created the world, etc. She spends one night with each
> man. She gets a husband but turns him mad with her infidelities
> and gets another husband. Her real lover is Diego Tsaaj (a* nawal
> acha *in tree form) who is very rich and lives inside a hill. Everyone
> is crazily attracted to her.*   (Tarn and Prechtel 1986: 177)

This provides another identity for Xinula in the Momostecan Tzulab Dance. Rather than a passive object of lust like Malinche in the Matachines Dance, she is active lust woman, a Magdalena or Castellana, and the Tzulab, like Maximon, are driven mad by her powerful sexuality. If Xinula is Magdalena/Castellana, the Nabe Mu's is her distracted husband and San Simón is her "real lover" in tree form as a foliated cross. This little story, recorded in a Tzutujil-speaking town, is the script for the dance!

When the Maximon in Santiago Atitlán is considered in its guise as the old defunct yearbearer (Ocel; the old Mam), then the young *mams* are represented by San Martín and his angels (Mendelson 1959: 59), the *dueños* of nature, symbolized by little wooden angels sewn onto an apron displayed as part of the festival of the San Martín sacred bundle (Mendelson 1965: 170). In Momostenango the young *mams* dance as the Tzulab for a full five days, and literally take the place of Maximon when he is immolated on Good Friday, thus explicitly enacting a part of the rain god cycle which is implicit, or at least not performed publicly in Santiago Atitlán.

Many of the dance elements in Momostenango appear to be ordeals, understood as tests of personal *costumbre*, as when the Tzulab dance with a snake or when animal impersonators in the Monkeys Dance do tricks while balanced on a tightrope seventy feet above the paved plaza in front of the church. The twenty Tzulab also have, at their *r'awas*, the performance described above in which they embody the Tzolkin. The Tzulab then link the *mams* to the twenty named days, enacting in the form of a divinatory ordeal their passage through the eternal recurrence of thirteen numbered appearances. This esoteric ceremony, performed in a secluded precinct, when combined with the death and resurrection skits performed in public may also link the Tzulab Dance thematically to the twentieth-century Ix-Balam Keh Dance performed at Rabinal, described as "a drama of the death and resurrection of the 13 days" (Edmonson 1965: 145). These linguistic and thematic clues suggest a relationship between the expressive culture performed in the dances and rituals of Quichean Holy Week and the story of the confrontation between One Death and the Hero Twins in the *Popol Vuh*, a relationship that is explored in chapter 6.

THE FLOWERING CROSS AND QUICHEAN TRADITION

San Simón's body in Momostenango is a flowering cross. There is an additional element in the iconography of San Simón that harks back to ancient Maya symbolism. Every Wednesday during Lent, the mask of San Simón is brought by the *cofrades* of Corpus to the *armita* of the *cofradía* that made the coastal pilgrimage that week. It is placed, facing forward, at the feet of the image belonging to the *cofradía*, and the flowers are presented to it by the *cofrades*.

The placement of his mask, staring forward from its position at the feet of a saint, is reminiscent of the faces peering forward from pedestals on which Maya dignitaries stand in Classic artwork, or even the heads from which the foliated maize cross grows in the famous Palenque panel. This formal resemblance is intriguing, though it does not demonstrate continuity of meaning. Eric Thompson argued that the pedestal faces represent Itzam Cab, or Itzam Cab Ain, the reptilian earth deity, an aspect of Itzam Na (Thompson 1970: 210, 226). More recently, some of them have been identified through epigraphy as Yax-Hal-Witz, or First-True-Mountain (Freidel, Schele, and Parker 1993: 138). While the details of the interpretations vary, there is general agreement that a fertile or sustenance-providing earth is personified. Hun-Nal-Ye, the maize god, emerges from the head or skull of Yax-Hal-Witz (Freidel, Schele, and Parker 1993: 139). Carlsen and Prechtel (1991: 33) identify the image as a "seed/skull." The possibility then arises that San Simón personifies last year's maize, the seed corn from which the new crop will grow. While this might be one of his many Momostecan meanings, and is consistent with the timing of his appearance at the end of the dry season when the seed corn is about to be planted, Momostecan cosmogony emphasizes another cosmological identity.

In Momostenango it appears that San Simón, in his cosmological as opposed to his sociological guise, is preeminently the personification of a season in the agricultural cycle, and as an aspect of that personification he is the *dueño* of wild vegetation, of the snake-infested coastal jungle and the desolate highland *cumbre*. He is associated with the vegetation that must be cleared to make room for the domesticated world of humans and Jesucristo, the *juyup,* as when a farmer says that the land where he plants his milpa was "puro juyup" in the old days before it was cleared. In the term *Juyup Takaj* used by the Quiché to refer to the Holy World, *Juyup* stands in complementary opposition to *Takaj,* the cultivated, fruitful land associated with human life. This opposition or tension is ordinarily perceived as balanced in cosmos, but in the liminality of Holy Week this balance is temporarily upset; cosmos is temporarily suspended.

San Simón links the *uayeb* homology in Holy Week, the sleep of Jesucristo, to the jungle, the bush, and to a fertility of the Mundo which is necessary to all life but which is also antithetical in many respects to a human cosmos. The bush is exuberant, but it must be cleared and burned to make way for the milpa, for the human realm of ordered nature, *takaj.* Simón and his flowers are not linked in any way to the economically important cultigens. The crosses flower during the inversion when the world is Xibalba and Jesucristo—probably personifying both the world-transforming sun of a new creation and the dormant maize—is in the underworld. These crosses, at this time, are not maize plants. The body of Simón, a world cross bursting into flower, dries out while seated at his table and is finally burned, just as cleared land is burned at the end of the dry season in preparation for softening rain and the planting of maize.

San Simón is, then, in some sense a vegetation god.[62] The *juyup* penetrates Momostenango for five days during Holy Week, and its *patrón*, San Simón, is in power for three days as part of a rite of renewal, a fertility rite, but he is not himself an apt symbol for fertility. He is old and spent, perhaps emasculated or homosexual, the exhausted world at the end of the dry season. His flowers wither and die in a few days. He sits under a branch of the barren willow tree, in a scant shade that gives sleepers nightmares. Jesucristo leaves a world which is barren. He returns to one that has been fertilized by burning the personifier of the dry season and its wild vegetation—a world that has also been fertilized by the visit of the young orgiastic rain gods. But this transitional world of flowering bush dying and withering, burned vegetation, and looming rains requires human labor and organization. In the domesticated world chartered by Jesucristo and reimposed when he is reborn, the liminal potential of Holy Week has energized and fertilized a cosmos, a Juyup Takaj.

This cosmological symbolism is critical to understanding the meaning of Holy Week and its participation in older Maya traditions. Yet there is another dimension that must also be considered, for Holy Week is a social and emotional phenomenon, a ritual that represents and transforms social experience and renews humans and their communities as it renews the world. An understanding of all these dimensions of Holy Week within a Maya tradition requires that it be seen as the paramount rite of renewal. It enacts the mythic charter of society and the world. This suggests that comparison of the fully developed Momostecan Jesucristo myth and the *Popol Vuh* should explicate a continuing Quichean tradition linking cosmological, social, and psychological renewal. This exploration of thematic continuity in Quichean expressive culture is the main purpose of chapter 6.

6. Continuity in the Quichean Expressive Culture Tradition

CONTINUITY

In the 1970s and early 1980s ethnographers and ethnohistorians reconstructed the intellectual foundation for investigating continuity in Maya culture. The new perspective, given seminal expression by Eva Hunt (1977) and Victoria Bricker (1981), argued that "deep generative principles, which are essentially metaphysical premises, underlie an extraordinary array of surface diversity in the expression of native Mesoamerican verbal and iconographic ideas" (Gossen 1986: ix).

This loosely structuralist thesis sees "Indians" as ongoing creators of a "reconstituted Indian culture" which, following Nancy Farriss (1984), is a cultural configuration that emerges through adaptation from a central core of aboriginal concepts and principles (Carlsen and Prechtel 1991: 25). Maya culture in this view has adapted and been transformed but has retained a distinctive Maya character. Not a search for survivals in the backward "traditional" society of modernization theory,[1] the continuity thesis attempts to identify the central aboriginal elements and themes in ethnographically described village cultures, and to explain how fundamental cultural patterns persist within and give coherent structure to changing institutions.

This thesis underlies McAnany's (1995) recent argument that "armatures" (following Hunt 1977) related to ancestor veneration were originally derived from the needs of nascent elite descent groups to control estates and can be identified in Maya cultures from the Early Classic Period to the ethnographic present. McAnany's theoretically important investigation relates the power of the ancestors to social and political dynamics, showing that at least some armatures persist by serving an ideological function, in this case legitimizing status and the control of estates. This chapter applies the continuity thesis to the

Momostecan case study, investigating the patterns of continuity and transformation in this particular Maya expressive culture understood as an adaptive embodiment of Maya cosmology, political ideology, and social philosophy.

Metaphors for the Undertaking

Two basic approaches, sometimes acting in combination, have characterized recent investigations of continuity in Maya culture. One, described above, tends to focus on expressive culture, like ritual or myth, and seeks to discover underlying morphologies or structures that may be retained over long periods of time, but with superficially variable expression, especially through substitution of elements. The other borrows extensively from historical linguistics. It is based on the premise that a single Maya protoculture existed in the distant past and that it is possible to reconstruct that protoculture from features shared by its descendants in today's local village cultures. Several metaphors illustrate how these approaches have been developed in the literature.

Maya Culture Is Like a Jigsaw Puzzle.   One metaphor suggests that a cohesive culture that existed in the past has been broken into pieces, with different pieces surviving in different local cultures. It implies a theoretical possibility of reconstruction, though noting formidable practical difficulties.

> *Each community seems to be a collection of jigsaw-puzzle pieces, but no collection ever amounts to a complete puzzle. The pieces suggest an archetypal puzzle now lost: in any collection pieces will be found in different places; sometimes pieces will be lacking; sometimes there will be two seemingly identical pieces kept together side by side.*
>
> (Mendelson 1967: 405)

Mendelson argues that traditionalists hold onto their status, offices, and cults by maintaining the mythic and ritual system, fragmented as it may sometimes be, in the form of *costumbre,* which they define as a legacy from the more powerful and glorified ancestral past. While Mendelson's approach, like McAnany's analysis of the role of ancestor worship mentioned above and my interpretations below, is explicitly ideological— the retention of selected expressive culture complexes serves the interests of those that maintain them—it calls attention to the possibility that formal elements, especially in public ritual, may be retained rather faithfully for long periods of time even as the understanding of what they mean changes or simply becomes irrelevant and is forgotten.

Maya Culture Is Like a Ceiba Tree. Using a different metaphor but with similar practical implications, Freidel and Schele have suggested that we envision contemporary Maya culture as a single tree with many branches in its varying community expressions (Freidel, Schele, and Parker 1993: 41). The tree becomes a phylogenetic branching diagram in which widespread homologous traits in the present—for example, world tree symbolism or the legitimization of leadership via visionary shamanic mediation with the ancestors—hark back to prototypical ancestral culture.

The branching tree metaphor, when it is interpreted historically as a phylogeny, is the underlying model of historical linguistics, where it has been used very effectively to diagram the Maya language family and many others. Its use as a model for reconstructing ancient Maya culture was first made explicit in Vogt's "genetic" hypothesis. Homologous traits that have survived in related Maya communities are derived from common cultural ancestors, and on a regional basis might reveal systemic patterns that could be used to reconstruct a protoculture (Vogt 1964: 11). Quichean communities offer an especially promising field within which to attempt such an analysis. Many have retained very traditional local social structures since the colonial period, and a major, though in several respects problematic, part of the archetypal "puzzle" has been retained in the *Popol Vuh* and related documentary sources.

Maya Expressive Culture Is Like the Russian Fairy Tale. The structuralist metaphor represents expressive culture,[2] the central symbolic or expressive media of myths and rituals, as being like language in possessing underlying syntagmatic structure.[3] This approach calls attention to the possibility that cultural continuity may underlie apparent changes. As the pioneer structuralist Vladimir Propp (1968 [original 1927]) noted in his study of Russian fairy tales, the same story is told over and over again, with the same dramatis personae enacting the same roles in the same sequence of actions, but by varying the attributes of the characters who actually embody the roles and the contexts of the action, the story can be made to appear novel and different. The same story can be adapted to different audiences and retained over long periods of time in an apparently changing tradition without significant morphological transformation through a simple process of substitution of elements.[4] For example, the role of donor of magical objects can be assigned to the mountain lord or the patron saint, and the mountain lord in turn can be depicted as a Ladino in the early twentieth century or a gringo in the late twentieth century.[5] Jun Ajpu or Jesucristo or Pedro de Alvarado can be the rising sun of a new world order.

Victoria Bricker's (1981) exemplary study of Maya history and mythology demonstrates that throughout the colonial period and on into modern times a millenarian myth[6] has been enacted in ritual and in nativistic uprisings and recurs throughout Maya history. It appears to be one of the "armatures" around which highland Maya expressive culture continues to be formed, along with the vegetative regeneration model (Carlsen and Prechtel 1991), and the cyclical myth of the *mams* identified by Stresser Paean and applied so suggestively by Mendelson (1967).

Little and Great Traditions and Continuity Models

Farriss identifies three views of Maya cultural continuity (1984: 7–8). One position conceives of Spanish traits as a veneer on basically unmodified aboriginal systems. This position is labeled "primordialism" by Watanabe, who rejects it as simplistic in not taking account of the dialectical nature of syncretism or the adaptive creativity of the Maya (Watanabe 1990: 132). Farriss's favored position, the reconstituted Indian culture model presented above, conceives of substantial change but with preservation of a central core of concepts that shape new patterns. Watanabe is supportive of this approach, giving it a complex dialectical twist in which the central core is not so much conceptual as social: Maya community persists, with syncretism as its mode of adaptation.

A third position may reject the significant persistence of aboriginal culture but allows for some survivals that have lost their original meanings. Redfield's discussion of the culture hero Tepozteco "passing through the nursery on the way to oblivion" (Redfield 1958: 173) is a good example of this kind of degenerationist thinking. While it would clearly be a mistake to depict Maya village cultures or the religion of

Costumbristas as a collection of degenerated fragments, it is also certain that living village cultures do, as suggested by Mendelson, include vestiges of earlier times that have lost their original functions or meanings but are nevertheless retained as *costumbre*.

Village cultures seem to be, at the same time, coherent functioning adapted and adapting wholes and assemblages of jigsaw-puzzle pieces, suggesting a prototypical whole that is now lost. This is probably an apt characterization of any village culture anywhere, but Maya villages seem to represent rather extreme cases, like those optical illusions that switch back and forth between a vase and two faces in profile: now it is Maya/now it is Hispanic; now it is aboriginal/now it is colonial; now it is structured and coherent/now it is random and arbitrary. It is this problematic feature of Maya and many other Mesoamerican village cultures that makes them so intriguing, and that has allowed this debate to continue for generations.

Anyway, in a situation where different regions and even different local villages have very different ecological settings, settlement systems, histories of epidemic mortality and population movements, and modes of articulation with national economies, no one model could possibly be an apt characterization of the totality. If Farriss's three positions are not thought of as general theories about the Maya—that is, as mutually exclusive hypotheses about an entire tradition (or a collection of related cotraditions)—they could be seen to represent the range of possible complementary mechanisms, all or any of which could be brought to bear on specific cases. For example, as will be illustrated below, the *cabawil* has persisted in Momostenango in either a primordialist or reconstituted mode in the cults of Santiago and San Antonio, but it also survives in a degenerationist mode in the stories of Ek' and Yegua Achi'.

There is an additional problem for those who employ versions of the primordialist or reconstituted Indian culture models. Our knowledge about the ancient Maya is largely based on the archaeological and written remainders of the traditions of their urban elites, while contemporary Maya traditions are carried by peasants and artisans in local rural village cultures. The researchable continuity, then, is between a vanished great tradition and a surviving little tradition. What are the implications of this? Farriss rejects what she characterizes as the "Redfieldian" depiction of village life as an "ossified remnant of the

Mesoamerican Great Tradition" (1984: 389–390) as if whole village cultures were mere survivals, and as if peasant cultures have always to depend on urban elites for creativity.

A classic statement of relevance to the highland Maya is found in a short essay by Stephan De Borhegyi (De Borhegyi 1956). He argued that southern Maya culture history embodied the repetition of a pattern in which peasants with an earth-centered fertility religion were conquered by warrior elites with a celestial cult. This was most clearly expressed in the establishment of Postclassic conquest states and the Spanish conquest. Thus the continuity in Maya culture would be the continuity inherent in the peasants' little tradition[7] while a series of elite cultures came and went cyclically.[8]

It struck me as I pursued my readings of Maya mythology, and then my field investigations in Momostenango, that native Quichean historiography over the past six centuries or so has been saying exactly what De Borhegyi said. The autochthonous deities of the local peasants become spooks or devils from the perspectives of the intrusive Quiché or Hispanic rulers and their ecclesiastical cults. The millenarian myth depicts older deities as periodically going underground, literally, in the light of a new sunrise.

But the authors of *Maya Cosmos* (Freidel, Schele, and Parker 1993: 47–51) argue that the little tradition/great tradition model does not apply to Maya cosmology because the continuities in ritual and cosmology that survived the Classic collapse, the conquest, and the colonial period to find expression today indicate that a single inclusive culture was shared by peasants and elites. Yet the continuities documented in *Maya Cosmos* do not seem to require that there was a single unitary Maya worldview or cosmology, only that there were shared understandings of some central ritual symbols. Farriss (1984: 511), for example, posits not two isolated belief systems but a single system with a difference in emphasis developed in class or status group subcultures. A Watanabean sort of enacted dialogue between the celestial rulers and their terrestrial subjects would probably have characterized the internal workings of pre-Hispanic cultures just as it did the post-conquest colonial order.

The potential for shared understandings are heightened in a case like that of the Classic Maya in which the great tradition is not carried by an ethnically distinct conqueror. Much of it would have been derived in situ by elite Formative and Early Classic thinkers, artists, visionaries, and politicians from the same roots as the coexisting folk culture, which would, in turn, have had its own local philosophers and prophets.

The legitimization of Classic Maya kingship through the ritualized calling up of the shades of deceased kings mediated by offerings of their descendants' blood was the product of centuries of ideological and ritual construction by elite specialists creating an esoteric overlay of limited relevance and meaning to the peasants. The peasants would nevertheless have understood much of it because of its origins as an elaborated and specialized version of their own local shamanic-ancestral cult, and because major parts of it were publicly enacted and thus part of general socialization. The torture and sacrifice of captured lords, the focus on mythology relating to the defeat of the lords of death in a mortuary complex supporting the immortality of kings, the elaboration of the ball game with its cosmological symbolism, and the development of complex astrology in order to legitimize successions and to schedule wars of conquest would not have been relevant to the peasants. Nor would any of them have had the time and specialized instruction needed to master this arcane knowledge. Nevertheless, it would all have been based on commonly shared perceptions of the human role in the world, the nature and importance of sacrifice, and the great cycles that were prior to any of the gods. The Classic Maya peasantry did not, by this line of thinking, carry either a degenerated version of the elite cosmology and mythology or a distinctively different system. Rather, the elite initially developed an elaborated version of the common Maya village culture that all had once shared, and then greatly elaborated specific aspects that supported their ascendancy and their own specialized institutions.

Local versions of Maya cosmology persisted, following the De Borhegyi protocol, through several thousand years of changes at the top, so long as maize-based farming by patrilineally organized corporate groups persisted. From the construction of "Star Wars"-based polities, through the collapse of the Maya dynasties and their city states, to the emergence of new elites with cosmologies legitimizing them as the heirs of the original civilization derived from Tula, the celestial lords rose and fell cyclically. Finally the Spanish came along. In the highlands, with their war captain Alvarado and their chief god Jesucristo, both identified with the sun by the Maya, and their god of war, Santiago, identified with Venus, they were indeed just a repetition of the pattern, a retelling of the story, another conquering elite carrying a new but familiar celestial cult.

Most of what is in the *Popol Vuh* would probably have been recognizable to adult Quiché of all status groups or classes in the fifteenth or early sixteenth centuries. It would not, though, have been equally relevant to all, and it would have elaborated issues of no practical concern to farmers and artisans, while probably omitting, or offering a distinctive and biased ideological gloss on, the supernatural beings and mythic charters that figured in family- and lineage- and *chinamit*-level rituals outside of greater K'umarca'aj (i.e., Utatlán).

The peasant's cosmos is not documented for the Classic or Postclassic Periods, and though a Maya elite persisted in the *cacique* class through most of the colonial period, their descendants have survived into modern times as wealthy and influential peasants rather than as a clearly distinct status group, and to some extent—at least in Momos—they were challenged beginning in the eighteenth century (Carmack 1979: 210) and largely replaced as leaders and ideologues by commercially successful commoner "traditionalists" in the nineteenth and twentieth centuries.[9] Thus the *Popol Vuh* is a problematic starting point from which to derive the Quichean tradition, because most of the modern culture's aboriginal roots were in the undocumented culture of the peasantry.

What is found at the core of an ongoing Quichean expressive culture tradition, and how is it related to its documented precursors? The first part of this question, which charts a fruitful area of investigation, underlies the ethnographic enterprise reported in the chapters above. It is now time to address the second part of the question, relating the expressive culture institutions of Momos to precursors in the pre-Hispanic culture and to the social and political aspects of context that are relevant to ideological construction.

SODALITIES, SAINTS, AND *CABAWILS*

Ethnohistorical and ethnographic findings about the cults of the saints were presented in detail in chapters 2 and 3. Though there are about twenty-one *cofradías*, only three major saint-based complexes are important in ethnographic Momostenango: the fertility complex of Niño San Antonio, the protective complex of Santiago, and the world renewal complex of the solar-maize god Jesucristo, who is also lord of the dead. The first two complexes duplicate or replicate, at an inclusive community-wide level, the functions of the clan or lineage segment (*alaxik*) altars called *winel* and *warabal ja,* and are organized around images that were *parcialidad* patrons during the colonial period. While these images may have had community-wide significance of some kind during the colonial period, this is uncertain. The local corporate group known as the *chinamit* was renamed *parcialidad* in the colonial period, and its patron *cabawil* was replaced by the image of a Catholic saint. The basic pre-Hispanic settlement pattern of decentralized local communities organized around the ritual cycle of a god house whose cult was controlled by an elite patrilineage seems to have persisted until the late nineteenth century, possibly until the 1920s when the saints were captured by an ascendant *cabecera* and placed in the new church. The *cofradías* were gradually reorganized, until by the 1970s their memberships were restricted to residents of the town center and the *cantones* of Tierra Colorado, Los Cipreses, Santa Ana, and Xequemaya. Prior to this centralization and the subsequent development of Santiago's festival in the town center, the only "Catholic" cult institution of universal significance to Momostecans was the Holy Week rite of renewal organized by the colonial period *cabecera*-based *cofradías* of Corpus and Santa Cruz. This ritual complex marked, and possibly ensured, the transition from the barren season to the fruitful season of germination, growth, and harvest in the fields.

The actual participants in the sodalities—the *cofrades* and dancers—are dominated by the urban acculturated elite but are not members of the elite. Detachment of the *cofradías* from their ancestral *cantones* has reduced their political importance, and the separation of the civil and religious hierarchies in Momostenango has meant that cargo system careers do not rotate between them and that the politically powerful urban traditionalist families are absent from the *cofradías.* The esoteric knowledge of the sodalities in recent times has been retained independently of the *cabildo*-based indigenous elite, except for some of the written dance scripts that are owned by elite families, and is passed on via transmission during rotation of offices and retained largely within the institutions, though there is also some transmission of lore within patrilineages that are especially active in a particular *cofradía* or dance over several generations.

Continuity in practices is institutionalized within the shamanic cult institutions of divination and the keeping of the calendar through apprenticeships and initiations, which are of sufficient length and intensity to transmit a coherent, detailed, and systematic theory of practice (see Tedlock 1982). At the communalistic level there is nothing comparable to this. *Cofradía* service and sacred dancing have initiatory aspects and are of sufficient duration to allow for the transmission of basic practical knowledge, but they lack the intensity of an apprenticeship and probably lack the capacity to transmit a complex, specialized theological or cosmological system. Continuity is maintained through the ownership and sale of ritual lore within the *cofradías*. The existence of the position of *deputado,* usually involving long tenure and mastery of the lore in the *cofradías* of the important saints, ensures that there will be formal continuity in the ritual as long as the institution is allowed to replicate itself in the traditional way.

The lore that is passed on, though, emphasizes how to perform rituals rather than elaborating cosmological and theological rationales or models. The dances are performed and the fiestas are sponsored to please San Antonio or Santiago or Jesucristo and to please the *primeros*. Saints and *primeros* are pleased by being remembered, invoked, and praised. The *primeros* are pleased by lively and entertaining spectacles that reenact the primordial festivals that they initiated for the saints in the liminal world. They all require feeding, on complicated schedules, through offerings of candles, incense, and liquor. While much of the symbolism and psychological force of this complex seems to project colonial period patterns of patronage, it is also continuous with the older Quichean principles that "sowing and dawning," the cosmological processes on which human life depends, are themselves dependent on the "providing and nurturing" returned by the human creations.

The persistence of Maya tradition in Momostecan sodalities does not appear to be that of a largely unmodified intellectual system with a veneer of Spanish customs, but rather that of Quichean themes expressed through ritual symbols with complex Spanish-Maya pedigrees that crystallized in a nineteenth-century adaptive pattern with subsequent rather self-conscious adjustments made reluctantly when needed. The traditions include rites and practices reproduced as *costumbre* without knowledge of, or much speculation about, their esoteric and prior meanings (*secretos*). Nevertheless, the Costumbrista communalistic ritual cycle focused on the saints and Jesucristo is a Maya ritual cycle. The basic justification of *costumbre* repeats the Postclassic justification of the human role as a maintainer of a received order and a sustainer of

the initiators of that order. Within this basic underlying thematic continuity, complex patterns of accretion and transformation have marked
the cults of the saints. Three important illustrative examples are now
considered: (1) Quichean idolatry, (2) the erection of the *axis mundi,*
and (3) the communal rite of renewal. The first case study, that of the
cabawil and the saint, suggests that status group ideologies have constructed and maintained coexisting alternative meanings for core ritual
symbols throughout Quichean history.

A COMPLICATED QUICHEAN TRADITION OF IDOLATRY

A speculative reconstruction of the history of the Quichean tradition
of idolatry begins with the idea that the Classic God K embodied as
the manikin scepter is a documented early version of the tutelary god-
image. The key to understanding the transformations that the god
image underwent between the Classic Period culture of the Western
Rivers Region and contemporary Momostenango is provided by De
Borhegyi's model of elite celestial cults and local peasant earth cults.
Postclassic and colonial highland cultures represented either two co-
traditions, one for the peasants and another for the elite, or two very
different perspectives on a shared tradition. The splitting of the identity
of God K that I hope to demonstrate below seems to represent conflict
between the interests and identities of intrusive elite lineages and local
people. The intrusive lineages legitimized their rule by keeping transportable power objects from Tula that gave their leaders direct access to
supernatural power. The local leaders received legitimization through
fixed ancestral shrines and through ancestors and foundation figures that
had become spirits of place.

The argument is complex, and so is summarized here as a guide and
then developed in pieces. The Classic Period God K became the *cabawil* in the Postclassic. The *cabawil* then underwent a complex process
of identification with and replacement by the patron saint. However,
God K also seems to represent an early iconographic version of the
c'oxol, the lightning dwarf and patron of shamans. And yet the *c'oxol* is
depicted in both Postclassic and modern texts as an enemy of humans
and as an adversary of the *cabawils* and saints. In other words, if God
K is prototypical, then by the Postclassic, God K had split in two and
become his own adversary!

Momostecan narratives posit two adversaries of Santiago in the liminal period when the saints walked on the earth. Yegua Achi' (Mare Man) is a nature personifier whose offer of natural bounty in return for access to the female saints is rejected. Ek' (Black) is a creature born from a mare. Called a *cabwel,* it is kept in a cave and fed human victims.[10] Black is clearly a *cabawil,* and as such represents a version of God K. Yegua Achi' also has links to the *cabawil* as a man-eater and woman-taker. As Robert Carmack pointed out to me years ago, this name is a corruption of the term used for the war captains (*oyew achi'*) who brought the *cabawils* from Utatlán into the highland communities in their campaigns of conquest.

The same kind of thing had happened before in the Quichean tradition. The *Popol Vuh* recounts the adversarial exploits of Wucub Caquix, Sipacna, and Cabracan, earth-associated prototypes for the modern liminal adversary of the celestial powers, Yegua Achi'. The *Annals of the Cakchiquels* recount an encounter with the *c'oxol,* demonstrating the antagonistic attitude of the elite prior to the introduction of saints and displacement of the *cabawils.* Thus a deity concept from the Classic appears to have split and evolved by the late Postclassic into two opposed kinds of supernaturals—nature spirits and image-based tutelary gods with celestial associations—a division that has been carried over into the modern period when Santiago and other tutelary saints coexist with the *c'oxol* and other nature spirits, having overcome the *cabawils* and Yegua Achi' in the foundation myth. The process may be outlined in three steps.

Step One: God K Becomes the Cabawil *and the* C'oxol

This speculative historical interpretation of the Quichean tradition of idolatry begins in the Classic Period. The gods of the Palenque Triad—GI, GII, and GIII—are now recognized as prototypes for characters in the *Popol Vuh* (Schele and Freidel 1990: 407–411). The first-born GI shares many attributes with the Classic god Chac Xib Chac and with the Headband Twin Hun Ahau, suggesting that both are cognates for the Hero Twin known as Jun Ajpu in the *Popol Vuh,* where he is clearly identified as a celestial deity with solar attributes. GI is also identified with Hun Nal Ye, the Classic maize deity (Schele 1992: 127), creating a bit of a problem since Hun Nal Ye is identified with Hun Hunajpu, the father of Hun Ajpu (e.g., Schele and Freidel 1990: 412; Freidel, Schele, and Parker 1993: 276). Complex personifications—fathers and sons, wives and mothers, maize and the sun—that have overlapping identities seems to be typical of the personified Maya embodiment of cosmogony in all time periods, and will be considered in more detail in connection with Jesucristo as a sun and maize deity later in this chapter.

The second-born, GIII, whose birth only four days later suggests twinship with GI, shares attributes with the baby jaguar companion of Chac Xib Chac and with Yax Balam, the firmly identified cognate for the *Popol Vuh*'s Xbalanque. Thus names and identities for the Hero Twins were established in the Classic. They have not persisted into the modern period in Momos as named gods or dramatis personae in living myth. However, there are echoes of twinship in the paired Jesucristos, Capitagua and Corpus, in the Momostecan *calvario*.

The third-born, GII, also known as God K, is identified with the manikin scepter, a representation of the deity called K'awil by the Classic Maya, which on linguistic grounds appears to be a prototype for the *cabawil* of the Postclassic Quiché. The epigraphic identification of K'awil as a dwarf, when combined with his iconographic depiction with an ax head in his forehead and the documented association among the Maya of stone axes with lightning, all link K'awil with the *c'oxol*, the red—or sometimes white—dwarf spirit of modern Quichean mythology whose little hatchet awakens the divinitory sheet lightning called *c'oyopa* in the bodies of daykeepers during their initiations, so that thereafter their blood will speak to them of otherwise hidden things (Tedlock 1982: 147, Freidel, Schele, and Parker 1993: 194–203).

The name Tahil associated with some Classic Period representations of this god (see Tedlock 1985: 175; Schele and Freidel 1990: 414) suggests that it was not only the prototype for a *cabawil* or "idol" in a generic sense but was the cognate for a specific named *cabawil*, Tojil, which was the chief patron deity of the Quiché polity during the Postclassic, given to their most powerful ancestral lineage before the first sunrise when they were gathered with the other tribes at Tula.

How and why did the manikin scepter, principally a symbol of rank during the Classic Period, become a *cabawil*, a god of conquest requiring its own temple and human sacrifice? An important philosophical insight is offered by Freidel and Schele in *Maya Cosmos* (Freidel, Schele and Parker 1993: 194–203). K'awil, which in Yucatec carries the meaning of "sustenance" or "alms," embodies the central contract between humans and the deities, a contract of mutual feeding in which maize and other sustenance is exchanged for blood and other precious goods offered by humans.[11] This contract is clearly expressed in the *Popol Vuh* requirement of the creators that their human creations be their "providers, nurturers," and in the later justification for human sacrifice in the specific requirement of Tohil that the human tribes pay for his gift of fire by being suckled under the arms (see Tedlock 1985: 73, 174).[12]

The Classic manikin scepter, often depicted with a serpent for one leg, was an emblem of *ahau* (or *ajaw;* i.e., "lord") status, and of kingship specifically, until the broadening of status symbolism of the Late Classic. Its serpent leg is its *way*, what the Quiché would call its *nagual* (or *nawal*), the vision serpent, a spiritual entity that was called up by the kings in bloodletting rites to act as a conduit for the manifestations of the shades of their ancestors (Freidel, Schele, and Parker 1993: 195–196). The Postclassic *cabawil* Tojil thus follows in this more ancient tradition by manifesting its spiritual essence as a young man of handsome appearance, perhaps an ancestral figure, when it is fed.[13]

In Momostenango the three red-garbed *c'oxols* are portrayed in the Conquest Dance (see chap. 4). They are said to be the sons of Tecum. The youngest of the three is a little doll that is carried by the eldest, Aj Itz. When father Tecum is killed, the doll is placed on his coffin to guard it, and retrieved by the older brother at the time of burial. Thus the third-born *c'oxol*, the GII of Momos, is a manikin that functions as a ritual symbol in a mortuary succession event and may serve as a repository or conduit for the spiritual essence of the deceased father.

There is a practical political reason why the manikin scepter might have become a *cabawil* as the Maya elites' theology and ideology adjusted to the new world of the terminal Classic. It would not be possible for peripatetic younger brothers carrying the secondary *cahal* rank, warrior dynasts called *oyew achi'* by the Quiché, to bring their grandfathers' tombs with them when they set off to found their own political domains. Their elder brothers, the *ahaus*, would remain in control of the monumental portals to the power of the ancestors, the tombs, and the ceremonial precincts at the major centers which became Tulans. How then could the *cahals* legitimize their rulership and provide themselves with the supernatural power they would need to overcome their adversaries by calling up their fathers' and grandfathers' ghosts? They could bring along the more portable manikin scepter, and thus remain in contact with the ancestral tutelary spirits. So at their respective Tulans the *ahaus* gave them *cabawils* to bring with them as they went off to found new dynasties.

Step Two: The Cabawil *Becomes the Patron Saint*

The modern lore of Santiago suggests that in some cases saints were identified as counterparts of *cabawils* according to the timing of their festivals: Santiago's festival, for instance, came during the *canícula* and close to the early August Wakan Chah Period, as indicated by the widespread associations of Santiago with the Milky Way in highland Maya culture documented in chapter 4. Similarly, the coincidence that Holy Week came at about the same time as the yearbearer festival in the eighteenth century (D. Tedlock 1993), and that both corresponded to the onset of the rainy season at that time, probably explains the central place of Holy Week in highland Maya communities and its lack of emphasis in Yucatán, where it does not correspond to the planting season. There village patron saints and sometimes the Virgin Mary are honored, but Jesus Christ and Holy Week are not important (Farriss 1984).

The Vicentes obtained the image of Santiago, the most important Momostecan saint, from a distant "City of Spain," as the ancient elite obtained the *cabawils* at Tula. There is, of course, some disagreement in Momostenango as to which elite family actually brought Santiago to town. Lineages of lesser status similarly obtained patron saints for their *parcialidades*. Thus even the descendants of the status groups that maintained the *cabawils* and benefited from their cults in the aboriginal period maintain histories relating that their ancestors rejected the *cabawils* in favor of saints. The Diego Vicente story suggests that maybe the elite tried to hedge their bets for a while, maintaining saint cults with *cabawil* cults on the side until intergenerational conflicts within the cacique lineages resulted in the younger generation enlisting wider community support—or wider community opposition resulted in the community's enlisting the support of the younger generation within the cacique lineage—to put an end to the *cabawil* cults.[14]

Yet the saints were also identified with the *cabawils*. Diego Vicente found Santiago on a mountaintop while his sister found Santa Isabel in a ravine near a river. This is a remarkable coincidence in light of the *Popol Vuh* account that while waiting for the first sunrise Tojil was hidden on a mountaintop, and Awilix, the patron of the Nijaibs (Vicente ancestors), was hidden in a ravine. Santiago, like Tojil, is a god of wind and storms, a war patron, and is associated with the planet Venus. Thus while the *cabawils* as such were rejected in favor of saints, the saints that took their places were probably remarkably similar to them in many ways and shared significant traits: the saints are power objects provided by the ancestors, they materialize their spirit counterparts in the dreams of those who feed and nourish them, and until recently most of them were kept in god houses on communalistic estates dominated by elite lineages.

Step Three: The Cabawil *as an Adversary* Overcome by the Patron Saint

The *cabawil* is also remembered as an adversary overcome by the patron saint. The story of the conquest has been assimilated into the millenarian myth of autochthonous powers overcome by celestial powers.

In the Diego Vicente saga, told by Vicente descendants of the elite Nijaibs who conquered the Momostenango territory, the semimythical founder of their lineage kept a *cabawil* named Black (*Ek'*) in a cave and fed it human victims until his own sons joined forces with his enemies and a little captain, probably Santiago, to destroy it. Another and more widespread tradition has Yegua Achi' turned away from Momostenango by Santiago, who rejects his offer of bountiful harvests in exchange for a female saint. He is eventually killed by the Cristo of Esquipulas with the help of San Cristóbal for seducing the female saints there. Elsewhere, in Cubulco, Yew Achi' is a red manlike being that lives in the earth and devours human victims until Santiago arrives to protect them (Shaw 1971: 55–56). Thus the *cabawil* is assimilated into folklore as the war captain, the *oyew achi'*, who originally introduced and carried its cult as a personifier of oppression, a devourer of people, and a stealer of women, and is generally remembered as a bogey from whom people are protected by the saints. Like Tojil (see Jose Chonay and Goetz 1953: 171), Ek'/Yegua Achi' as remembered in folklore is willing to accept either women in marriage (here "seduction" may be substituted for "marriage") or human victims as food.

This is a typical illustration of De Borhegyi's hypothesis that imported celestial cults of predatory elites come and go cyclically, while the peasant religion just continues. From the perspective of the peasants — the Postclassic nonelite people of the seven "tribes" (Wuk Amak) conquered by the expanding K'umarca'aj polity — the late Postclassic's introduced gods (*cabawils*) were enemies. The cult of the saints for them would have represented the welcome vanquishing of the *cabawils*. Similarly, the Postclassic elites, whose myths have survived because they were recorded in writing, tell us of their antagonism toward the earth-associated tutelary spirits of the peasants.

The *c'oxol* and the *cabawil* were clearly distinguished from each other in the Postclassic. The Zaquic'oxol (White C'oxol) was known to the Quiché and Cakchiquel in the Postclassic. He is mentioned in the *Popol Vuh*, where he is either turned to stone at the first sunrise "with the other enemies of man" (Recinos 1950: 188), or escapes into the trees to live on in hidden places as a nature guardian (Tedlock 1985: 182, 305–306, 368). The *Annals of the Cakchiquels* describes the White C'oxol as a spirit of the volcano, a maker and guardian of the roads, who is intimidated by the paired founders of the leading Cakchiquel lineage (Recinos and Goetz 1953: 61–62). The Postclassic elite defined the *c'oxol* as a spirit associated with volcanoes and animals, a nature personifier. Like Yegua Achi' in the Momostecan mythology of today, the Cakchiquel White C'oxol was a roadbuilder and lord of animals. Like the Cubulco version, Yew Achi', the Cakchiquel White C'oxol, once he is dressed in his wig, breastplate, and sandals "the color of blood," is a terrifying red apparition that kills people.

The modern Momostecan understanding of the *cabawil,* as explained above, links it to this evil apparition that already existed as a being separate from the *cabawil* in the Postclassic. As saints replaced the *cabawils,* the folk memory of the *cabawil* dwelled on its oppressive aspects as a demander of human sacrifice, and it came to be assimilated into the already existing *c'oxol.*[15] Preexisting fearful aspects of the *c'oxol* were then rationalized by understanding it as the surviving displaced spirit-essence (*nawal*) of the *cabawil.*

The *c'oxol* in Momos today—invariably called K'ak'ic'oxol (Red C'oxol)—remains a fearful apparition. The mere sight of it can cause death or be a sign of one's destiny to die in the near future. Yet it can also provide riches, and is seen as an assistant to the most powerful *mundos,* the Tecumes or Principales del Mundo, who live in the mountains and who keep treasures and the original magical dance costumes that could transform their wearers into spirit-beings. Thus the *c'oxol,* like the *cabawil,* serves a mediating role between people and ancestral or quasi-ancestral powers. The *c'oxol* is the patron of diviners, the source of the power that awakens their blood (B. Tedlock 1986: 135).

The *c'oxol* is an ancient Maya notion of deity. It was probably the personifier of power in the shamanic religion of local peasants from the Classic Period or earlier throughout the Maya area. It was elaborated in the dynastic cults of the Classic elite into the God K/manikin scepter, but it also survived in the nature cults of the peasants. In that guise it was at least partially redefined as a bogey by the invading Quichean warriors, who had defined their own evolved and transportable descendant of God K as greater than the animistic God K variant—perhaps a surviving little-tradition ancestor of God K—of the local priest-shamans. The mythology of current times has attached most of its fears about the abuse of supernatural power to its degenerated folkloristic Ek' and Yegua Achi' versions of the *cabawil,* the imported god which demanded human victims and symbolized oppression to the peasants. The peasantry, in this case supported by Christian clergy and the power of the Spanish empire, was mobilized on the side of saintly *cabawil* counterparts that did not thirst for blood. From an emic point of view, the *cabawils* as such were deposed and degenerated into folklore, while from an interpretive functionalist point of view they survived through transformation into saints, new patrons of *parcialidades,* with new and more wholesome food preferences.

The *cabawils* and the patron saints that succeeded them served as tutelary gods representing and protecting the elite lineages and the *chinamits* that were their power bases. The portion of the *Popol Vuh* that deals with the Quichean emigration from Tulan, the wait for the sunrise, and the post-sunrise establishment of the Quichean polity is the setting for these deities who are protectors in war, and personifiers of wind and storm and bringers of rain. Yet in Momos, as in the *Popol Vuh,* the tutelary gods coexist with another family of deities: those that personify the sun/day and the maize, and whose cosmogonic actions in the liminal period and the rituals that reenact them embody the agricultural cycle as the birth, sacrificial death, and rebirth of deity. Knowledge of the aboriginal Quichean pattern is derived primarily from conflict between the Hero Twins and Xibalba in the *Popol Vuh,* while the Momostecan pattern is expressed in Holy Week. Table 4 summarizes how the *Popol Vuh* pattern and the Momostecan pattern are related.

WORLD TREES AT MOMOSTENANGO AND PALENQUE

In 1976 I learned that San Simón was a flowering cross. I was intrigued by the possibility that Momostecan Holy Week might offer clues to the interpretation of the iconography of Palenque with its foliated cross icon and its depiction of God L as a cigar-smoking old man, as if the

Table 4. Popol Vuh *and Momostecan Divinity Correspondences*

The solar maize complex is described in chapter 5 and in the discussion of the rite of renewal below. The tutelary complex is found in chapters 2 and 3, with discussion immediately above in this chapter.

Solar-Maize Complex

Popol Vuh	Momostenango
Jun Jun Ajpu	Jesucristo
Jun Ajpu and Xbalanque	Corpus and Capitagua
One Death	San Simón
Xquic	María Concepción
Cabricán	Yegua Achi'
Vagabond dancers	Tzulab
	(Nabe and Ucab Mu'us)

Tutelary Complex

Tojil (Cawek patron)	Santiago
Awilix (Nijaib patron)	Santa Isabel
	(later, María Concepción)
Pizom Gagal	*Título*
Cabawil (generic)	Saint (generic)
	Ek' and Yegua Achi' also seem to represent aspects of the *cabawil* as it "degenerates" into folklore.

artists at Palenque had seen San Simón (Cook 1981: 602). My lack of expertise in Maya archaeology and the complexity of Maya iconography were daunting obstacles, and though I hoped at some point to follow up on this lead, my life took another course. The issue here, though, is not one of offering an original interpretation of Classic iconography in light of ethnographic data, but rather of summarizing some commonalities that suggest continuity in a Maya tradition reaching back to the Classic, especially at Palenque.[16]

Recently, epigraphic and archaeoastronomical breakthroughs[17] have opened up the meaning of the Palenque complex. An intriguing ethnography-based interpretation (Carlsen and Prechtel 1991: 33–35) links modern Quichean symbolism of vegetative renewal and flowering crosses to Palenque's iconography. Symbolism of ancestral renewal founded in the life cycle of plants is central to Santiago Atitlán and Palenque. In the altarpiece at the church and in Santiago Atitlán's creation mythology, a world tree is a central motif, as it is in the group of the cross at Palenque. In both traditions the world tree exists in two guises, a tree proper and a maize tree. In both Santiago Atitlán and Palenque there is a conception of human immortality based on descent in which vegetative metaphors abound; for example, the ancestors are likened to trees and their descendants to leaves, suckers, and so on.

Freidel and Schele (Freidel, Schele, and Parker 1993: 144–146) argue that the three temples in Palenque's group of the cross represent the three stones of creation. A pattern of three temples in the central plaza is also found at the Quiché center of K'umarca'aj. There is no clear parallel arrangement of sacred structures or precincts in Momostenango. The church and its plaza, located north of the world's center at the Paklom, seem to have a functional and spatial relationship to Palenque's Temple of the Cross, while the *calvario* and the shrines located in the cemetery and on a nearby hilltop lying east of town have a functional and spatial relationship to the Temple of the Foliated Cross. The shrines of Paja', Pasabal, and Chutisabal lie west of the Paklom, but I am unable to link them to the symbolism or iconography of the western temple in the Palenque complex.

On the east in the Palenque group of the cross, the Temple of the Foliated Cross depicts the world tree as a maize plant giving birth to twin maize personifiers at the ends of its arms. The *calvario,* where paired images of Jesucristo are kept in a cave, is located on the eastern side of Momos. This is the staging place for the emergence of the re-born Jesucristo at Easter. Jesucristo has interconnected sun and maize associations. These associations include Monte Cristo, a hill rising above the cemetery on its eastern side where an altar called Cruz Pasión marks the "mountain place" of Jesucristo (*Ujuyubal Katat*). Holy Week begins when the sun and full moon as observed from there rise at a particular spot. This event, which may be understood as the conception of the maize personifying Jesucristo (see chap. 5), marks the transition from the dry season to the agricultural season, and links the maize cycle to the solar and lunar cycles. A large cross stands in the cemetery today near the *calvario* and is "foliated" during Lent and Holy Week each year. This cross, however, used to stand in the central plaza near the church, so this apparent replication of Palenque's spatial iconographic arrangements seems coincidental rather than a representation of historic continuity.

The central panel in the Temple of the Cross, at the northern apex of the group of the cross at Palenque, represents the world tree. This may have been the prototype for the Momostecan plaza cross mentioned above that was moved to the cemetery in the 1950s. From the south-facing portal of the Temple of the Cross, the dazzling Milky Way could be observed twice each year when, shortly after the solstice, it embodied the Wakan-Chah arrangement representing the world tree. The world tree is erected in Momostenango in the plaza just outside the church doorway in a ceremony that takes place every other year, establishing the ground for the Monkeys Dance, the Momostecan version of the Deer Dance. This ceremony occurs during Santiago's fiesta, linking it to the Milky Way in its Wakan-Chah arrangement, as explained in chapter 4. A rope running from east to west crosses the vertical axis of the "tree" and permits spirit-animals to descend from the roof of the church to the dance ground where an old couple, cognates of first mother and first father, officiate in a dance depicting offerings at the cardinal points and the killing of a deer.

Even though the large plaza cross was moved to the cemetery, there is still a flowering cross in the central plaza during the crisis period of Holy Week. San Simón, whose hidden body is a flowering cross, is seated in the plaza on Thursday and Friday mornings during Holy Week. His attributes as a cigar-smoking old man with a tendency toward both sterility and exaggerated sexuality link him and the church-plaza complex in Momos and to the Classic Period God L and the Temple of the Cross at Palenque, where God L is represented in a large carving in the threshold to the inner sanctum on top of the pyramid. It seems plausible that a rite of renewal was staged at Palenque in which performances involving the eastern temple and the northern temple enacted a Classic Period version of the defeat and resurrection of the maize and sun personifiers and their overcoming of the powers of death and sterility to inaugurate the maize planting season.

CONTINUITY IN THE CENTRAL RITE OF RENEWAL:
THE HOLY WEEK COMPLEX AND QUICHEAN TRADITION

Two cosmogonic myths are widely employed in Momostecan communal rites. The millenarian myth depicts world transformation as a sunrise. This myth has obvious ideological implications, for example, in legitimizing the conquest as a completed sunrise in which Alvarado is the new sun, or delegitimizing it as an incompleted sunrise in which

Tecum has gone underground to await rebirth as the sun, in which case Alvarado is a Xibalban or San Simón presiding over the sacrificial death of the true sun. Christmas and Easter are both sunrises of this type, in which Jesucristo's birth or rebirth defeats devils. The Momostecan version of the liturgical year, however, also embodies another cosmogony, one that is less explicit, in which the burning of the jungle and the coming of rain and the germination of the maize are implicitly represented and a successful agricultural season is ensured by the rituals of the *cofradías* and dancers. In this section, these two interrelated cosmogonies are explicated more fully than in chapter 5 and are related to possible aboriginal prototypes.

The Maya Millenarian Myth and Its Morphology

That the central ancient and modern cosmogonic myths and rites of the Quiché tell versions of the same story follows from the morphological analysis of Maya tales. This approach conceives of a story as a sequence of actions called "functions," each of which may be represented by a noun, for example "instruction" or "flight" (see Propp 1968; Dundes 1963, 1968). A tale type is a sequence of functions expressed over and over again in actual tales. Among the stories that constitute a type, each presents a selection of the sequence of functions from the inferential and prototypical type tale and always in the type order, though sometimes with omissions. The dramatis personae — protagonists, allies, villains, etc. — remain constant as represented in the functions, though actual characters may be highly varied from tale to tale. For example, the villain may be a father, a giant, or a king in different embodiments of a single tale type. Similarly, the context of the action may be varied from tale to tale. Thus a single type may, by omitting episodes or repeating episodes, by varying the characters that embody the roles of the dramatis personae, and by varying the settings, produce a large number of distinctive stories. Independent attempts to employ Propp's approach to investigate the same Maya tale type (see Cook 1981: 457–467, the millennialistic myth; Pickands 1986, the Maya hero tale) have yielded similar findings about the sequence of functions and the central role of an imprisonment motif.[18]

A condensation of the tale type,[19] suited to the argument here, identifies a sequence of defining functions:

1. A. Journey
   B. Engagement or Contest (may be integrated into the journey, making the journey a pursuit)
2. Imprisonment or burial[20] (implied or actual death)
3. Emergence (rebirth)
4. Reengagement (repetition of contest)
5. Defeat (of adversaries)

The Mesoamerican life of Jesucristo, who is pursued by the Jews or devils, is captured and killed, is reborn and then ascends, erasing his persecutors from the earth, embodies the tale in its complete form. The Momostecan texts I have collected omit the imprisonment motif from the Jesucristo story, but such motifs do occur in Maya stories of the life of Christ (see Thompson 1930; Oakes 1951; La Farge 1947).

The Xibalba episode of the *Popol Vuh* also embodies the tale type, though in a more complex form than the modern tales. In the *Popol Vuh,* function 1 is a journey to Xibalba, with a contest via the ball game between the lords of death and twin brothers who are children of the creator couple. The Twins lose and are killed and buried in the ball court (function 2). There is a partial resurrection (function 3), which is sufficient to allow the living skull of one of the Twins to impregnate Xquic, a daughter of the lords of death. She flees to the upper world (a return to function 1 in its pursuit variation, as in the sun/moon folk tales). At this point other material is inserted, but soon the nuclear plot reasserts itself. Function 1 is repeated when the twins born to Xquic are called upon to play against the lords. They play a series of ball games during the day, are imprisoned in houses of punishment at night (function 2), and are eventually killed (function 2 completed). They are reborn (function 3), revisit the lords (function 4), and then defeat them with a trick and kill them (function 5).

The Momostecans, like other Mesoamerican communities, found in a folk version of the Jesucristo story—probably learned in part from enactments of the apocryphal gospels—a life of Jesucristo that familiarly embodied the Proppian morphology or mythic structure, if not much of the detailed contents, of their own sun/moon cycle. This basic Mesoamerican millenarian myth, which had previously been embodied in the Twins at Xibalba episode of the *Popol Vuh,* was then retained as a story of the sun-Christ and the moon-Virgin.

A basic difference between the Jesucristo myth and the *Popol Vuh* is the highly developed series of flight and pursuit episodes in the Jesucristo myth and its absence in the Xibalba account. At the same time, the imprisonment function often found in Maya millenarian myths is elaborated in the Xibalba episode, where the Twins are imprisoned within Xibalba in the "houses of punishment." They are finally doubly imprisoned, taking refuge inside their blowguns in the house of bats, and eventually undergo the ultimate transformation of being sacrificed and reborn before defeating the lords and emerging from Xibalba. These imprisonment motifs are absent from the Jesucristo texts that I collected and are only weakly developed when present in other recorded Maya texts of the life of Christ. A useful way to approach this change at the heart of the mythological tradition is to follow Joseph Campbell's (1949) analysis of the hero myth and view these as morphologically homologous but culturally specific images of initiatory ordeals.

Ancient and Modern Rites of Renewal

Culture heroes are the prototypes or models for the carriers of the tradition, and their stories are cosmogonic myths providing models for rituals (rites of passage and rites of renewal) through which the participants are able to enter mythical time and re-enact the cosmogony (Eliade 1963). The substitution of flight and pursuit motifs for ball game and imprisonment motifs in the narrative myth, then, should be related to changes in the basic forms of initiatory ordeal and collective ceremonies of renewal, the cultural performances for which the narratives provide cosmogonic charters.

The sunrise episode in the *Popol Vuh* served as a charter for an elite rite of renewal, probably an elite version of the yearbearer rite, the Quichean new year.[21] In examining the relationship between Jesucristo and the Hero Twins, it is possible to make an argument for a transformed expression of the cult of the yearbearer in the *Popol Vuh* in much the same way that the Jesucristo/Simón/Tzulab complex in Momos may be viewed as an expression of a yearbearer-like myth, as one that is transformed but carries many of the same central meanings.

The Twins' Xibalba episode, read as a script for a performance, is the prototype for a major Quichean rite of renewal. It begins, like a rite of passage, with the Twins' separation from the ordinary world by their trip to Xibalba, the underworld. There, as in the margin phase of a rite of passage, they are forced to suffer and attempts are made to humiliate them. They undergo an ordeal for six days and nights, in which each night is spent in a different house of punishment and their days are spent playing ball against the lords. At the end of the six-day ordeal, they are sacrificed; actually, like the Mexican sun deity, they sacrifice themselves by leaping into a fire.

It is at this point that the episode manifests traits of the yearbearer mythos. The Twins remain "dead" for a period of five days. During these five days the evil lords of death rule over the world. Then the Twins return, and in the form of vagabonds (like the Tzulab dancers in Momos) they entertain, deceive, and finally destroy the lords. The rightful, legitimate powers thus undergo a five-day period of regeneration before reentering the world, deposing the false and evil tyrants, and restoring or perhaps completing the cosmos. The Twins ascend to heaven where they are given the sun and the moon. If the Xibalba episode served as the charter for a yearbearer-like rite of renewal, it also served as a model for a rite of passage for the sons of the Quiché warrior elite. Like their counterparts, the Twins, they would be expected eventually to avenge their fathers by overcoming their fathers' enemies,[22] and in preparation they would die as boys to be reborn as warriors.

Las Casas' account of the Quiché of Vera Paz, who still maintained an aboriginal culture when he went among them in the sixteenth century, describes a rite of passage of the type I am suggesting. The young men were instructed in seclusion at a special building. Marriage was postponed for men until age thirty, suggesting the need for some alternative road to adulthood for the young men of the elite (Las Casas 1967: 515). During the "Lent" of the Indians, which occurred near Easter when he observed it, men and women were kept separate, and the men and youths went out to crossroads and mountain peaks to make blood offerings.[23] If the youths were timid, the adult men cut them (Las Casas 1967: 218), a typical element in a rite of passage involving humiliation, pain, and fear for the youths and helping to define the adult male role. Corresponding closely to its Xibalba prototype, the fiesta proper followed a period of fasting and separation of the sexes, lasted for three to seven days—like the six- or seven-day ordeal of the Twins in Xibalba— and involved a ball game each afternoon (Las Casas 1967: 220–22).

The initial separation of the fasting men and boys reenacted the journey of the Twins and their twinned father and uncle to Xibalba. The fiesta centering on the ball game was a reenactment of the liminal period set in a reconstituted Xibalba. Las Casas does not mention the Uayeb (five unlucky days) or any period of danger or suspense following the fiesta. He mentions, however, that sacrifices were made at altars to the sun and moon that were located at the cardinal points. These altars suggest the two altars at each of the four entrances to the town that figured in the yearbearer ceremonies in Yucatán (Tozzer 1966: 137). All the above suggests an enduring complex linking the sun and moon, the Hero Twins, and the yearbearer to each other as central symbols in an annual rite of cosmic renewal and of transforming boys into warriors.

The ball game was repressed after the conquest, and this hypothetical rite of passage probably was too. It no longer exists in its original form. It is not needed in peasant village cultures where a warrior elite has ceased to exist, where warrior status is established by basic training and service in a national military, and where manhood is clearly marked in village culture by marriage and fatherhood at an early age. The Indian Lent described by Las Casas, though, has not vanished entirely. The reenactment of the Xibalba story now occurs in Holy Week.

Lent and Holy Week constitute the principal rite of renewal for Momostenango.[24] Small groups of men and women in the *cofradías* undergo a number of ordeals. A version of the vigils in the houses of punishment has perhaps been retained in the two-night vigil of a group of *cofrades* with the image of San Simón and in the all-night vigil of all the *cofrades* with Corpus in the *calvario*. San Simón must have a cigarette burning at all times, which may relate to the motif of the cigars associated with the house of gloom in Xibalba. It also helps to identify San Simón as having descended from the cigar-smoking God L, the Classic prototype for One Death in the *Popol Vuh*. These vigils are ordeals. It is very dangerous to lose concentration, regret the time or expense, or fall asleep (see chap. 2). In preparation for them, sexual abstinence and *costumbre* are required.

The major ordeals, however, are the trips to the coast for the greenery used to decorate the town crosses and the cemetery. The coast is the modern counterpart of Xibalba. Saler (1967) has shown that highland Indians perceive the coast as a place of evil where witchcraft and evil transformers called *wins* are endemic. On the coast, plantation work is encountered that serves as the model for a contemporary Maya conception of hell, service to a *dueño* on his plantation inside the mountain. The coast is a place of unbearable heat, dirty undrinkable water, disease, death, and humiliation.[25] San Simón, among many other things an embodiment of evil, the Ocel of the Momostecan Uayeb, is dressed and treated as a parody of the Ladino *patrón.*

The journey to the coast for flowers also corresponds to the Hero Twins' journey to Xibalba in that one of the tasks set for the Twins was to pick flowers for the lords from the underworld garden. Collecting flowers on the coast, the garden of Xibalba, and presenting them to San Simón recapitulates this *Popol Vuh* motif faithfully. The journey is an ordeal because it is fraught with supernatural dangers and signs. If anyone in the party has had sexual relations during the period of abstinence, snakes may appear in the jungle and bite someone, or the greenery itself may be transformed into serpents. The greenery may wilt before the decoration of Momostenango is completed. This sign (*retal*) would show that the *cofrades* had failed in their *costumbre* and might presage a hot and prolonged dry season. If the *costumbre* is not perfect, the party might be arrested by the police for transporting the greens without a license, potentially inserting the often-absent imprisonment motif in exactly the right place in the story.

Transformation of the Ordeal

The Lenten–Holy Week journey is a form of pilgrimage called a *visita* by Momostecans because they visit the shrine of the *cofradía's* saint in Momostenango and its cognate at the other end of the journey in El Palmar. There are additional significant ordeals in the form of *cofradía* journeys associated with the images of San Antonio and Santiago (see chap. 3) that are also called *visitas.* In these, private houses as well as *aldea* chapels are visited for fiestas.

In such *visitas,* a prototypical role for Jesucristo as culture hero is apparent. The saints travel through the Momostecan world, blessing those who treat them properly and cursing those who receive them badly. Thus the ordeal of Jesucristo as a traveler through a liminal world beset by enemies is familiar to Momostecans not only as a description of life but also as the prototype for their own individual participation in the sacred journeys of the *cofradías* or in personal pilgrimages.

Mendelson (1967: 410) suggested that correct *viaje,* which he defined as correct movement between places, is a central theme in the ritual of Mesoamerica. In Momostenango the most significant form of *viaje* is the *visita*. The confrontation between a person or persons and a supernatural power object is the goal of the trip, and, furthermore, the trip is an ordeal. It is a test of one's power or grace. It is an opportunity to be given signs of one's fate or destiny. It seems to have replaced the pre-conquest model of an ordeal, which was a period of fasting and bloodletting in seclusion in the mountains, the temple, or the houses of punishment. The *viaje* as an ordeal is the form taken by Proppian function 1 in the Momostecan mythos, in both the stories of Yegua Achi' and the life of Jesucristo. Both can be read as cosmogonic prototypes for the pilgrimage-*visita* complex.[26]

The Dance of the Vagabonds, Then and Now

The Momostecan dance called Grasejos or Tzulab links Lent and Holy Week clearly to the Xibalba episode in the *Popol Vuh*. The Tzulab of Holy Week are the dancers of Jesucristo in his guise as Corpus or Señor Resurrección, but for the first two days of their performance they dance for San Simón because this is his fiesta and Corpus is dead. Although the Tzulab dance at the cemetery while San Simón is seated in the plaza, a smaller image of San Simón is seated under their marimba. Late in the afternoon the Tzulab dance with this little Simón, carrying him on their backs.

In the Recinos translation of the *Popol Vuh*, the dancing of the Twins before Xibalba is described as follows:

> *And the following day, two poor men presented themselves with very old-looking faces and of miserable appearance, [and] ragged clothes, whose countenances did not commend them. So they were seen by all those of Xibalba.*
>
> *And what they did was very little. They only performed the dance of the* puhuy *[owl or churn owl], the dance of the* cux *[weasel], and the dance of the* iboy *[armadillo], and they also danced the* xtzul *[centipede] and the* chitic *[that walks on stilts]. . . .*[27]
>
> *Presently they cut themselves into bits; they killed each other; the first one whom they had killed stretched out as though he were dead, and instantly the other brought him back to life. Those of Xibalba looked on in amazement at all they did, and they performed it as the beginning of their triumph over those of Xibalba.*   (Recinos 1950: 156)

Xtzul (centipede) is the diminutive or feminized form of *tzul*. The relationship of the Tzulab to a centipede is clearly seen when the Tzulab perform one dance in the form of a leapfrog in which a dancer passes down the whole length of the kneeling dancers, takes his place at the head, and is followed by another and another, while the entire group resembles a centipede or millipede crawling slowly across the plaza.[28] The Tzulab are dressed in rags and have unattractive faces. They manipulate stuffed weasels (called *sacbin* rather than *cux* in Momos) during the dance, and they resurrect each other (see chap. 5). The Tzulab Dance enacts this *Popol Vuh* episode. The Twins and One Death have been replaced by Nabe and Ucab Mu'us (First and Second Ladinos [or "Dandies"]), the two dance leaders, and San Simón. There may be other vestigial traces of the Twins in the way in which Jesucristo is represented by both Corpus and Capitagua in the cemetery chapel and perhaps even in the way in which the cult is maintained by the cooperative activities of the two *cofradías* called Corpus and Santa Cruz.[29]

The Tzulab dance and San Simón is defeated and removed from power on Friday at noon. The following morning, on Saturday, Jesucristo is returned to life. The Tzulab continue to dance, now in front of the church. As the Hero Twins have a last meeting with their partially resurrected father at the ball court after defeating the lords, the Tzulab are present for the resurrection of Jesucristo. After the unseating and the destruction of the body of San Simón, the homologue for the defeat of One Death, they mediate in the resurrection as rain mediates in the germination of maize.

The dance still plays its Postclassic cosmogonic role as the accompaniment to the defeat of liminal adversaries and the world-transforming emergence from the earth of a solar or celestial culture hero. Emergence from the earth may be the key idea. This would explain why the *xtzul* was danced when the Cakchiquel culture heroes emerged from the volcano Gagxnul with fire for their people (Recinos and Goetz 1953: 71), and why the Tzulab is also the dance at the festival of the Momostecan Niño San Antonio, a fertility deity who emerged from a cave in Pologua.

The Tzulab is a fertility dance linking the solar culture hero myth to peasant concerns with the agricultural season. A Maya fertility dance would have been discouraged by the Christian overlords, but the Matachín Dance element (see chap. 5), probably attached to the dance early in the colonial period, provided a pretext for continuing the dance and probably made it more entertaining. The Matachín motifs, though, were brought into conformity with the fertility theme and with the identities of the Tzulab as the orgiastic young godlings of the Stresser Paean/Mendelson rain god cycle.

As symbolized in Momostecan linguistic usage in which grandparents and grandchildren refer to each other as "my replacement" (*nu c'axel*), the Tzulab—young and fertile grandsons and rain bringers— replace their grandfather, the old Mam, San Simón, who ends his career as the used-up husk of the vegetative world, burned to prepare for the planting. In the rain god cycle, the young *mams* grow old with the year and are replaced in their turn. Jesucristo here personifies the maize, and his birth, death, and rebirth mark the critical phases of the maize cycle within the solar year.

The Two Myths of Renewal

The Momostecan Costumbrista Holy Week observances, then, integrate versions of the millenarian solar mythology and of the vegetative renewal/rain god complex, and represent a version of an underlying armature, a Maya model for the renewal of the world, that may not have seen fundamental change since the Postclassic horizon and that had roots in the Classic and perhaps the Formative. Dennis Tedlock (1985: 251) finds that the metaphorical linkage of sowing and dawning is basic to the *Popol Vuh*. A similar integrated complex is expressed in the iconography of Palenque, with its seemingly inextricable mixing of imagery of kingly accession, the sun, the maize cycle, vegetative generation, life, death, and human ancestry (Carlsen and Prechtel 1991: 35, 36).

Though Carlsen and Prechtel argue convincingly that the interweaving of solar and vegetative symbolism, and of the political and cosmological frameworks, is central to the meaning and function of the renewal complex, I will try to tease the threads apart a little bit. In the Momostecan tradition the solar component tends to be emphasized in oral narratives, and in the Quichean tradition it is embodied explicitly in the actions of named characters, for example, Jun Ajpu and One Death or Jesucristo and San Simón. The Quichean version of the vegetative renewal myth in Momostenango embodies the seasons of the milpa cycle, understood as stages in the life of a personified year in ritualized performances, but is enacted without an explicit narrated charter.

In his solar deity culture hero guise, Jesucristo is born at Christmas and journeys to the underworld at Easter, while liminal beings released from the underworld, San Simón and the Tzulab, reenact the defeat of the lords of death by the vagabond tricksters. Six sodalities[30] make pilgrimages to the coast, the modern counterpart of Xibalba, during Lent and Holy Week to return with "flowers" for San Simón, as the Twins collected flowers in Xibalba for Lord One Death. The *cofrades* complete individual rites of passage as pilgrims within the framework of a community rite of renewal. When the images of Jesucristo, the Virgen, and the little angel San Miguel accompany the sun to the central plaza at dawn on Easter Sunday, the cosmogonic sunrise is reenacted.

While it lacks an explicit, narrated charter, the vegetative renewal complex can be deduced from a substantial body of evidence. Holy Week begins on Palm Sunday, which is timed to fall approximately on the first full moon after the vernal equinox. Momostecans watch the sun and moon rise over a hill above the cemetery on the eastern side of town. When the sun and full moon are both seen to rise at a marked location, it is time for Holy Week, the ritualized transition from the dry season to the planting season. Cakchiquel informants conceptualize an ideal model of celestial paths in which the sun's and the moon's paths cross at the equinoxes (Remington 1977: 77), so this event when the moon turns full at the onset of Holy Week represents one of two possible encounter points during the year. This encounter initiates the planting season and may be understood as a celestial conception, a prototype replicated by the placing of seed in the earth, which is also understood as being like conception and is correlated with the full moon.[31]

The celestial encounter/conception complex is replicated on the ground in the meeting and journeying together of María Concepción and the reborn Jesucristo, "our father the sun," before dawn on Easter morning. The moon is often referred to as "our grandmother" (*Katit*) in her role as the mother of "our father" Jesucristo. Yet there is also a tradition, embodied clearly in the Kekchi sun/moon mythology described above, that the sun and the moon are a couple that eloped when the sun stole the moon from her kinfolk. Thus Jesucristo is potentially both the husband and the son of the moon. In the Momostecan enactment of this cosmogony, it may be that as the mature year-ending sun he impregnates the moon at Easter to initiate the planting season, and nine months later, after gestation in the fields, he is born as the maize, the Baby Jesus, ending the harvest season at Christmas.[32] Momostecans say that the maize is born when it is harvested (B. Tedlock 1992).[33] Thus, with the Baby Jesus as harvest patron and the life cycle of maize likened to human gestation, it makes sense that the Niño San Antonio became the Momostecan fertility deity.

As a personifier of maize, then, Jesucristo is conceived by the sun and moon, undergoes a gestation during the growing season, and is born at the harvest when the birth of the maize is linked to the birth of the sun, the Baby Jesucristo, born when the sun reverses its drift to the south at the winter solstice and begins its journey to the vernal equinox and the planting season, its rebirth. Perhaps, in a very Maya take on being the son of God, Jesucristo is cyclically reborn as his own son, fulfilling literally what Jun Jun Ajpu's skull confided to Xquic when she was impregnated in the ballcourt of Xibalba: "The father does not disappear, but goes on being fulfilled. Neither dimmed nor destroyed . . . he will leave his daughters and sons" (Tedlock 1985: 114–115).

Matters become confusing when the Jesucristo cosmogony is compared to that in the *Popol Vuh.* Jesucristo plays two roles, one as the son of María, and the other as the regenerator of the agricultural cycle, as her husband acting to make her conceive at the beginning of the planting season. Jesucristo thus plays cosmogonic roles that were divided between Jun Jun Ajpu and his son Jun Ajpu in the Postclassic myth.

Echoing this complication, it appears that GI in the Classic Period Palenque triad may be either Hun Ahau (Jun Ajaw)—that is, the Classic prototype for Jun Ajpu—or Hun Nal Ye, the maize god and, as the counterpart of Jun Jun Ajpu, the father of Jun Ajpu.[34] How then can a deity be its own father? It is here that a custom recorded in Santiago Atitlán takes on explanatory significance. There "the *k'exel,* as the grandparent's 'replacement', becomes the symbolic parent of the biological parents. Consequently one's child is sometimes actually addressed as 'parent' and males always address their fathers as *nuk'jol,* or 'my son.' Likewise, a woman will often call her father '*wal*' which translates as 'my child'" (Carlsen and Prechtel 1991: 29).

There is no comparable role or identity confusion in the narrated Jesucristo story, nor in the basic folk-type myth of the rain god cycle as presented by Mendelson. The ancient mythology and the current enactments of the vegetative renewal myth in Holy Week depict a more intricate and complex social and sexual world than the generic folk-type myth, with its focus on life cycle themes or the simple story of the lone Jesucristo pursued through a primordial world by devils.

In his guise as the dying and reborn sun, and the vanquisher of the liminal beings of the pre-creation chaos, Jesucristo is also the lord of the souls, a role he enacts in part by allowing them to visit their living relatives every time the day Ajpu comes around, thus referring back to his pre-conquest counterpart. Yet in the vegetative renewal guise, his own soul or spirit is abroad in the world, passing through various temporal forms in constituting the annual cycle of importance to those who would derive their lives from maize.

A logical splitting of the cosmological identity of Jesucristo occurs as he represents both the maize and the sun. Although his annual birth, death, and rebirth identify him with the maize growing toward its new birth in the fields, he is also the rain sun—the sun that enters the church (*rochoch Tiox*, "God's house") on Easter morning and marshals the four rain bringers, Santiago, San Felipe, San Miguel, and San Francisco. As he embarks on this phase of his solar career, the orgiastic young rain gods, the Tzulab (i.e., *mams*), dance in the plaza, cracking their lightning whips in imitation and preparatory celebration of the coming storms that will renew the world. Jesucristo as the rain-sun then seems to be like the father of the maize.

This vegetative renewal guise of Jesucristo is tied up with the symbolism of San Simón as the embodiment of the flowering cross of Holy Week and the patron of the flowering crosses of Lent. San Simón, in the symbolism of this complex, is patron of the dry season, or agricultural off-season. He is lord of the growth of wild vegetation in the resting fields, and of the growth of jungle (*juyup*) which is cleared and burned to create new fields (*takaj*) that are fertilized by the ashes. Thus, Juyup Takaj refers not only to the world of mountains and plains, of wilderness and cultivated lands, but is also the year with its seasons of milpa cultivation (*takaj*) and of agricultural dormancy when the wilderness reasserts itself (*juyup*). San Simón personifies *juyup*. He is lord of the period during which the maize is absent from the fields, when the dry stalks stand rustling until the rains come again and the earth is turned to bury them. San Simón's body, a cross of bunchgrass harvested in flower, dries while he is seated in power in the plaza during Holy Week. It is burned at noon on Good Friday in preparation for the moment of germination or conception when the life force of Jesucristo returns, renewing the world and reinvigorating the seed corn, at dawn on Saturday.

While San Simón clearly has underworld connotations and his mythic charter portrays him as an enemy of Jesucristo, he is also, in terms of the Stresser Paean/Mendelson rain god cycle, the old Mam, the personification of the sun or year whose vitality has been used up in the rainy season when it nourished the maize and who, like any human father who has raised his family, is in decline during the dry and sterile final phase of his life. He is now the grandfather of the maize and of the living world, the old Mam, having fulfilled his rain-sun role as father.

The sun ages and eventually, as old Mam Simón, becomes grandfather to the maize, his *c'axel* or replacement.[35] The old Mam dies and is burned before the sun is reborn on Saturday morning, and before the reborn sun promenades with his wife/mother the moon to the plaza at dawn on Easter Sunday morning. Perhaps the conception of Jesucristo in his maize guise is then a reincarnation, the recycling of the spiritual essence of his grandfather, his older self, the Mam Simón who was sacrificed at noon on Friday as the *c'axel* of the maize.

An intergenerational drama of replacement linked to the renewal of the agricultural cycle, with complex intimations of reincarnation, seems also to inform the expressive culture of Santiago Atitlán. There it has been clearly articulated as an implication of the *jaloj k'exoj* complex by Carlsen and Prechtel (1991) in an essay that served, with the Mendelson (1967) rain god cycle, as inspiration for the complex interpretation above.

The pre-Hispanic Quiché surely also embodied millenarian and vegetative myths in their expressive culture. The *Popol Vuh*, the product of the memory and concerns of a descendant of an elite status group, presents an elite version of Quiché mythology. It focuses on the sunrise, on the charter for the social and political aspects of civilization, and emphasizes the millenarian sunrise myth variant. Even today this variant is emphasized in the oral narrative tradition and in much of the enacted expressive culture—for example, the Conquest Dance, which was given during Holy Week until the 1920s, the Devils Dance at Christmas, and the text-driven explication of Holy Week as an expression of the Jesucristo story.

The vegetative myth—the rain god cycle and the regeneration of the maize—is expressed in Momostecan ritual and embodied in core ritual symbols, but is encountered in round-about ways, seen out of the corner of one's eye, constructed on the basis of linguistic leads and iconographic interpretations and the fitting together of other puzzle pieces in other towns, like Santiago Atitlán. In this variant of the mythos, as in the Stresser Paean/Mendelson rain god cycle, the Quichean deities, the *mams,* are seen in various stages of a life cycle. They are orgiastic and chaotic in youth, like the jungle or violent spring rainstorms. They are orderly and fertile in their prime years, like the milpa and like Jesucristo as a transformer creating a domesticated world. They are old, spent, and even vindictive at the end of life, perhaps like the sun-Christ in the dry season and certainly like San Simón. The Jesucristo myth in its entirety, as told in stories and enacted in sodality performances, is about all of this. Its perpetual reenactment unites the human or cultural and natural worlds, *takaj* and *juyup,* and through this conjoining moves the human community with nature through the maize cycle.

Societal Models in Holy Week

Holy Week also embodies Maya social theory about the cyclical alternation of authority and power, good and evil. For several days each year during Holy Week, legitimate authority is terminated, and chaos— both in the form of the Tzulab dancers and as overly rigid, restrictive, and illegitimate "authority" on the part of San Simón—intrudes into or temporarily replaces cosmos. In this guise it is another rite of renewal concerned with the breakdown of cosmos and its reinstitution. It is concerned with the safe passage of the community through a dangerous time, as, for example, in difficult transitions between political regimes.

On Thursday afternoon the staffs of office (*varas*) of the town's officials and the silver standards of the *cofradías* are replaced by large candles from Antigua at mass, and the staffs and standards are placed in the sacristy. San Simón, who has been seated in the plaza in front of the church since dawn, is now in complete power. Chaos or liminality seems to peak by Thursday night, which is a night of licentiousness or *communitas,* depending on your values. Bands of unmarried youths of both sexes, Maya and Ladino, roam the streets of Momostenango unchaperoned by their elders.

On Saturday morning Jesucristo is called back, and with his return the souls of the dead are also returned to the living in a day of liberty. Given the importance of the dead as part of the Momostecan "trinity,"[36] the absence of the dead for these five days, and their fiesta on Saturday when their lord has returned to power should not be underestimated as a key to the meaning of the five days. At mass on Saturday morning the emblems and staffs of office are returned to the officials. By noon on Saturday order has been restored.

In Holy Week the opposition between fertile chaos and sterile hierarchy, symbolized by the opposition of the Tzulab and San Simón, is resolved in the reestablishment of the cosmos of Jesucristo. During Holy Week's dissolution of cosmos, while the community as a whole is entering a phase of antistructure or *communitas,* also symbolized by the surrender of the differentiating emblems, a myth of cosmogonic struggle is enacted at the church and cemetery.

San Simón is clearly a Ladino and is sometimes also referred to as a gringo.[37] He is said to be a world traveler and a foreigner. He is said to be a *patrón* and the *cofrades* who care for him during Holy Week are his peons. He is also a shopkeeper on whose behalf the *cofrades* attempt to sell the dried maguey leaves which are his fish. In these roles as *patrón* and as storekeeper and even in his simple association with money itself, he personifies the Ladino (or gringo, the powerful and wealthy alien) as he is perceived by Momostecans. He is dressed in Western-style clothing including glasses, black oxford-style shoes, and an ascot or tie.

The Tzulab, in spite of the fact that in the dance the "woman" is named Xinula (Ladina) and the leader is called Mu's (Ladino), are clearly Indians. They are dressed as Momostecans but not as urbane urban *indigenas.* They are shepherds, the most rustic of Momostecans. The woman wears a man's hat as only a woman tending sheep in the *cumbre* would do. Like the Mam in the Origins of Costumbre narrative,[38] they are shepherds with whips slung over their shoulders.

Viewed as a statement on indigenous/Ladino relationships, the Holy Week mythos is a wish-fulfillment fantasy. The Ladino only briefly penetrates the community during the five days, which could not happen if Jesucristo were in power. The Ladino's peons are able to insult him and make jokes about him with impunity as long as they maintain a formal appearance of respect and keep him supplied with cigarettes and drinks. After a couple of days of service, they can strip him and burn his body. Meanwhile, the Tzulab take his place and survive the return of Jesucristo to dance at his fiesta on Saturday and Sunday. Jesucristo is pleased with them, and by inference with the peasant shepherds they represent, perhaps, as one dancer suggests, because "God likes the sound of the lash."

The type of domination represented by the Ladino and other foreigners is thus symbolically linked to Xibalba and is erased by Jesucristo, who establishes or reestablishes cosmos each year. The power of Jesucristo protects the community from penetration by alien tyrants and allows the Momostecans to act out their fantasies of insubordination.

What theories or models of society are embodied in the Costumbristas' Holy Week symbolism?[39] Three different potential world orders are represented: the worlds of Jesucristo, of San Simón, and of the Tzulab.[40] The mythos enacted in Holy Week depicts the resolution of an opposition between the sterile hierarchy of San Simón's world and the fertile chaos of the Tzulab, a cosmogonic struggle out of which cosmos is reborn. This cosmogony can be analyzed as a dialectic in both syntagmatic and paradigmatic terms.[41]

The syntagmatic analysis is inspired by the insights of Eliade (1963) and Turner (1968, 1969). We humans experience community life as a cyclical alternation of ordinary time and sacred timelessness, of mundane structure and therapeutic antistructure. The world of Jesucristo, a "societas," is interrupted by a chaos embodying two opposed worlds, the orgiastic dance of the Tzulab and the dominance of the emasculated paymaster San Simón. A chaos-cosmogony-cosmos sequence is publicly enacted by the sodalities, and the chaos-cosmogony crisis in the sequence is accompanied by a liminal period "on the ground" in community life. It is this syntagmatic structure that has been described and discussed in detail up to this point. Yet a paradigmatic analysis is also possible. This would recognize that at least insofar as theories of society are concerned, the three "worlds" can be arranged with a rigid, formalized, hierarchical, and sterile social structure at one extreme (Simón) and an exuberant, chaotic, contrary, and fertile antistructure at the other (the Tzulab). As in the crisis period of Holy Week, human history, like the agricultural year, seeks a balancing of these contrary forces that may allow the societal analogue of *takaj* to flourish in its season. The sodalities that unite the human or cultural (*takaj*) and natural (*juyup*) worlds in their great rites of renewal in order to effect positive movement through the seasons also harness the forces of nature—as personified by Jesucristo, the saints, the Tzulab, and even San Simón—to model and effect a balance of social forces within which human community is possible.[42]

Societal Models in the Quichean Tradition

The Hero Twins episode of the *Popol Vuh* posits these same two sorts of threat to cosmos. On one hand it is threatened by the "underdifferentiated" nature-associated tricksters, Cabrican and Zipacna. On the other hand it is threatened by the illegitimate, tyrannical, restrictive, and alien power structures represented by Wucub Caquix and Xibalba. So it is possible to find within the enacted mythos of Momostenango, as within the narrated mythos, a dialectical structuring that is also a theme in the larger Quichean tradition running back to the *Popol Vuh*. Rituals of renewal and cosmogonic narratives establish polarities between nature and culture, indigene and alien, earth and heaven. In Holy Week this dialectic is mediated by Jesucristo and the souls of the dead. Their return ends the period of chaos and tension associated with the Holy Week crisis, with the lewd dancing and violence of the underdifferentiated and chaotic Tzulab and the sterility of Simón, who combines senescence and a Ladino-gringo identity in a symbol of authoritarian dominance. The central myth of the Quichean tradition unites nature and community as expressions of a single underlying theme of alternation and succession which is seen in the yearly alternation between seasons, in the historical alternation between presidents or regimes with dangerous but creative periods of transition, and in the perpetually recurring replacement of the old by the young.

Notes

CHAPTER 1

1. Here and below in this section I am relying on the interpretations of my mentor Robert Carmack (1995: 7, 1981: 53) and my colleague and friend John Fox (1987: 181) to reconstruct the late Postclassic situation when the Epigonal-Toltec Quiché conquest state expanded in the highlands. For a more detailed interpretation of the Quichean sociopolitical system at the time, see Fox and Cook (1996: 811–815).

2. Terms that lack accurate and commonly used English cognates and that reappear in the manuscript are given in Quiché or Spanish. For convenience, and to allow for fuller treatment, they are listed and defined in the glossary. As a stylistic convention, the plurals of Quiché nouns are formed according to the rules of English usage; for example, *porobals* rather than *porobalab*. The only exception is in the case of a few proper nouns like "Tzulab Dance," in which "Tzulab" is used rather than "Tzuls," or in citing a term given in the translation of a transcribed text.

3. The description of the colonial period social organization of Momos here, and in an expanded version in chapter 2, is based on Carmack 1995. A clear description of the very similar Cakchiquel pattern of the seventeenth century has also been published (see Hill 1992: 38–47). Hill's description calls attention to the problems of social integration that developed during the seventeenth century when independent *amaks* were thrown together in the *congregación* process to form pueblos. Carmack's work focuses more on the political struggles during the eighteenth and nineteenth centuries, when the traditional caciques in the *parcialidades* were increasingly opposed in effective political struggles by commoner political blocs utilizing the centralized *cabildo* government of the pueblo as a springboard to power.

4. The *Popol Vuh* first came to the attention of European civilization when a copy and Spanish translation was made by Father Francisco Ximénez at Chichicastenango (Ch'uwila) in the early eighteenth century. This copy remained unknown to a larger public until it was independently rediscovered in

the University of San Carlos archives in Guatemala and published by Carl Scherzer and Abbe Etienne Brasseur de Bourborg, the latter with a new French translation from the Spanish, in the mid-nineteenth century (See Recinos 1950: 16-61, Edmonson 1971: viii, Tedlock 1985: 28-30, Himelblau 1989: 1-15). The most influential subsequent translations, all made from the Quiché, have been those of Adrian Recinos, originally in Spanish in 1947, the Spanish later translated into English by Delia Goetz and Sylvanus G. Morley (Recinos 1950), and those of Munro Edmonson (1971) and his student Dennis Tedlock (1985), both translated directly into English. I have relied primarily on the Recinos and Tedlock translations, though Edmonson's discovery that the *Popol Vuh* makes extensive use of couplets is one of the major breakthroughs in its literary interpretation, and the supplementary dictionary that he compiled (Edmonson 1965) is an invaluable reference for critical reading of the translations.

Dennis Tedlock, responding to those who have found evidence for syncretism in some of the *Popol Vuh*'s motifs, has argued persuasively that the *Popol Vuh*, though written "within Christendom," represents a distinctive Maya alternative to the biblical creation account and should be considered as an expression of aboriginal culture (D. Tedlock 1986). The troubling thesis that the *Popol Vuh* was written by a Spanish cleric, Domingo de Vico (Acuña 1975, 1983), is effectively refuted by the discussion of motifs in Dennis Tedlock's hermeneutical approach (1986) and by the detailed morphological analysis of Jack Himelblau (1989). The *Popol Vuh* is thus here considered to represent a Quiché-Maya cosmogonic and historical account intended to preserve the traditional knowledge of Quichean origins so they would not be lost, in spite of the loss of their traditional media of expression, under Spanish rule.

5. A successful adaptation always refers to conditions in the past. When environmental, demographic, or economic conditions do not permit the maintenance of a traditional way of life, it will change. Cultural crystallization, a term coined by George Foster (1960: 227-234) to refer specifically to the colonial cultures of the Americas, refers to the process of institutionalization in which a new, but subsequently stable, and eventually "traditional" way of life precipitates out of historical tumult.

6. Oliver La Farge (1940, 1956) suggested a workable framework for the sequence of Maya cultural "crystallizations" in Guatemala, although he did not use that term. He postulated a nativistic Recent Indian Stage that developed in response to the nineteenth century attacks of the post-colonial social and political order on the privileges and protections that had been enjoyed under the crown by Indian communities (see Carmack's 1995: 125-222 discussion of the transitional Early Republican Period for a description of this transformative period in Momostenango). Early-twentieth-century Maya village cultures embodied this Recent Indian Stage crystallization and attempted to defend it

from, or to adapt it to, sometimes hostile liberal regimes and the evolving Ladino nation-state. It persisted, as an ideal at any rate, for the majority of Momostecans on into the 1970s, but under increasingly strong pressures from "ladinoizing" acculturated Maya and from an increasingly alienated Maya proletariat attracted to Catholic Action and to evangelical Protestant sects (see Carmack 1995: 223–414 for a comprehensive description of the recent Indian stage and its internal factions and conflicts in Momostenango).

7. "Costumbrista" is the term used by Momostecan traditionalists to refer to practitioners of the syncretized Maya-Catholic religion. They call their religion "Costumbre" (from the Spanish word for custom) or "Poronel" (from the Quiché word for burning). In this work, *costumbre* (lowercase italic) is used to indicate rituals carried out in the practice of Costumbre.

8. This pattern was disrupted for a period of several years during the violence and oppression of the 1980s when an *intendente* system was temporarily restored, with rule by an appointed local Ladino representing the governor.

9. When speaking Spanish, Momostecans refer to those of Maya ancestry as *naturales* or *indígenas*. The term *indio,* sometimes used by Ladinos, is considered a demeaning pejorative.

10. The story of the emergence of this acculturated sector and its rise to power, always in competition with the traditional native caciques and the local Ladinos, is the major theme of Carmack's (1995) detailed social history of Momostenango.

11. In a provocative essay John Watanabe (1990: 131–132, 146) has defined two points of view about Maya syncretism. The primordialist perspective that he associates with Eva Hunt and Victoria Bricker sees an "essential Mayaness" in contemporary syncretised culture, while an opposed historicist position sees syncretism as a colonial construction. The Indian in this latter view is created by oppression in the colonial order, rather than being a survivor carrying a Native American tradition. Watanabe criticizes both of these positions as guilty of reification, and argues for a mediating position in which syncretism is understood as a conditional adaptive on-going process in which traditional symbols—earth lords, for example—are used to construct meaningful social identities in the process of maintaining local moral communities.

I am in sympathy with Watanabe's view of the process, and it informs the interpretation of Quiché expressive culture offered below. I have tried to go beyond the Indian versus Ladino dynamics of identity construction in Watanabe's approach to also consider the identities and ideological needs of opposed traditionalist Indian factions in Momostenango. Unlike Watanabe, though, I don't see mystical essentialism in Bricker's work, or in other theoretically similar works that identify Mesoamerican themes in colonial and modern Indian cultures (e.g., see Gossen 1986), and I think Bricker's study is eminently historical. Consequently, I prefer the less metaphysical terminology of continuity (for primordialist) versus discontinuity (for historicist) models offered in a critical discussion by Carlsen and Prechtel (1991: 23–24).

12. Foster (1960: 232–233) noted that a restricted set of the possibilities from Spanish culture was transplanted to the New World in a fluid period early in the conquest/colonial process when the new colonial order was being constructed. Once the colonial pattern had "crystallized," it was so resistant to change that later immigrants from northern Spain were not able to influence the pattern to any great extent. Similarly, it would seem that any elements of the indigenous pattern that were incorporated during this fluid period would also tend to endure within the "crystallized" culture.

13. In a critique of materialistic adaptationism, Barrett (1991: 118) asks: "[I]s it common to find enduring sociocultural traits whose persistence has almost nothing to do with adaptation—in the sense of adjustment to environmental conditions—but has very much to do with their 'place' in a constituted social pattern?" He goes on to amass evidence in support of Veblen's thesis that cultural inertia is a very real phenomenon derived from the social power of vested interests, or to put it another way, from the amount of prior investment in social and material infrastructure that supports the existing cultural pattern.

14. Malinowski (1944) defines institutions as organized groups of people performing culturally defined tasks. Each institution has a charter, including legitimizing mythology, as well as personnel and capital. Wallace (1966) defines religions as collections of cult institutions of several types. His model is presented in more detail early in chapter 2.

15. This alphabet is used in the linguistic sources that I worked with in studying Quiché (Fox 1973: 15–18, Mondloch and Hruska 1975: 1.1–1.6), and by Barbara Tedlock (1982: 213) in her monograph on Momostenango. It pronounces vowels as in Spanish. Consonants are also pronounced as in Spanish, except *x* is pronounced as English *sh*, *w* is like the English *w*, and *k* is articulated further back in the throat than the English *k* and is slightly glottalized. *K'* is a full glottal stop, and an apostrophe means to glottalize any consonant or vowel that it follows. In spoken Quiché, words are normally accented on the last syllable.

This is largely consistent with the more recently developed official Guatemalan Maya alphabets as established by Acuerdo Gubernativo Número 1046–87, of November 23, 1987. The main differences are that where I would use *k'* the 1987 system has substituted *q'*, and where I would use *qu-* or *c-* in initial position depending on the following vowel, as in Spanish usage, the new alphabet uses *k-* (as in k'ak' [red] going to q'aq' and Quiché going to Kiché).

16. An *aj mesa* is a high-ranking priest-shaman who followed his initiation as an *aj vara*, or *aj patan*, a diviner with a bag of *tzite* seeds, with a second

initiation at a special altar called a *mesabal* or *mesa,* dedicated to the Holy World. Among these altars the most important are located on the Paklom at the center, and on four lesser and four major mountains located in the cardinal directions. Only initiated *aj mesas* may perform offerings at these *porobals,* which are usually marked with a cross. *Aj mesas* perform an important role as curers and defenders against witchcraft, especially in those cases where intervention by the shaman-priest of one's lineage has been ineffective, or in those cases where a diviner identifies the *mesa* as the cause of a problem.

17. I mentioned this remarkable narrative to Barbara Tedlock, who later recorded it in Quiché and published an English translation (Tedlock 1982: 180–187) and a translation with an extensive commentary under the title "Ojer Tzij" or "Ancient Word" (B. Tedlock 1986). Since Tedlock used the raconteur's actual name, and especially since there are no texts by Don Vicente published in this work, I have retained his name rather than a pseudonym.

18. *Alcalde* is usually pronounced as *alcalté* in Quiché texts.

19. Deputy is a position of lesser status than *alcalde,* but often held for many years, leading to a role as the chief expert on *cofradía* lore and *costumbre.* The pronunciation *teputado* is most commonly used when speaking Quiché. In a more extreme case, *mayordomo* has become *mortoma,* and so this latter term is used in this work.

CHAPTER 2

1. The two community-level festivals that are scheduled by the Maya calendar—the yearbearer's festival, when the Mam is welcomed at the beginning of the new solar year, and 8 Batz every 260 days, when daykeepers are initiated—have been documented (see Tedlock 1982). The present work seeks to supplement and complement B. Tedlock's approach to contemporary Maya religious thought through an ethnographic description of the sodalities that are touched on only superficially in her work.

2. Hill and Monoghan (1987: 9–10) elucidate the semantic difference between *aldea,* an officially recognized territorial subdivision of the municipality, and *cantón,* a traditional territorial unit that may not correspond exactly to an *aldea.* The *cantones* are the settings for *cofradías* (17–18) and are descendants of the *chinamits* (24–42). In similar fashion, Carmack (1995: 296) notes that Momostenango is broken down into modern rural districts (*aldeas*) and traditional rural subdivisions (*cantones*) that are usually coterminous, but that there are *cantones* (Pueblo Viejo in Aldea Tunayac and Pologua in Aldea Pasajoc, for example) located within *aldeas* and yet recognized as independent *cantones,* while some *cantones* are composed of two recognized *aldeas* (for example, the *aldeas* Tzanjon and Tierra Blanca are lumped together as one *cantón*). I will argue below that both Pueblo Viejo and Pologua were *parciali-*

dades during the colonial period. In Momos, as well, the cantonal organization is derived from the earlier *parcialidad* system.

3. The recent publication of a history of Momostenango by Robert Carmack (1995) makes it possible to relate the origins and development of the *cofradías* to a documented context. Except where another source is indicated, the historical reconstruction here relies on Carmack's book.

4. Carmack (1977: 12) reconstructs the Postclassic pattern as one in which an *amak* was a hamlet dependent on a *tinamit,* that is, it was a *chinamit* as the terms are defined here. Quichean sociological terms may often have lacked specific jurisdictional or scale-based references but were more relativistic. Thus a *chinamit* of Chuwa Tz'ak might be called an *amak* by the resident lords there, but Chuwa Tz'ak itself would be considered as an *amak* from the point of view of the lords at K'umarca'aj. See Fox and Cook 1996: 811–812 for an expanded discussion of how the same term was applied in a graded fashion, sometimes with associated qualifying terms (*chuti amak, amak tinamit, amak tecpan, nima amak, ajawarem amak,* and *onojel amak*) to designate larger and smaller territorial units within the Quiché polity.

5. As described in Carmack (1977: 12) and Hill (1992: 39).

6. *Ah pop (Aj pop)* and *calel* seem to correspond to the Classic Maya political positions of *ajaw* and *cahal,* that is, ranked offices in a system of bipartite rulership. *Ajaw* means "lord," while *aj pop* means "he of the mat," a term that had connotations of kingship for the Postclassic Maya.

7. A colony of K'umarca'aj like Chuwa Tz'ak would have been a *calpul* from the perspective of the capital. Such *calpuls* within the K'umarca'aj sphere of influence would each have had resident at least one political and one military officer representing each of the two moieties at K'umarca'aj (Carmack 1977: 13). Since one moiety linked the Cawek and Sakic lineages while another linked the Ajaw and Nijaib lineages (Wallace 1977: 31–39, 47), the Cawek/Nijaib rivalry was built into the administrative structure of Chuwa Tz'ak. As will be argued below, it may have played itself out during the early colonial period in a struggle between the Herrera and Vicente lineages for control of Momostenango and its patron saint.

8. The descent of the Vicentes from the Nijaibs is documented in native *títulos* (Nijaib I [Recinos 1957: 70–76], and Alvarez Arevalo 1987: 9).

9. A summary of this text is available in Fox and Cook 1996: 820–821, while the complete translation of the text is in Cook 1981: 678–684.

10. The mountain and spring altar complex is described in B. Tedlock 1982: 54, 76, 80.

11. The pattern of a male patron saint and a Virgin Mary or other female saint as village patrons that is attested for Yucatán (Farriss 1984: 311) may, then, have been the early colonial pattern in the highlands as well.

12. Carmack opts for Xequemaya, located in *tierra caliente* northeast of the town center, as the location of the sixth early colonial *parcialidad* (Carmack 1995: 79). The only difficulty in identifying San Antonio as the sixth seventeenth-century *parcialidad* appears to be that the documents refer to it as a *cofradía* (Carmack 1995: 110). But that might not mean that it wasn't a *parcialidad*, since contemporary Cakchiquel communities used the terms interchangeably (Hill and Monoghan 1987: 34).

13. The term *wachibal* in modern orthography is given as *guachibal* in colonial documents.

14. This reconstruction is based on numerous interviews and is consistent with Carmack's 1995 description of this historical period.

15. The *auxiliatura* keeps a list of all of the *cofrades* and the *aldeas* or *barrios* in which they live. A series of these lists would be the ideal starting point for a social anthropology of the *cofradías*. Unfortunately, the leaders of the *auxiliatura* would not allow me to see the list(s). I relied on the cross-checked testimony of two knowledgeable informants—one who was the deputy of the *cofradía* of Santiago for almost twenty years and one who was the sacristan for a longer period of time—in order to sketch out recent changes in the *cofradía* system.

16. The original *parcialidad* of Santa Catarina was located south of the town center and corresponded in territory to what is today recognized as the *aldea* of Los Cipreses (see Carmack 1995: 57).

17. I take this to mean three households with a wife in each.

18. The Chanchabacs were not a cacique family, but they had gained control of the colonial image of Santa Catarina, perhaps having established one of the "progressive clan based parcialidades" described by Carmack (1995: 80). Like many other dynamic and forceful descent groups left out of the *cabildo*-centered power bloc of this century, they opted for a leadership role in the Catholic Action movement in the 1960s and 1970s.

19. Presumably, it had been somewhere to the south in the territory of the older *parcialidad*, perhaps at one of Francisco's other houses, since *wachibal* cults are usually located in the houses of leaders of patrilineages.

20. The sense of this seems to be that the Chanchabacs living today in the *barrio* Santa Catarina are a lineage segment that broke off from the lineage in the original (Los Cipreses area) *parcialidad*. Whether Francisco transferred the *parcialidad* image to his new estate, or whether he acquired a new image, as in "the first man to have the image," is unclear.

21. In the typical and ancient pattern, there was both an image and a sacred bundle/*título* to legitimize Chanchabac social position and claims to an estate.

22. The implication, allowing an average of twenty years for a generation,

until the last one which is now coming to manhood, is that Francisco established this community with its *wachibal* about 140 years before 1976, or sometime in the 1830s.

23. That is, in Pueblo Viejo, Tunayac, the site of Chuwa Tz'ak. The church may be the *armita* constructed during sixteenth-century *congregación*, as noted above.

24. The concept of cultural crystallization was originally developed by George Foster in an effort to explain why colonial Latin American culture was so resistant to change (Foster 1960: 227–34). In developing a critique of the continuity model in Maya studies, Wilk (1991: 234) argues that today's traditional village cultures are actually "crystallized" versions of adaptations to colonial and neocolonial situations. An older interpretation, less hostile to the continuity thesis, suggests that a nativistic or resurgent Maya "Recent Indian Stage" emerged from the "Colonial Stage" during the fluid period of the collapse of colonialism and crystallized in response to opposition during the nineteenth-century liberal period (LaFarge 1956). The more recent scholarship and findings reported in this chapter seem to confirm the continued viability of the LaFarge thesis. Costumbre, the Recent Indian Stage religion, has been attacked by Catholic Action and Protestant evangelists.

25. For additional descriptions of the Momostecan *cofradías,* see B. Tedlock 1982: 36 and Carmack 1995: 320–321.

26. The pronunciations *alcalté* for *alcalde, teputado* for *deputado,* and *mortoma* for *mayordomo* are normal in spoken Quiché. After a long period of indecision about style for this work, I opted for use of the Spanish phonology for the first two terms. I retained *mortoma,* though, since it is used by Momostecans even in Spanish speech.

27. That is, a noncostumed recreational dance. The men dance with men, and women usually watch kneeling on the floor, though they may dance with other women.

28. Barbara Tedlock (1982: 37) argues that there is, nevertheless, a civil religious hierarchy in Momos, since elders (i.e., *principales*) are also "initiated priest shamans." This seems, though, to lack the expected rotation, since a position in the *auxiliatura* may be held during tenure as *chuch kajaw* of a lineage with concurrent service. In some *aldeas*—for example, Pitzal or Tunayac—there are *auxiliatura* officials and *principales* who are members of Catholic Action (i.e., non-Costumbristas), just as there are increasing numbers of *cofrades* who are not Costumbristas. Many *cofrades* are also initiated daykeepers, just like the majority of *auxiliatura* officials and *principales.*

29. In 1976 a quetzal was equal to an American dollar and was the standard payment (with lunch) for a day's work by a field hand.

30. The main church is built over the colonial period cemetery, and is said

to have catacombs beneath it. The *calvario* is built in the current cemetery and has a "cave" in its eastern end that is a symbolic entry to or exit from the underworld. In both cases, the bones of the dead and the abodes of the souls are understood as being below the floor. One needs to recognize them with invocations and offerings, since one is passing above them.

31. Paklom, a hill just south of the central plaza, is the location of Wakchob, the Six Teams, a major altar that is the center of the Momostecan sacred cosmos. Joyam is a ridgetop in the bunchgrass highland south of town on the border with San Francisco El Alto that marks the divide between the north-tending Momostecan watershed that flows into the Usumacinta and the watershed that flows south to the Pacific through the pass near Quetzaltenango. At Joyam, where the road crosses the ridge, one can see Santa María Volcano, and men tip their hats.

32. A refusal must be made within twenty-four hours. It is only approved if the nominee identifies and takes the flowers to an assenting replacement.

33. An *arrova* is twenty-five pounds, one-fourth of a *quintal.*

34. Barbara Tedlock (1982: 42–43) describes this affair as it was presented to her by a member of the *auxiliatura* and interprets it as a case of the Quichean tendency to convert a problematic dualism (traditionalists versus catechists) into complementarity (sexual abstinence and abstinence from alcohol). While the structuralist elegance of this interpretation is attractive and reasonable on the basis of Tedlock's information, it does not work very well if, as according to Ixc'oy, the *cofradía* ends up completely staffed by Catholic Action members.

The Ixc'oy account implies that the *principales* were outmaneuvered by the priest and his Catholic Action allies. The fact that within a year or so the *principales* chartered a new indigenous *hermandad* for Santiago suggests that they lost a battle but continued the war. These differing accounts illustrate the role played by political spin within Quichean culture.

35. Many *cofrades* of Don Pablo's generation are not only illiterate but also have a limited knowledge of Spanish, the language used to keep the inventory. When an item is read off the list, they randomly hold up objects and bundles until the *auxiliatura* secretary nods assent.

36. The term *itzel* (usually translated as "evil") in this context means touchy, dangerous, and powerful—ideas connoted by *delicado,* the translation recommended by Julian Ak'abal, my research assistant. The term *itz,* when viewed within the larger context of several centuries of pan-Maya cosmology, carries complex meanings related to supernatural power, rather than only the connotations of morality suggested by the English word *evil* (see Freidel, Schele, and Parker 1993: 210–213, 411–412).

37. *Mais* are groupings of the souls of the dead as cohorts according to

successive units of time. Momostecans do not agree on the precise translation. Some translate *jun mai* as a generation of the dead; others say a century of the dead.

38. They invoke the dead by calling the *mais* into which they have been grouped.

39. Chance and Taylor (1985: 2) call this the Wolf-Nash interpretation and trace its origins to 1950s functionalism. The hierarchy acts like a thermostat: it stops economic differentiation when it heats up and distributes prestige according to public expenditures, thus making have-nots of all (see Wolf 1959: 215).

40. It is also clear that during the colonial period *cofradía* service often provided tangible rewards to leaders who had access to *cofradía* capital (Chance and Taylor 1985, Rojas Lima 1988: 61–65).

41. Bunzel (1952: 425) describes the *palo volador* in Chichicastenango, Paret Limardo (1963) describes Quichean deer dances, and Mace (1970) describes some dances of Rabinal. McArthur (1972) demonstrates that the dances of Aquacatán, like those of the Quiché area in general, figure in a "cult of the dead."

42. The Conquest Dance was moved from Holy Week to Santiago's fiesta in the 1920s by order of the *caudillo* Teodoro Cifuentes.

43. *Malinches* are named after the famous mistress of Hernán Cortés, the conqueror of Mexico, and lack specific relevance to the Quichean conquests by Pedro de Alvarado. Their parts are played by prepubescent girls. Aj Itz Chiquito is understood to be the younger brother of Aj Itz, a red-garbed shamanic figure who represents the Mam, the Quichean version of the Yucatecan Chac.

44. That is, the narrator understands that females do not ordinarily participate in the sacred dances, and that this is an unusual exception worth noting.

45. This behavior of the Tzulab, even including the insulting of other supernaturals, like images of the saints, is typical behavior in a Native American contrary society, as for example has been reported among the Sioux (Lowie 1954). During the final week of Lent in 1976, the Tzulab in front of the cemetery would not make way for the image of the Virgen Dolores. When the *cofrades* set the *anda* down, the dancers lifted the virgin's skirts with the handles of their whips, and made lewd remarks, treating her as they would Xinula (Ladina), the "woman" in their dance.

46. "Tzul" is understood by Momostecans to refer to anyone who exhibits contrary, impolite behavior, especially swearing. The dance is also called Grasejos, probably a corruption of the Spanish word *graciosos*, meaning "jesters" or "clowns." The dance itself is described and discussed in detail in Chapter 5.

In forming the plural of "Tzul," the Momostecans with whom I spoke used "Tzulab." In his Quiché-English dictionary, Edmonson (1965: 128) gives "Tzulub."

47. *Wachibal* cults continue to exist in rural *parajes,* usually for images of Esquipulas or other crucified Christs.

48. Sam Pras—i.e., San Francisco El Alto—is a nearby market town frequented by Momostecan merchants. In the 1970s, with the quetzal tied to the dollar, a hired farm laborer earned from one to two quetzals per day.

49. *Mu'us* also means something fancy or pretty (*jelic*). Probably the closest translation into English for use in this context would be a dandy. The old woman in the deer-hunting skit of the Monkeys Dance is also called Xinula.

50. This was the beginning of the portion of a longer interview in which the Monkeys Dance was described. I asked if we could arrange to meet this man and see his book. Don Florentino reported five days later, at our second interview, that he had invited the man to come, but that he was suspicious and did not trust foreigners and so declined to participate in the project. The word "story" here is my translation of the Spanish *historia* used in a Quiché language text. It actually refers to the words spoken by the dance characters; that is, it is a script.

51. Thus twenty dancers make one team, but there are two teams that alternate in the performance, hence forty dancers in all. The Tzulab also has twenty dancers on a team.

52. This is exactly how a saint is adored at its annual *cofradía* festival.

53. In 1976 one quetzal was the day's wage for a field hand.

54. This narrator was a Costumbrista and a priest-shaman of *mesa* rank, with the calling, training, and initiation needed to make offerings at the four sacred mountains. He had experimented with other religions, including a period as a Protestant, but had come back to Costumbre because of health problems that seemed to require supernatural intervention. A certain amount of drinking is prescribed within ritual settings. Many Costumbristas drink excessively, and binge drinking is common among dancers during fiestas. Don Tino's negative reaction to excessive drinking, though, is not unusual among leading Costumbristas. Many view drunkenness during a ritual as disrespectful to the saint and the *primeros.* If one's *costumbre* is effective, one can drink without becoming drunk.

55. This is the third reference to problems with dancers who are not from Xequemaya. The dance team and sponsor are from there and do not trust outsiders to complete their obligations.

56. Thus *costumbre* for the important saints may grow in complexity over time. New offerings and rites may be added to adjust to changes in circumstances, but the existing ones will still have to be maintained as long as they

are remembered and can be maintained without encountering severe counter-vailing pressures, like the destruction of an altar complex or intimidation by the authorities.

CHAPTER 3

1. The image used to go to Totonicapán, Zunil, San Pedro Almalongo, San Francisco El Alto, San Andrés Xecul, and San Cristóbal. An attempt was made to steal it in San Andrés Xecul, and that provided the rationale for the *auxiliatura*'s decision that it not be allowed to leave Momostenango without official permission.

2. This text is presented in full in Cook 1981: 654 - 677, and another version obtained from the same raconteur has been published by Barbara Tedlock (1982: 180 - 187, 1986).

3. There is actually little sleeping done, since all-night dancing and prayer sessions are held. The *cofrades* sit on benches and occasionally doze, but the image gives them a shove and wakes them instantly if they begin to fall asleep.

4. The Patrón is similarly brought out on days Ajmak and Quiej, but also on Noj and Camé.

5. Note that this would total seventeen, but he has stated that there are eighteen. Here he omits mention of the altar in the *armita* that was mentioned just above. There is also a second *armita* in Pasajoc with a *porobal* inside, which may or may not be included among the thirteen altars in Pasajoc. What is important is not the actual number, but that the official count is given as thirteen and eighteen. The thirteen is especially important in light of the alter-nate term for the *cofradía* system as the thirteen teams, and the thirteen tradi-tional divisions (*amak'*) of the ancient Quiché polity.

6. In other words, the incident was a sign. The immediate question is, whose fault is it? The idea of fault in this context implies a lack of preparation. *Mak* appears frequently to connote this idea of some lack, of a sin of omission more than commission.

7. Thus reenacting in microcosm the entire *costumbre* of the image. Also note in chapter 5 a similar custom among the Tzulab or Grasejos dancers. They burn copal on thirteen *tejas* as part of the *costumbre* during their rehear-sals. The Monkey dancers, described in chapter 4, burn copal on nine *tejas* surrounding the tree selected as their dance pole.

8. Pologua is located on the Pan American Highway, so it is a convenient place for pilgrims from other communities.

9. This supervision is comparatively recent, having started in about 1960.

It was ordered by the municipal government to control the business activities of the *cofrades* and to keep the image from being stolen.

10. As, for example, when a piece of flat fallow land that has grown up into bush prior to clearing is called "puro monte, puro *juyup*."

11. Historical reconstruction related to these complexes was presented above in chapter 2, in the section on the origins of *cofradías*.

12. Thus it seem that a historical pattern reasserts itself. The four colonial *parcialidad* patrons have been reduced to three. Similarly, in the *Popol Vuh*, of the four ancestors and four *cabawils* that figure in Tula, only three figure in the story of the rise of the Quiché state. Iqui Balam and the *cabawil* called Mahucutaj disappear somewhere along the way.

13. Like Santiago, the yearbearer (Mam) has a secretary, as do the munici-pal *alcalde* and the *síndico segundo* or *alcalde* of the *auxiliatura*. A *chuch kajaw* is often accompanied by an *aj bix* (speaker) to chant from the missal. Other dualisms include the coexistence of a municipal *alcalde* and an Indian *alcalde*, and the two official *chuch kajaws* for the pueblo whose *costumbre* protects the municipal officials. Although the dualistic Santiago and Mam complexes may plausibly be seen as reflections of colonial administrative organization, it is worth noting prehispanic prototypes in conquest period Momostenango's bi-partite rule by brothers Francisco and Juan Izquin Nihaib, with ranks of *aj pop* and *calel* and the earlier *ajaw* and *cajal* ranks of Classic Period kingship.

14. Santa Isabel has a foundation myth association with the sister of Diego Vicente that closely parallels Diego's association with Santiago. Santa Isabel was the colonial patron of the *parcialidad* that contained Chuwa Tz'ak and later became the *cantón* Pueblo Viejo in the *aldea* Tunayac. Isabel was later the center of a *wachibal* cult in the *barrio* Santa Isabel of the *cabecera*. In 1925 or 1926 she was transferred to San Vicente Buenabaj, and now figures as the image of the "unofficial" *cofradía* of Buenabaj.

15. There seems to be a pattern in this account of paired messengers of the Mundo. This punishment seems to be at least as much for lack of *costumbre* at the altars as it is for the absence of the image of Santiago.

16. The 1920s mark a period of intense change in the cults of the saints in Momostenango. Santiago was removed from a private house and placed in the church. Some informants referred to this period as "the time of the centraliza-tion of the images under Teodoro Cifuentes." This was the last phase of the transition from *parcialidad* or *cantón* control of major images to centralized control by *cofradías* in the *cabecera*, and so by the *auxiliatura* and the priest. This centralization both embodied and symbolized the ascendancy of the ac-culturated militarist leadership of the Quiché people of Momostenango. *Ca-bildo* control of the *parcialidad* saints represented further loss of authority and status for the cacique lineages.

17. Most of the population of Pueblo Viejo, led by the Herreras, has converted to Catholic Action.

18. K'anil, Ajmak, and Noj are also days for masses called *wa' ja'*; i.e., *tamalito-atole* (maize dumpling–maize gruel), given around harvest time.

19. The Ordinance is said to contain the land titles, and Santiago is said to have been associated with the title of Momostenango. San Gaspar, although not referred to as a secretary, seems to be associated with secretarial records—lists of names (Siegel 1941: 68). San Felipe, like the Gaspar chest, has an ambiguous role in town ritual, honored highly with the Patrón but lacking a cult in his own right.

20. There are several indicators of the status of an image in Momostenango: the treasures (cloaks, blankets, mirrors, etc.) that belong to it, the frequency with which *costumbre* must be performed for it, the number of *porobals* (altars) at which *costumbre* must be performed, and the number and size of its fiestas.

21. The pattern of rotation between *cofradías* and dance teams is common among the men that keep these traditions going. It is motivated by a desire for supernatural patronage to protect health and business endeavors.

22. The meaning here is that the *costumbre* performed by the narrator had the effect of opening the hearts and purses of the many who provided donations to make the clothing drive successful.

23. Don Juan decided to sell twelve of the blankets he makes to get the forty-three quetzals for his share of the cost of the Patrón's new clothing, but, because of the efficacy of his *costumbre*, he obtained such a good price that after he made his donation he still had eighteen quetzals left. This was a reward sent by Santiago.

24. This whipping is meant literally. Arms and legs are whipped with a switch to energize them when fatigue has set in. In this case there may also have been a touch of penance in the whipping. As Juan Ixc'oy notes in describing the Tzulab Dance, God loves the sound of the lash.

25. San Antonio can make skinny pigs look fat, and *costumbre* can keep police from noticing the transportation, without a license, of masses of foliage from the coast tied on the outside of a bus.

26. This is a typical example of fright sickness, or *susto*. The sickness came from either the image or the *primeros*, who were angry for an undisclosed reason. The explosion at the fiesta was a sign both of their anger and of the coming punishment.

27. This is being-of-two-hearts and is explained by Pablo Itzep in chapter 2.

28. That is, at the *armita*, the *cofradía* house, where the dance shaman, sponsors, and dancers present themselves before the image of the Patrón and formally agree to dance.

29. These are the four sacred mountains of Momostenango, recited in

clockwise order from the east, and the Spider Monkey Stone, the sacred altar of the dance he had promised.

30. He called the names of the dancers themselves. There are twenty roles in the dance and two teams of dancers who dance on alternate days.

31. There is no such image. There is a San Bartolo. In this case, the patron saint of San Bartolo Aguas Calientes is clearly intended, but it has been feminized and called a sister. San Bartolo has passed in and out of the control of Momostenango, but since 1951 has been a separate municipality (see Carmack 1995: 279 – 81, 355 – 66, 371 – 72). Does this identification as a sister reflect twentieth-century ideological construction or a folkloristic survival of an aboriginal or colonial structural model?

32. Malacatancito is properly the name of an archaeological site, while the neighboring township is called Malacatán. There was a San Raimundo in Malacatán, a colonial image which the Maryknoll father in Malacatán reports was stolen in the early 1970s. Thus, in both cases of sisters, the informant has feminized the names of male images in other towns. Malacatán, like San Bartolo, lies north and west of Momostenango but is a Ladino town with a large Mam population and numerous Momostecan immigrants since the 1860s. Another informant, in a text related below, has Diego Vicente and the first *principales* of Momostenango buy the land on which the town was founded from Malacatán. The symbolism seems to suggest that within the Momostecan sphere of influence, *cantones,* which are subordinate to the *cabecera,* are like wives, while more equal communities, other municipalities, are like sisters. This might reflect the past presence in these other towns of ruling cacique patrilineage segments derived from the Nijaibs who ruled Momostenango at the time of the conquest. A junior lineage segment controlling a nearby *tinamit* might be represented as a younger brother or as a sister, marking a community whose elite were too closely related to be bound to Momostenango by intermarriage. This line of reasoning could prove very fruitful, but needs to be investigated with additional fieldwork and archival research.

33. Translations of the Momostecan myth texts that describe the liminal period are found in Cook 1981: 625 – 694. The Yegua Achi' story is an updated version of the Cabrican and Wucub Caquix episodes of the Hero Twin story in the *Popol Vuh* (Cook 1981: 517 – 531 and Cook 1983: 140 – 145, 150 – 153).

34. More detailed summaries of the foundation accounts are readily available in Fox and Cook 1996: 820 – 821. The complete texts are in Cook 1981: 678 – 690.

35. These are moths whose larvae eat the kernels on the cobs, but Momostecans traditionally saw this as a kind of spontaneous generation of moths: the corn turns into moths.

36. Ixbatz and Castillo present agreement on the day names, but not on the numbers associated with *costumbre.* Similarly, there was a discrepancy in

comparing Castillo's account of the yearbearers with the account given by Vicente de Leon: they agreed on the names of the *alcaldes* and the secretaries, but not on their directional associations. Two possibilities come to mind. One is that there are different local traditions about these things within Momostenango. Another is that Domingo Castillo wished to explain his world to me, but that he intentionally misrepresented some of the details both to protect me and to prevent the misuse of his knowledge, since he knew that I was not an initiated daykeeper. I strongly suspect the latter case.

37. The original *wachibal* cults, the unofficial *cofradías* that proliferated within mature colonial society, seemed to have functioned to permit the cacique class to pursue its economic goals within the colonial context. The post-*parcialidad cofradías* of the twentieth century seem to work in Momostenango to legitimize both economic differences within the community related to entrepreneurism and the emerging power of the acculturated sector in opposition to the traditional status claims of the caciques.

38. The symbolism in folklore of Santiago and his assistant, San Felipe, seems to replicate this older dualistic authority structure, while the assigning of roles to other patron images as his women or kin seems to reflect, perhaps even to model, the political relationships among communities during the colonial or even prehispanic periods.

39. At the new year or changing ceremony in a *cofradía* today, the incoming and outgoing *cofrades* refer to each other as *nuc'axel,* a term meaning "my replacement" and ordinarily used between grandparents and grandchildren within a lineage.

CHAPTER 4

1. The discovery that the Classic Maya cross represents the world tree, the king, and the mythical creator and father of the Palenque Triad and has a celestial counterpart in the biannual Milky Way–ecliptic alignment called Wakan Chah is summarized in Schele 1992: 118–153. These discoveries are applied to the interpretation of the Group of the Cross at Palenque in Maya Cosmos (Freidel, Schele, and Parker 1993: 144–146).

2. It has not been possible to present the corpus of Momostecan mythology in this work. In Momostecan texts, Jesucristo escapes from the Jews by climbing a tree (Cook 1981: 629, 635) and the primordial Principales hide in a tree all night while awaiting the dawn and the yearbearer (Cook 1981: 661–662).

3. In Quichean astronomy the "rising of the Milky Way around Christmas" predicts cold weather, and its rising at another (unspecified) time (perhaps July?) predicts dry weather (i.e., the *canícula?*) (see Remington 1977: 83–84).

4. The female impersonator playing the part of the woman in the Tzulab Dance during Holy Week is also called Xinula.

5. This was the beginning of the portion of a longer interview in which the Monkeys Dance was described. I asked if we could arrange to meet this man and see his book. Don Florentino reported five days later at our second interview that he had invited the man to come, but that he was *envidioso* and did not trust foreigners and so declined to participate in the project. The word *story* here is my translation of the Spanish *historia* used in a predominantly Quiché text. It actually refers to the words spoken by the dance characters; that is, it is a script.

6. Twenty dancers make one team, but there are two teams that alternate in the performance, hence forty dancers in all. The Tzulab Dance also has twenty dancers on a team.

7. Socop is the sacred mountain of the west. Barbara Tedlock (1982: 103) associates Socop with the Mam (the yearbearer; lit., "grandfather") called Ik', the most dangerous Mam, having strong associations with death and destruction. My informants disagreed about how the yearbearers were assigned to directions and mountains. Here I am relying on the discussion and chart on pages 99–101 in Barbara's fine study, reinforced by Robert Carmack's (personal communication, 1980) comment that if the Mams didn't rotate from mountain to mountain, which might help explain the different accounts, then Quiej had an eastern and Ik' a western association. I use the spelling "Quiej" for the yearbearer called "Quej" by Tedlock, since this is phonologically more accurate given current pronunciation in Momos.

8. That is, the lord of Socop, possibly the Mam Ik', is owner of these animals. The day Ik' is the day for ceremonies related to prehispanic idols. It is the day when such idols are most active in human affairs (Tedlock 1982: 128).

9. The rope is a thick cable made by braiding together about forty ropes, each of which measures about fifty feet in length. It extends from the roof of the church to the top of the pole and then down to the ground. Elsewhere Don Florentino reports: "Each of the dancers brings a length of rope, and the cable is made of these. The author must provide two. Each measures twelve arm's breadths in length. After the dance it is used for, well, whatever. New rope is bought for each dance. Before, they used a rope of leather, but it has decayed and no longer exists."

10. This is clarified in a story told to me by Julian Ak'abal, my research assistant, at this point in the transcription:

A man was a great hunter, and the owner of a large flock of sheep. He had one hundred sheep. One day he told his wife that he was going hunting on the mountain Pipil.

Late in the day he saw a very large buck with a beehive in its antlers. He prepared to shoot the animal. He heard a voice that said:

"Don't shoot my horse!"

He looked around but there was no one there. He took aim again and he shot the deer. When it died, all of the bees flew away. He was very happy and he brought the meat and honey home.

That night Pipil spoke to Tamancu:

"Lend me your dogs."

In the morning the man discovered that only one sheep out of four in his flock was still alive. The rest had been torn apart by coyotes. The coyotes are Tamancu's dogs. There are some on Pipil, but more on Tamancu.

The deer with the beehive appears to be a Quiché cognate for the Yucatec Zip, the supernatural protector of the deer which takes on the form of a deer with a wasp nest in its antlers (see Thompson 1970: 308). In Cakchiquel-speaking Comalapa, there is a story of a deer that rescued the community from dire consequences when a young woman vomited up the host in a bathing pool after communion. The deer saved the day by lifting the petrified and enlarged host in its antlers and carrying it to the church (Paret Limardo 1963: 41).

11. Although the account up to this point has not mentioned it, the dance pole was erected prior to the dance. Thus the sequence is this: (1) erect the pole, (2) go to the four corners, (3) attach the rope (the umbilicus-ecliptic) to the pole, and then finally (4) animals descend the rope to the world. This is reminiscent of the performance mentioned in the preamble of the *Popol Vuh,* a "fourfold siding, fourfold cornering . . . halving the cord, stretching the cord in the sky, on the earth" (Tedlock 1985: 72).

12. These four sacred mountains of the cardinal directions are associated with the yearbearers. Only shamans of *mesa* rank have the authority to make offerings at these four mountains.

13. The Spanish word *pruebas* was used here, in the sense of proofs of power, commitment, and faith but referring specifically to tricks performed on the rope. A *prueba* is a sign (*jun retal*) and a test for the dancer, who may be fearless and unhurt or who may freeze in fear, be badly cut and burned by the rope, or even fall. A troupe of Hungarians, circus performers or gypsies, camped in tents and caravans in Momostenango for a prolonged period during the 1940s, according to other informants. This probably recounts a Momostecan understanding of an actual event.

14. C'oyabaj (Spider Monkey Stone) is a rugged angular boulder about four meters high perched on the edge of a chasm with a sheer drop of about

one hundred meters to the western end of the most popular bathing pools just east of the town center on the road out to Xequemaya.

15. *Katit kamam* (lit., "our grandmother our grandfather"; i.e., "our ancestors"). Following the reference to the *warabal ja* (lit., "sleeping house"), a shrine for the souls of the ancestors, this reinforces the point that each dancer must be in harmony with his *alaxic* (patrilineage), including its deceased members. The dancers come from Xequemaya and probably broadly represent the lineages in that *aldea*. Dancing tends to run in families, and so among the ancestor's shades at the *warabal ja* there would be many who had danced in the past, that is, *primeros*. A new dancer is the replacement, *ru caxel,* for one who retires, for a dancer who is probably his father, grandfather, or uncle. The new recruit is a new link in a very long chain.

16. This is the sacred mountain of the east associated by Tedlock with the Mam Quiej (Deer), as noted above.

17. This mountain of the south is associated by Tedlock with the Mam E.

18. The mountain of the west is associated with Ik', as noted above.

19. The mountain of the north is associated by Tedlock with the secretary Tziquin. While some *aj mesas* report that they visit the mountains for clients in a cruciform sequence (e.g., N-S-E-W), the dancers here utilize a clockwise sequence starting in the east and ending in the north. Thus the pattern of visiting the mountains in preparatory *costumbre* is replicated in the pattern of visiting or establishing the corners of the dance ground.

20. The text says *xoculok* (they enter) the time of the fiesta; that is, this final visit to a sacred mountain comes on a good day in late July.

21. A pole is erected on an unspecified date in January and another is erected in late July. Presumably, these dates are precisely six months apart. These dates arrive slightly before the critical two days of classical creation, February 5 and August 13 (see Freidel, Schele, and Parker 1993: 96–99), when celestial events appear to replicate the setting of the three stones of creation and the erection of the world tree. I do not know the precise date in January for the erection of the pole.

22. There is a widespread Mesoamerican tale about a poor man who wishes to dance but cannot afford to rent a costume and receives one from a *dueño del cerro.* See, for example, the legend of Cerro Chicutuya from Comalapa in which the *dueño* is a native Maya man (Paret-Limardo 1963: 43). Here is one version of the tale told by Julian Ak'abal at this point in the transcription of the Ixbatz interview:

> A man was very poor but he wanted to dance, and he agreed to dance, but I don't know which dance, the Vaqueros or the Conquista. The day came when the costumes were arriving. He could hear the *bombas,* but he still had no costume, he had no money. He went to the bathing place at

C'oyabaj, and he was crying. He kept crying there on the ridge above the baths. He could hear the *bombas*.

Then he looked up. A tall man was standing before him, very tall, a gringo.

[Aside by Don Julian:]

Because the *mundos* represent themselves as gringos.

[Don Julian continues:]

He asked him, "Why are you crying?"

At first the man would not answer. He kept crying. But the gringo kept asking, so finally the man stopped crying and explained:

"I want to dance, but I am poor. I don't have money for a costume."

"But you do want to dance?"

"Yes, but I am too poor."

"Very well, then, close your eyes!"

When he opened his eyes he was in a different place, in a palace all of gold. The pillars were gold. And huge, but really huge, snakes were twined around the pillars. There were boxes full of money all around. A different man was there. He showed him a whole room full of costumes and told him to take his pick. He gave him lots of money. Then he told him to close his eyes. He was back at the baths!

The gringo said, "All right, but there are two conditions. You can't tell anyone about this until after the dance, and after the dance you have to come here with the costume and return it."

He went to the dance and he had the finest costume, but it was strange, covered all over with strange designs. The people all stared at it. He kept his word, and because of the money he became a rich man.

Don Julian explains that the house was inside the earth, the *mundo* was a *nawal* (*nagual;* shape-shifting spirit), and the custodian inside the mountain was K'ak'ic'oxol, the red dwarf who is represented as Tzitzimite or Aj Itz in the Conquest Dance.

23. Momostenango lies largely in a highland oak and pine forest zone where monkeys are not to be found. This monkey, then, must have been called from or sent out of C'oyabaj.

24. The dancers are from the eastern *aldea* of Xequemaya, a three-hour walk from the town center, and so must arrange for housing in the town center during the period of performance.

25. A spring-side *porobal* near the base of the western side of the Paklom is the "water" of the altar of Santiago, a *porobal* located on top of the Paklom. Thus over the years this altar grows larger, as nine tiles are added to it each time this dance is performed.

26. Don Julian Ak'abal likens this to the *costumbre* performed at the four corners when a new house is erected.

27. Mayanist lore has the number thirteen carrying celestial connotations, while nine has underworld associations (see Farriss 1984: 513; Thompson 1970: 280–282). In Momostenango, wax candles are offered to the celestial powers, saints, angels, Jesucristo, and the Eternal Father. There appears to be an inversion, with celestial candles buried in a hole while nine little *porobals* ring the pole seated on the celestial candles. Perhaps until the pole is seated, the sky has not yet been raised. Perhaps the seating of the pole creates an inversion of some kind, with up and down reversed. Unfortunately, the meaning of this symbolism also escapes Don Florentino.

28. In the mid-1970s, while Allen Christenson was undergoing training to become a daykeeper in Momostenango, he had to learn prayer texts containing archaic terms and phrasings that he did not understand. His teacher, a formidable Costumbrista ritualist, explained that he didn't know what the phrases meant himself. As he advised Allen, "You just have to learn them because they are in the prayers."

29. This myth, which I call the Origins of Costumbre, has been referred to several times above. Two versions are available: see Cook 1981: 654–677, and B. Tedlock 1982: 180–187, 1986.

30. The Niño San Antonio is brought forth in a cave by the Mundo in this same episode, thus also having a post-conquest but autochthonous origin.

31. A prominent Costumbrista ritualist and *principal* identifies the Devils in the Devils Dance at Christmas as an ancient people called Xibalba who went naked except for feathers and didn't bury their dead. These people were led by three kings, including Tecum Uman and Tecum Cakchiquel, and were "erased" by Jesucristo. I believe the third Tecum is the Tecum or Rey that Momostecans call Witzitzil, that is, the Tzutujil king. Thus Xibalba for Costumbristas today has an historical identification in a fuzzy "folk memory" of the conjoined prehispanic Quichean polities and does not necessarily mean the underworld, as it seems to in the *Popol Vuh*. In Quichean and broader Maya cosmology, races and beings from earlier suns or epochs often survive in the earth.

32. Only six are given here. Later, Francisco Carrilas (Carillo?) and Juan de León y Cárdenas (Cardona?) are mentioned.

33. The four yearbearers also have secretaries, and Santiago is served by his secretary, San Felipe. While this appears to reflect the structure of colonial *cabildo* and modern municipal administration, dualistic leadership with the offices of *aj pop* and *calel* held by brothers in the Nijaib lineage is also documented for the pre-conquest *tinamit* of Chuwa Tz'ak (Alvarez Arevalo 1987: 39, 42).

34. This account by Don Miguel contradicts Barbara Tedlock's (1986: 134) description of Aj Itz and the little *c'oxol* as brothers to Tecum. The source of her information is not cited. There appear to be different coexisting traditions.

35. On the yearbearer's mountain associations, different informants gave different accounts to me, and I was not able to determine whether this represented intentional deception, errors, movement of the yearbearers, or the coexistence of several versions in different local traditions. For interpretive purposes here, I am relying on Barbara Tedlock's (1982: 100) depiction in the expectation that, as an apprentice in training for initiation as a daykeeper, she was not misinformed.

36. Here is a cosmological model reminiscent of the ideology of Classic Maya kingship in which living descendants of powerful deified kings acted as mediums for their spirits, materializing them through vision serpents in bloodletting rites (Schele and Freidel 1990).

37. This derivation of the prototypical *mundo* from a historical figure who is buried in the earth seems to be a typical Quichean doctrine. Mendelson (1959, 1965) finds that the most important *mundos* in Santiago Atitlán, beings called *nuwales* who figure among the Companía del Mundo, are the spirits of actual charismatic leaders whom he calls prophets, about whom historical accounts have been maintained. The Late Postclassic custom of burying important chieftains and lineage heads in little underground chambers with treasure, and erecting shrines to mark the locations in the mountains for offerings (Las Casas 1967), is evidence that a similar belief was part of the prehispanic mythos. This old mortuary custom provides a prehispanic prototype for the *mundos* called *dueños,* treasure-owning spirits that dwell inside the mountains.

38. This identification was suggested to me by informants' comments, and was also documented by Barbara Tedlock (1986: 133).

39. Redfield and Villa Rojas (1964: 328; also see appendix, tales 4–6) used the term "millenarian myth" to refer to Yucatec accounts of vanquished races that have gone underground in preceding world transformations, but that will reemerge to usher in a new world order.

CHAPTER 5

1. The Costumbrista Holy Week in Momos, concerned primarily with two related cosmogonies—the millenarian sunrise and a vegetative succession complex—is resonant with the finding that the *cofradías* in Santiago Atitlán are concerned primarily with effecting the smooth movement of the seasons and the sun (Carlsen and Prechtel 1991: 36).

2. *Tzulab* is the Momostecan plural form of *tzul,* a term that Momostecans translate as a strange or contrary being. It appears to come from the same

root as the Yucatec *dzul* which means "foreigner" (see Bricker 1981: 166 for a discussion of the evolution of *dzul*).

3. The identification of Maximon with Pedro de Alvarado is attested to by O'Brien (1975: 140) and Mendelson (1959).

4. As noted above, the Kekchi, a non-Quichean people of the northeastern highlands, moved their yearbearer's festival to Holy Week. The Kekchi depict the old yearbearer as a bound god buried in the earth whose struggles cause the earth to tremble.

5. Perhaps the most convincing attempt to deal with the etymology of Maximon notes that "Mam shimon," a construction meaning "bound grandfather" in Tzutujil, could be the original term, as had been suggested by Lothrop in 1929 (see Mendelson 1958, fn. 8: 7, and 1959: 59, where he states noncommittally and without further comment that there is a "present day etymology" of Maximon as Mam-Shimon).

In his Holy Week incarnation, San Simón has definite prototypes in Hispanic civilization including the burning of straw dummies of Judas (see Foster 1960: 180-181) and also the complex of straw-filled dummies called *monigotes, peleles, entroidos,* or *mecos.* They preside over the bawdy celebration of Carnaval only to be "killed" and burned or buried, to mark the transition from Carnaval to Lent (Foster 1960: 173-174).

6. More recently this interpretation has been questioned. Since the Mam identity in Atitlán actually overlaps with Jesucristo, "Mendelson's separation of the three icons now seems shallow" (Tarn and Prechtel 1986: 175).

7. *Ts'oloj che* or *sauco* is a type of willow. Its flowers and bark are brewed to make a tea to fight fever. One who sleeps in the shade of the *ts'oloj che* will have very vivid dreams and courts nightmares.

8. Momostecans are mystified by the fact that cigarettes placed in Simón's mouth do not go out. Guatemalan cigarettes in general burn more slowly than North American cigarettes, and in the high altitudes around Momostenango they will go out if they are left burning in an ashtray. This miraculous trait of the image is one that I cannot explain.

9. Here is an example of the mixture of veneration and contempt, since in ritualized drinking the highest status person is ordinarily served first.

10. The local radio station, Radio Momostenango, broadcasts in Quiché but uses broadcasters from the neighboring town of Totonicapán, where a slightly different dialect of Quiché is spoken and where usage of many terms is different. A number of urban Momostecans were incensed at the use of the word *tziquin* over the air by these broadcasters and demanded that it be replaced by the Spanish word *pajaro* for "bird."

11. The old Mam in Santiago Atitlán is often associated with homosexuality and any sexuality not related to procreation. Since it is both male and female, no one knows what its sex organs would be like. There is also a story

that Maximon was castrated by a woman from the coast (Tarn and Prechtel 1986: 183–184).

12. That is, where no one has performed functions of elimination or of a sexual nature.

13. Unlike the other saints' altars, which are closed during the period when Jesucristo is dead from dawn Wednesday through dawn Saturday, the altar of San Simón is open; his spirit is thus abroad and in power.

14. That is, his body is complete and his mask is placed on his head. He is seated as a completed entity for inspection by the thirteen teams.

15. A reference to the *cofradía* house of Señor Resurrección, highest ranking of the three chiefs of the *cofradías*. This *cofradía* is also called Corpus because, though it is responsible for the colonial period image of Señor Resurreccion, it is also the official custodian of the far more important *calvario* image of Señor Sepultado and has its new year or changing ceremony at the time of the festival of Corpus Cristi. The *cofradía* of Santa Cruz has overlapping responsibilities for this important image, washing its clothes and removing it from its cave and returning it to its cave under the supervision of Aj Señor. On Wednesday, when Corpus is officially dead and its altars are closed, San Simón is constructed in its *armita* by Santa Bárbara under the supervision of Aj Señor. Thus the *cofradía* of Corpus basically oversees and supervises the entire Holy Week complex, though it is not itself directly responsible for most of the activities. It does carry the little image of Señor Resurrección from the *calvario* to the church at dawn on Easter representing the sunrise that ends the liminal period and restores cosmos.

16. A testimonial: The image is actually smoking or the cigarette would go out! As noted above, Guatemalan cigarettes will go out if they are laid down in an ashtray, so this really is a mystery.

17. A weakness of Costumbre, as it becomes ever more embattled by Catholic Action and Protestant sects, is that, on the contrary, these permissions may be and are withdrawn. Most altars, shrines, and sacred places are on private property where the owner can destroy them or close them to the worshiping public if the owner doesn't fear supernatural punishment or comes to believe that Costumbre is devil worship. Shrines are not protected from public works either. A major one at Joyam was destroyed in building the road to San Francisco.

18. The keeping of Simón by the sodalities is quite complex. The mask is kept year around by Aj Señor, but the construction of the body and seating of the image, as well as the custodianship of the image during Holy Week and its final burning, are all by Santa Bárbara, but supervised by the alcaldes of all the *cofradías,* headed by the *c'amal be* (five chief *cofradías),* which again includes Aj Señor (as described in chapter 2).

19. "Two Heads" is the name of a monument located at the official en-

trance to the *cabecera* where busts of Diego Vicente, the indigenous cacique credited with founding Momostenango, and Teodoro Cifuentes, the Ladino *caudillo* who reorganized the town during its initial period of modernization early in this century, are displayed.

20. The *cofradía* of Santa Bárbara is responsible for the trip to El Palmar to get the flowers during Holy Week. The *alcalde* accompanies them to the *cumbre* (highland bunchgrass plain) and remains behind there to make offerings and collect bunchgrass to form the body of San Simón. All have observed twenty days of sexual abstinence. The *cofrades* return from the coast on Monday night, sleeping at the cross in Los Cipreses and decorating that cross and the Two Heads monument on Tuesday. On Tuesday night the flowers are presented to the mask of San Simón, facing forward from its resting place at the foot of the statue of Santa Bárbara, at her *armita*. On Wednesday they decorate the cemetery cross and the church altar; then, on Wednesday night, they construct San Simón and keep an all-night vigil. On Thursday they seat the image in the plaza and guard it all day, which they follow with another all-night vigil on Thursday and then the guarding of the image until noon on Friday. Thus the flowering of the crosses and the presentation of San Simón is an ordeal for the *cofrades,* which they undertake on behalf of the entire pueblo in order to effect the renewal of nature, which is the central cosmogonic purpose of the Costumbrista Holy Week. While I have separated San Simón and the coastal journey and "flowering" of the cross for purposes of description, it is clear that to the Costumbristas it is all one thing.

21. I am reminded of the Classic Period stelae at Copán and Quirigua which often depict a holy lord (*chul ahau*) standing on a forward-facing head. The latter, usually interpreted as a personification of the earth, is here represented by the mask of Simón.

22. There could not be a clearer statement that the period of Lent and Holy Week represents and reconstitutes the liminal period before the rising of the Jesucristo sun.

23. San Jorge, a Cakchiquel-speaking village, is a shrine center often visited by Quiché pilgrims. It is on the road to Panajachel. There is a cave known as Ujuyubal San Jorge with twenty altars. There is a church with many images and a *cofradía* house dedicated to Don Pedro, that is, the conquistador Pedro de Alvarado, seemingly a kind of alter ego for Maximon. Worshippers there can visit an ancient Conquest Dance outfit and shrouded mask. The eyeglasses and twisted cigars in the case with the outfit make a clear allusion to Maximon. San Jorge is where Vicente De León Abac reported that he read an ancient book that contained the myth text I have called the Origins of Costumbre (see Cook 1981: 654–677) and that Bárbara Tedlock has also published as Old Words (1982: 180–187) and *Ojer Tzi* (1986).

24. November 30. As noted by Mendelson (1959: 57), San André's day was

a traditional festival for Maximon in Santiago Atitlán in the 1950s. Since San Andrés is the patron of people who fish (Pasinski 1990: 44), it is not surprising that his festival would have become important in the lakeside communities, though when and why Maximon came to have this association with San Andrés remains a mystery.

25. As in the case of the mask of San Simón, the *cofradía* of Señor Resurrección is again a director and custodian. Another *cofradía*—here Santa Cruz, or in the case of San Simón, the *cofradía* of Santa Bárbara—performs most of the actual tasks involved in the cult institution.

26. The contemporary association of the day Ajpu with the freeing of the souls of the dead and the role of the *Popol Vuh*'s Jun Jun Ajpu and his son Jun Ajpu in defeating the lords of death suggest an enduring linkage. Here is the clearest cosmological evidence that Jesucristo has retained the functions of Jun Ajpu.

27. The images of Santiago, Niño San Antonio, Corpus, and San Simón are referred to as *delicado* in Spanish. In Momostecan Quiché, this is usually rendered as *kaxlic tiox* or *kaxlic santo,* a painful god or saint, but sometimes as *itzel ri tiox,* an evil or powerful god.

28. A spring located near the slaughterhouse across a little stream from the western base of the Paklom hill is the site of this altar, which is called Blessed Water (*Agua Bendita*) in Spanish.

29. The name *Wak Chob'* means "Six Teams" and refers to a single altar on the Paklom hill, but also to a larger complex of six holy places, including the Paklom altar, where offerings are made in Momostenango in connection with many important undertakings. The six teams may actually be the *primeros* or spirits of the dead priest-shamans who established the altars and those who have used them over the centuries. Possibly this originated in the colonial period when Momos was composed of six *parcialidades,* as described in chapter 2.

30. Chutisabal is "Little Swept Place," an altar complex of broken pots where *tzolkin* (260-day almanac) ceremonies are performed in the *barrio* Santa Isabel a couple of kilometers west-southwest of the Paklom hill.

31. Note the agreement here with B. Tedlock's findings about numbers and shrines utilized by diviners on behalf of their families or private clients (1982: 108). This informant, however, refers to Paja' as Pa Cho and possibly includes the entire Wak Chob' complex, with the Waquibal altar on Paklom as a place of visitation on the days numbered six. During the course of a year of service this pattern would repeat almost forty-six times, with a total of about 137 days of *costumbre.*

32. *Quimbec pa qui wi' ri Dios Animas* means "I go to at their hair the Holy Souls," that is, to a position near the center of the church where tallow

candles used to be burned for the dead. This is referred to as "at their hair" because the church and market are said to be located on the colonial period cemetery, above the heads of the dead.

33. That is the *auxiliatura,* or *alcaldía indígena,* keeps a copy of the inventory and supervises the transmission of the image's wealth to the new *cofradía.* If anything is missing, the outgoing *cofradía* is held responsible.

34. An interesting observation. Perhaps in spite of the religious divisions in the community in the 1970s and since, population increase may provide for a large enough Costumbrista faction to maintain a traditional *cofradía* system. Of course, intentional disruption of the system by reform Catholics in league with clerics is a different story. However, in brief visits to Momostenango in the 1990s I observed that Costumbristas are again being allowed to burn candles on the church floor above the Holy Souls as they did up until the 1950s, an innovation that recognizes and legitimizes Costumbrista rights to the church.

35. As noted in the text above, this happened in the 1950s as a result of disagreements between the Maya and Ladinos over which image to crucify.

36. This hilltop complex serves as an observatory for the timing of Holy Week. Holy Week begins when the sun and the full moon rise at the same spot.

37. That is, these altars are closed during the three days that San Simón is in power seated in the plaza. His reign ends at noon on Friday. During these three days Corpus is dead, his altars are closed, and neither the image nor the souls of his deceased *cofrades* have any power.

38. Thus the *cofrades* are accompanied by Jesucristo and by the *primeros,* the deceased *cofrades* who have maintained the cult over time, on their symbolic reiteration of the journey to the gardens of Xibalba. After they have returned and presented the flowers to the mask of San Simón the *primeros* and the spirit of Corpus are themselves called away, their altars are closed, and they have no power during the three days of the construction, reign, and immolation of San Simón. The interpretation of this complex is expanded below under "Corpus and the Souls."

39. The paired crucified and entombed Cristos are also a prominent element at the shrine of Maximon in Santiago Atitlán. A pan-Quichean ritual symbol links the two Cristos as lords of the dead and the liminal world to Simón. I suspect that this is the main iconographic remnant of the Hero Twins/Xibalba symbolism in Momostecan culture.

40. This interpretation of Holy Week and San Simón advanced by Mendelson on the basis of his investigation of the complex in Santiago Atitlán has been presented in detail in this chapter in the section on Mayanist interpretations of Maximon and so is not repeated here. The Quichean Holy Week complex is paralleled by the yearbearer complex among the Kekchi, who hold

that the Ocel—the patron of the five evil days and called the old Mam—is kept bound in the underworld during the year, released for the five days, and then returned to bondage (Thompson 1930: 133).

41. Momostecans identify San Simón as a Ladino, and the resemblance of the tableau in which he is displayed to a paymaster's table on a coastal plantation is not coincidental. In Zinacantán (Vogt 1969) and elsewhere in the highlands, there is a vision of purgatory as a *finca* within the earth where the soul must work until it has worn out a pair of iron sandals.

42. In his seminal article on Mesoamerican myth and ritual, Mendelson (1967: 410) identified *viaje*, which he defined as "correct movement," as one of the central themes of ritual concern.

43. A tentative depiction of the Quichean pilgrimage complex, based on ethnographic data from Momostenango, was presented at a conference (Cook and Fox 1994) and is awaiting publication in the Palenque Symposium Series from INAH.

44. That is, each *cofradía* that makes the trip represents a saint whose image is found in both Momos and El Palmar. These "flowers" are the blossoms, fronds or leaves, and fruits of a lowland palm tree called both *c'oyol* and *mop' (Acromonia mexicana)*. The fruits are hard-shelled spheres that turn yellow when they are ripe, the blossoms are yellow with a very strong scent, and the fronds are long—up to five or six meters in length—and spiny.

45. That is, the four chief *cofradías* are followed by San Francisco (Momos was a Franciscan mission) and Santa Bárbara, the *cofradía* whose *alcalde* is the *alcalde* for San Simón during Holy Week.

46. Several hundred Momostecan families colonized land in the *boca costa* region above Retalhuleu by the second half of the nineteenth century, received title to the land in 1871, and became an independent municipality in 1873 (Saler 1960: 25–34, B. Tedlock 1982: 20, Carmack 1995: 126, 147–149). The account here indicates that the Momostecan colonists replicated the central Momostecan *cofradía* structure. Perhaps at that time it was still more of a *calpul* or *parcialidad* organization in which intermarrying groups of families from a specific territorial division within Momos had settled together in El Palmar, bringing with them a privately owned image of their ward's, *aldea's*, or *calpul's* patron image in Momos. So the major holy images of Momos also are found to be central to El Palmar. For the *cofrades* the trip is a visit to another image of their patron saint, replicated in a daughter colony with a daughter *cofradía*.

47. As in Atitlán, this journey was left up to the younger men, but with oversight and authority by the highest-ranking elders still active in the *cofradía* system. This also suggests an initiatory function.

48. This combination or equivalence of serpents with greenery and flowers in the "foliating" of crosses is resonant with the discovery that the cruciform Classic Period world tree mixes and substitutes serpents for flowers in icono-

graphic transformations of the bell-shaped elements at the ends of its branches (Freidel, Schele, and Parker 1993: 183). For Momostecans a specific snake, the fer-de-lance (*canti'*) is involved. Also see note 44 above.

49. That is, the days numbered 1, 6, or 8. See the description above in the narrative "The Service of Corpus," by Pedro Contreras. Also see the discussion in note 31 above and B. Tedlock 1982: 108.

50. The tree is also called *mop'*, a palm tree (*Acromonia mexicana*) whose fruit is sold in the market during Holy Week. The association with Holy Week and the thorny fronds suggest that this may be the tree in which Jesucristo hid himself from the Jews. A tied bunch of dried spiny branches is displayed under San Simón's table.

51. Santa Cruz decorates the top member and the crossbar, while María decorates the lower member.

52. *Tzul* appears to come from the same root as the Yucatec *dzul*, which means "foreigner," but in one interesting thesis has come to mean "member of the dominant foreign ethnic group" (Bricker 1981: 166).

53. The Momostecan dancers perform somersaults called *pitzcai*, suggesting a possible alternative etymology for *patzcar*.

54. Children are not officially a part of this dance, but a dancer who has made a vow and then become ill or who is otherwise unable to dance may send a son, even a child, in his place.

55. The weasel, called *sacbin* in Momostenango, is the animal spirit companion (*nawal*) of drunks and seemed a likely candidate, considering the drunken and unruly behavior of the dancers.

56. Although these particular images are not held in any special respect by Momostecans, this shows that the Tzulab are a good example of a contrary society of the form described for North American Indians (Lowie 1954), including the trait of cursing and reviling some supernaturals.

57. Two dance teams alternate, each dancing every other day. If each of the two teams has twenty members, that would yield the forty that he refers to here. I have never witnessed more than sixteen Grasejos dancing at any one time, so twenty is probably the ideal number but may be only rarely attained. It is possible that the twenty dancers personify the named days, since the year-bearer (Mam) is depicted in Momostecan stories as a shepherd with a whip (see B. Tedlock 1986: 130–131). The two teams numbering forty correlate nicely with the forty days of Lent, and the forty days of *costumbre* that must be observed by the dance sponsor.

58. The social organization of this dance, including the named roles, is described in chapter 2. Nabe Mu's is First Ladino, the leader of the dance.

59. A little piece of copal is burning on each tile. Here the twenty dancers become the twenty named days of the *tzolkin*, each passing through its thirteen numbered occurrences, so that the entire team embodies the 260-day almanac.

60. Edmonson (1965: 136) reports an eighteenth-century definition of Tz'ul Xahoh as "sword dance" or "Matachín Dance." He also found that one late-seventeenth-century lexicon reported *tzulunik,* a verb, to have the meaning "make love to," an appropriate referent considering the libidinous behavior of the dancers.

61. The Mam is described as a shepherd boy with a whip in a myth text that I have called the Origins of Costumbre. It is presented (Cook 1981: 654–677), and discussed (Cook 1986: 143,145) elsewhere. Also see a published version of a variant of this myth, called "Ojer Tzib" (B. Tedlock 1986).

62. Thompson (1970: 299) sees the Kekchi San Simón as a vegetation deity because the underworld reaches up to just below the earth's surface, thus affecting the plant world and crop fertility.

CHAPTER 6

1. A thesis that the postcolonial highland Maya culture (or Mesoamerican village culture) is a creation of conquest and colonialism lacking significant institutional continuity with the prehispanic past has informed the work of Eric Wolf, Severo Martinez, Marvin Harris, and others (Carlsen and Prechtel 1991: 23–24). This discontinuity thesis, which seeks to counter naive notions of aboriginal cultural survival in remote villages, is derived from dependency theory (see the critical discussion in Wilk 1991: 21–23) in which the "traditional society" of modernization theory has been redefined as the "peripheral society." Peripheral society is characterized by "partialism," in which rural workers who receive wages below their costs of living must retain subsistence production as part of their economic strategy, giving them an appearance of traditionality that disguises the fact that society has been transformed in order for them to play an economic role as exploited labor. According to dependency theory, then, this transformed society lacks meaningful continuity with the primordial precapitalist culture from which it was in part derived.

Though a corrective was needed for naive conceptions of traditional society in early modernization theory and dependency theory was valuable in providing the remedy, I believe that the empirical support offered to the continuity model in the recent past (see, e.g., Tedlock 1982; Gossen 1986; Hill and Monoghan 1987; Carlsen and Prechtel 1991; Freidel, Schele, and Parker 1993; MacAnany 1995; Carmack, Gasco, and Gossen 1996; Fox and Cook 1996) has by now made any theory-based rejection of the possibility of substantial continuity untenable.

2. The term "expressive culture" refers to song, narrative, dance, and other arts and ritual, that is, to behaviors and artifacts that have a primary function in representing a culture's symbols and themes to an audience, often

mobilizing emotional states. These events may be called cultural performances (Singer 1959).

3. Syntagmatic structures are the basis of morphological analysis that identifies types of tales or rites based on recurrent sequences of elements or events (see Fischer 1963, Dundes 1968). Syntagmatic structural analysis is empirical and inductive and its operations are replicable (Dundes 1968: xii).

4. Propp himself did not engage in cultural analysis, focusing rather on the identification of a formal tale type. Nevertheless, he made a distinction between morphology based on predicates ("functions"), actions in the story that may be represented by nouns ("deception," for example), and themes, which are varied by varying the attributes of the subjects and objects or characters (Propp 1968: 113). Thus a morphological analysis identifies the recurrent tale type, while a derived thematic analysis shows how it has been modified to fit different cultural contexts.

5. Las Casas (1967) reports that Quichean kings were buried in small tombs on hilltops accompanied by jewelry, thus providing a prototype for the lord of the hill as treasure owner. Classic kings at major centers were buried in pyramids, which we now know represented mountains. Highland Maya cultures today recognize ancestral mountain lords (called *witz* or *nuwal*), largely benevolent community protectors and enforcers of morality, and *dueños del cerro*, who take the forms of Ladinos or gringos and must be paid for the use of resources (see Cook 1986: 152–153).

6. The Maya millenarian myth was identified as such by ethnographers as early as the 1930s when it was abstracted from Yucatecan accounts of surviving races and beings from earlier creations poised to return (Redfield and Villa Rojas 1964: 328).

7. This basic dichotomy between little and great traditions, popularized in the 1930s and 1940s by Robert Redfield (see Redfield 1941; Redfield and Villa Rojas [1934] 1964) has continued to inform the work of Mayanists engaged in historical reconstruction (e.g., Thompson 1970; Farriss 1984).

8. The so-called Star Wars complex, reconstructed from Peten Maya archaeology, iconography, and epigraphy, in which a new kind of interpolity warfare timed by celestial events and deriving much of its iconography from Teotihuacán emerged early in the Classic Maya Period (Schele and Freidel 1990), represents another example of this pattern unknown to De Borhegyi but supporting his argument. It is doubtful that the new celestial cult of the warrior ruling class at Tikal had much impact on peasant village cosmology or ritual forms. The rural communities simply had to adjust as best they could to heightened warfare and to the emergence of more competitive conquest states, and probably to more demanding and socially and spatially insulated elites.

9. Carmack (1995: 396–405) provides an expanded description and anal-

ysis of political conflict in Momostenango from the colonial period through the present. Conflict between the rural *caciques* and the urban *cabildo* (municipal corporation) was significant between the 1650s and 1750s. From then until the end of the colonial period commoner *principales* checked the power of the caciques and controlled the *cabildo,* even instituting a new *"cacique"* status based on charisma and military achievements early in the nineteenth century. Traditional conflicts over succession to offices and over land, water, and forest rights have remained endemic within and between kin-based factions, but these local conflicts could be resolved within the *auxiliatura* system. Separatist movements organized by "ancient status groups whose roots extend all the way back to the prehispanic period" (Carmack 1995: 402)—i.e., the original cacique lineages that had controlled the *parcialidades*—reflect opposition to *cabecera* domination by Ladinos or non-cacique Indians. That is, though they have been outmaneuvered politically by commoner alliances during the past couple of centuries, cacique lineages were still active players in community-level politics throughout the colonial period and on into the Recent Indian stage. Even though they might constitute a seemingly united group vis-à-vis the reform Catholics, the Costumbristas and the traditional communities idealized in their worldview were deeply factionalized before reform Catholicism or evangelical Protestant cults arrived on the scene.

10. The Yegua Achi' and Ek' stories are presented and analyzed more fully in Cook 1983: 135–146. For the transcribed texts, see Cook 1981: 640–647 (Yegua Achi') and 683–685 (Ek').

11. Dennis Tedlock (1993: 15) notes that *k'ab'a* in Quiché means "to open up the mouth."

12. Perhaps the manikin scepter is shown as a serpent-legged baby because it requires this kind of suckling (Tedlock 1993: 18). Part of the clowning in the Conquest Dance involves the presentation of the little Aj Itz doll at the breasts of female tourists.

13. Chan Balam, the Palenque king who built the group of the cross, is depicted in a painted stucco relief in the Temple of the Inscriptions as an infant with the smoking celt and serpent leg attributes of the god K'awil or manikin scepter, apparently representing his transformation into that god as a sign that he would be heir to the throne. The Maya kings are also sometimes depicted after death with the smoking celt in the forehead attribute (Freidel, Schele, and Parker 1993: 193–194). Thus the Classic Period K'awil/manikin scepter seems to have represented both a conduit for materialization of the ancestors and an alter ego for the kings as divinities.

14. An abridged version in English of the Diego Vicente saga is in Fox and Cook 1996: 820, where the possible significance of the intergenerational conflict as evidence for segmentary lineages is developed. It exists in a Spanish

abridged version with a discussion relating it to the Epi-Toltec migration saga in Cook 1983: 136–140, and is transcribed in full in Cook 1981: 678–685.

15. Dennis Tedlock (1993: 42–43) argues for similarities between the *c'oxol* and Tohil. They are both associated with fire and thunderbolts, and Tohil has one leg, while the *c'oxol* has one shoe.

16. The selection of Palenque as a model here and in the section above is based on the fact that it is a well-documented site and that there seem to be parallels. Palenque may be an especially appropriate model, though, if the Western Rivers Region of the Classic lowlands where Palenque is located turns out to be the homeland from which the archaeological Quichean cultures are derived (cf. Sabloff and Willey 1967; Thompson 1970; Carmack 1981; Fox 1987). In an important critical article, Price argued that archaeological inference from analogies must be based on either historical connections or ecological similarities. Unwilling to deal with vague notions of generalized Maya culture, she asked: "Where are the descendants of Tikal's population?" (Price 1974: 448). Perhaps some of the descendants of Palenque's population ended up in Momostenango.

17. The discovery that the Maya cross is both the world tree and the Milky Way/ecliptic arranged in the special biannual Wakan Chah arrangement is summarized in Schele 1992: 118–153. These discoveries are applied to the interpretation of the group of the cross at Palenque in *Maya Cosmos* (Freidel, Schele, and Parker 1993: 144–146).

18. A Proppian morphological analysis focusing only on the Hero Twins episode of the *Popol Vuh* (Himelblau 1989: 49–64) concludes that it follows Propp's syntagmatic model for the morphology of the Russian fairy tale precisely. An implication of this closeness of fit, according to Himelblau, is the universality of the Proppian morphology of Aarne-Thompson tale types 300–749: "I believe that Propp has discovered, if not the archaic syntagmatic deployment of narrative functions, then at the very least one of the basic morphologies of the narrative" (Himelblau 1989: 67).

Joseph Campbell's (1949: 245–46) depiction of the monomyth of the hero also clearly follows this same pattern. He explains the recurrence of departure, supernatural adventure motifs with helpers and donors, and return and apotheosis in the world's hero myths as the application to the narrative form of the psychodynamics of the rite of passage. The only significant difference that I can find between the Campbell generic hero tale and the Propp generic fairy tale is that in Campbell the marriage function (marriage to the goddess) occurs while the hero is in the other world, while, as would be expected in a good fairy tale, Propp has marriage at the end. In this regard the *Popol Vuh* is, appropriately, closer to the Campbell than to the Propp model, since Xquic is impregnated in Xibalba.

What follows from this universality is that the recognition of a recurrent tale type at the level of Proppian functions may not be taken as a proof of historical connectedness or of the existence of a tradition in the usual sense of the term. It may be a reflection of psychological principles embodied in all heroic narratives. If the myth of Jesucristo, then, is seen to embody the same syntagmatic structure as the Hero Twins episode in the *Popol Vuh*, what are we to make of this? It has no real bearing on the interpretive-historical argument made in this work. One hero tale can replace another just as one hero can replace another. It is at the thematic, rather than the morphological, level that culture becomes salient. The relevant issues for understanding the Quichean cultural tradition will be related to how the themes attached to a more or less universal tale type have developed, and what we may infer about continuity in the process from that mode of development.

19. This tale type is given partial expression in various Maya hero tales, for example, the Negro of Panchoy (Correa 1960: 63–65), other giant tales (Thompson 1930: tale 16; LaFarge 1947, tale 3) and a Yucatecan story about an ancient king who tries to overcome a boy (Redfield and Villa Rojas 1964, tale 14). In a truncated version of this tale type, the action does not go all the way to completion: the protagonist is defeated and imprisoned (in the earth) or is buried and has not yet reemerged. In this truncated form, the tale type is millenarian in the full proper sense and often nativistic, because the reemergence of the hero will transform the world. Thus, for example, there are tales in Yucatán of ancient races who have been defeated and driven underground, but who will return and usher in a golden age (Redfield and Villa Rojas 1964: 328). The Costumbrista gloss on Tecum as the leader of the *mundos,* discussed in chapter 4, is another example of this.

The tale type is also expressed in contemporary folk tales in the eastern region of the southern Maya area, especially, it seems, in Kekchi and Mopan-speaking communities, in stories about the sun and moon (see Thompson 1930 and Shaw 1971). The sun, as a young man, journeys to the underworld to obtain his wife from a tyrannical father. They are forced to elope, with a pursuit and magical flight motif. The woman may be killed and revived during the elopement, providing the charter for lunar phases. The young man or young couple eventually kill the pursuers. This basic plot exists in many variations, though it is not always clear that it is the about the sun and moon (e.g., Shaw 1971: 187–192). In a unique but still recognizable version, the tale has also been recorded in Mitla (Parsons 1966) as "The Barren Woman." Here the sun and moon are male and female twins being raised by an evil and tyrannical pair of guardians.

20. Comparative research on Maya myths shows that imprisonment and burial may substitute for each other in nuclear plots. Evidence is cited in detail in Cook 1981: 461–475. Momostecans conceive of their own burials as impris-

onments, during which their souls are periodically allowed visits by their living relatives on days Ajpu, on the Day of the Dead, and on Saturday of Glory, "just as prisoners in jail are allowed visitors on Sundays."

21. The Jacaltecan version of the founding of the pueblo by its ancestral couple (see La Farge and Byers 1931) establishes the custom of blood sacrifice for the yearbearers on a ridge near town at the same point in the plot where the four ancestors in the *Popol Vuh* establish blood sacrifice and then human sacrifice for their patron images, the *cabawils*. The four idols or *cabawils* appear to be elite culture substitutions for the peasants' yearbearers. Tojil, the most powerful of the *cabawils*, is identified with Quetzalcoatl in the *Popol Vuh:*

> Even though Tohil is his name, he is the same as the god of the Yaqui people, who is named Yolcuat and Quitzalcuat . . . the Yaqui people whose dawn was there in the place called Mexico today.
>
> (Tedlock 1985: 183)

In late Postclassic Yucatán the rulers of Mani convened at their temple for a five-day vigil in honor of Kukulkan (the Yucatec Quetzalcoatl) each year. They believed that Kukulkan descended from heaven and entered his temple on the fifth day (Tozzer 1966), a seeming reference to the five day *uayeb* or gap between solar years associated with the yearbearer's festival. Thus it seems reasonable to see the peasant's yearbearer and the elite warrior's feathered serpent/*cabawil* as versions of the same deity.

22. The Twins play ball against the lords of Xibalba. These killers of their father are also their maternal grandfathers via Xquic. The Twins ultimately defeat them. Perhaps part of the message here is the illegitimacy of authority when claimed by matrilineal relatives. I think that the generation gap itself may be more significant. Even today grandfathers and their patrilineal grandsons, often namesakes for each other, refer to each other as *nu c'axel* in Quiché, "my replacement." This is suggestive of the yearbearer complex, because the yearbearer is called Mam (grandfather). It suggests a rite of passage in which coming of age is symbolized as taking one's rightful place as a young adult, replacing one's grandfather. In fact, this reading of the symbolism even suggests that the psychological meaning of the yearbearer may lie in the anxiety attached to the alternation of authority between generations, of the delicacy, danger, and hostility associated with the replacement of the old by the young in a society in which the old are venerated and powerful.

23. If the yearbearers are not perfectly synchronized with the solar calendar because there is no leap year correction, then the highland yearbearer ceremony drops back one day in each four years, or twenty-five days in each century. This reasoning allows Tedlock (1993) to explain the Maximon linkage of Judas and the Mam by the occurrence of the yearbearer during Holy Week when Antigua was destroyed by earthquake in the early eighteenth century. By

this same reasoning, the yearbearer's festival would have been in June in the mid-sixteenth century and probably would not have been described as a Lent (*Cuaresma*) occurring at about the same time as Easter. The Postclassic cultures probably had a planting season festival timed by observing the sun or the constellations. B. Tedlock (1992) identifies survivals of such an almanac in Momos. The Postclassic civilization may have observed several new years in each solar year, just as Momostecans do today with their celebrations of Easter, Christmas, Santiago's festival, and the yearbearer as major rites of renewal. The linkage of the elite's rite of passage to the planting-season rite of renewal suggests that this was the most important festival in the highlands and probably the one at which the Xibalba myth was most prominently featured as a cosmogonic charter.

24. Community-wide world transformation or new year symbolism also occurs at Christmas, Santiago's festival, and the yearbearer's festival. Each *cofradía* also celebrates a new year festival on its saint's day.

25. One need only read the relevant portions of *A Mayan Life* (Gonzalez 1995: 37–53, 67–77) or the autobiography of Rigoberta Menchú (Menchú 1984: 21–27, 33–42) to experience first-hand accounts of the hellishness of the modern highland Maya encounter with the coast.

26. That the Yegua Achi' story is a charter for the pilgrimage complex is quite clear. He built the roads, he built the cathedral at Esquipulas, he was killed there, and signs of his life are seen along the route from Momostenango to Esquipulas.

27. Tedlock (1985: 150) omits reference to the centipede dance, replacing it with "only swallowing swords," thus finding a translation that grammatically parallels the idea of walking on stilts to make a sort of couplet at the end. Edmonson (1965: 136) gives "Tz'ul" as "sword dance" or "*matachín* dance," and "Ix Tzul" as "centipede dance." In Momostenango, the Tzulab perform a skit clearly derived from the Matachín Dance, and also perform a leapfrog-over-the-line that causes the company of dancers to resemble a great centipede crawling across the plaza, thus uniting both definitions in one dance but without any sword swallowing. I suspect that the centipede dance is the appropriate prehispanic gloss, and that a *matachín* motif was added to the dance in the sixteenth century to give it a Hispanic-Christian character and thus facilitate its ongoing public presentation.

28. As noted in chapter 5, the most reasonable etymology for *tzul* is the Quichean borrowing of the Yucatec term *dzul*, which means foreigner.

29. *The Annals of the Cakchiquels* (Recinos and Goetz 1953: 70–71) has an interesting parallel to this episode. Gagavitz, an ancestral culture hero, and his companion, Zaquitzunun, clothe themselves in green cornstalks and foliage. Carrying water they enter the erupting volcano, Gagxanul. They extinguish its eruption and bring fire to their kin. The celebration when they return with the

fire features the performance of the Xtzul Dance. This parallels the *Popol Vuh*'s Xibalba episode in that paired (though not twinned) heroes enter the underworld, vanquish its antihuman forces, and ascend again to the human world. In the *Annals'* scaled-down human version, they return with fire. In the *Popol Vuh* they are given the sun and moon. The prehispanic Quichean cultures found this mythic structure of twinned heroes descending and ascending with fire or sun to be compelling and worthy of repetition as the charter for major cosmogonic events. The Tzulab Dance is a recurrent element in the human replications of the pattern, perhaps as a facilitator of the process based on the *Popol Vuh* prototype.

30. As noted in chapter 6, these are Corpus, Santa Cruz, Santiago, María Concepción, San Francisco, and Santa Bárbara. That is, four of the five "chief" *cofradías* known as the *c'amal be* (excluding Capitagua) plus Santa Bárbara and San Francisco. Recall that Momostenango was composed of six *parcialidades* during most of the colonial period. Unfortunately Corpus and Santa Bárbara cannot be reliably traced back into the colonial period as either *parcialidades* or *cofradías*. The sociopolitical and cosmological rationales for the roles of these particular sodalities in the complex are unclear.

31. The planting can begin at the next full moon, or any subsequent full moon once the rains have started. D. Tedlock (1985: 46) believes that the sun and full moon represented the Twins, while the moon in other phases represented their mother, Xquic. Similarly, I was very recently informed that Yucatec Maya lore assigns a male identity to the full moon (personal communication from Nancy Forand and Miguel Aguilero). If Momostecans make this association, then the Easter full moon's rise could correspond to the ascending of the Hero Twins at about the same time as the death and rebirth of the two *calvario* Cristos. I have nevertheless interpreted the moon in contemporary Quichean folklore as having female associations because of the moon-bride in sun-moon tales, the association of the moon with the Virgen in Momostenango and elsewhere in the Maya area (e.g., see Gossen 1974), and the clear associations of the moon with menstruation (Furst 1986). The full moon is clearly related to conception, because Momostecans explain that planting and sexual intercourse are timed to be most fruitful when the moon is full. Nevertheless, it seems that Maya moon lore and Maya understanding of the transition at Easter are variable and probably far more complicated than my interpretation would suggest. Holy Week in Santiago Atitlán may, according to Robert Carlsen, involve both the symbolic impregnation of the Virgen by San Juan, and of Jesucristo by Maximon (Canby 1994: 331–333). Sexually active transgendering deities may be critical to Maya understanding of the forces that move the annual cycle, and in complex permutations that go far beyond the simple model suggested in my account. Planting lore is also probably more complex than my information suggests. In unidentified Quiché and Cakchiquel villages, Rem-

ington (1977: 80–81) recorded planting scheduled from the third day of the waxing moon through the waning quarter moon, that is, a planting period that bracketed the full moon. During this time the moon is "tender." Harvesting may only occur after the full moon, as the moon moves from its "tender" to its "seasoned" mode.

My interpretation, then, is consistent with some evidence but probably also inconsistent with some. This is a well-intentioned working hypothesis that probably needs some correcting to adequately render an understanding of underlying Maya solar/lunar myth(s).

32. The nine-month period from planting to harvest, incidentally, suggests that for the Quiché the *tzolkin* (260-day divining almanac) has relevance to both the human gestation cycle (Furst 1986: 70) and the agricultural cycle. Maize in the western highlands is ready to harvest about one full *tzolkin* cycle after planting, as a child is born about one full *tzolkin* cycle after a missed period.

33. Also consider Linda Schele's discussion of *yih,* a Yucatec and Tzotsil term that can be glossed as both "to be born" and "to go to seed" (Schele 1992: 164).

34. As discussed above in connection with the Palenque Triad, this overlapping of identities is documented in Schele 1992: 127, Schele and Freidel 1990: 412, and Freidel, Schele, and Parker 1993: 276.

35. *C'axel* is the Momostecan cognate for the Tzutujil *k'exel.* In the construction *nu c'axel,* meaning "my replacement," it is the term used by a grandfather for his patrilineal grandson, especially a grandson named after him according to custom, and may also be used by the grandson to refer to this grandfather.

36. The Momostecan trinity of Dios Cielo (Sky God), Dios Animas (Souls' God) and Dios Mundo (World God) is described in detail in Cook 1986.

37. Momostecans point out that the *dueños del cerro* used to appear as Ladinos, but now are more likely to appear as gringos.

38. As noted several times previously, this text is not included in the present work. One version, recorded by Barbara Tedlock, is readily available in both B. Tedlock 1982 and 1986, while the text that I recorded is presented in full in my dissertation (Cook 1981: 654–677).

39. The central question asked about expressive culture by the structuralist school of British social anthropology is how it embodies alternative theories of society. In Leach's writings, for example, this takes the classic form of an argument that social structure is given cultural form and ritual expression by societies, and that any society will contain a series of alternative models, ideal modes of life, or theories about how the social system works (1964: 4). Mary Douglas sees what she calls "natural symbols," that is, quasi-universal symbolisms based on the natural and universal experiences with human anatomy and

physiology as elements used "for acting out theories of society," and further argues for a dialectical ritual/anti-ritual "idiom" in which this acting out occurs (1973: 179). Turner (1974) contrasts "communitas" and "societas," antistructure and structure, but beyond this he argues for an interpretation of a society's symbolism as ideological, as an arena in which competing metaphors or paradigms are enacted by a community.

40. Unlike Mendelson, who saw three "worlds" in Atitlán of the 1950s, I am not arguing for coexisting Maya (Martín), Spanish (Jesucristo), and syncretized (Maximon) worldviews. Influenced by the De Borhegyi (1956) hypothesis, I am inclined to believe that these three worlds have existed as potentials in Maya social experience and collective imagination since the rise of village life and a dependence on cultigens, or certainly since the emergence of rulers, who like Seven Macaw (Wucub Caquix) in the *Popol Vuh*, or San Simón, or any modern dictator, have the potential to impose illegitimate and hence oppressive authority. The villager, the peasant farmer, seeks a balance in nature and in society, a balance between natural fertility and human order, a balance between freedom and conformity, a balance between the needs and powers of the young and the old.

41. Fischer (1963) argues that drama is a human universal created through oppositions. When oppositional structure is worked out in a narrative dramatic form, that is, when the order of events or syntax of the symbolism is considered, he refers to syntagmatic structure. When the logical model of oppositions or relations is abstracted from its chronological narrative presentation and syntax is ignored, as in French structuralism, he refers to paradigmatic structure.

42. This is reminiscent of Leach's (1964) analysis of highland Burma, where the Kachin have two basic opposed ideal political models: *shan*, a feudal hierarchy, and *gumlao*, an anarchistic egalitarianism. Leach argues that actual communities oscillate historically between these two extremes, striking an ideal compromise principle of social organization called *gumsa*. I am not, however, suggesting an exact parallel. The Momostecan polarity projected in expressive culture is mythical. Neither pole represents an "ideal political model" in the sense in which *shan* and *gumlao* do, in the sense in which the models are ideological statements of what for some are positively valued political philosophies. The Momostecan Holy Week polarity is a bizarre and exaggerated version of the opposed tendencies of order and anarchy, hierarchy and egalitarianism. They are theories of what may happen when cosmos breaks down, rather than alternate versions of cosmos.

Glossary

aguardiente: Literally, "burning water." This is a rumlike liquor made by distilling alcohol from fermented sugar. *Aguardiente* is produced and sold commercially in Guatemala, and is also produced in substantial quantities at illegal stills. It is also called *guaro* and *cuxa*.

aj itz: A practitioner of *itzinel* (the use of supernatural power). Most Momostecans use the term synonymously with *brujo* (sorcerer or witch). As a proper noun, Aj Itz is another name for Tzitzimite, the hatchet-bearing diviner dressed in red who opposes the Spaniards in the Conquest Dance accompanied by a little Aj Itz called Aj Itz Chiquito. Also see *c'oxol*.

aj mesa: A priest-shaman who has been initiated at a *mesa* altar and who consequently has special powers to combat witchcraft, the responsibility of making offerings at the *mesa* on certain days C'at, and the right to visit the *mesa* altars on the four sacred mountains on behalf of clients.

aj patan: Literally, "one who carries a burden"; that is, a *cofrade*.

aj vara: Literally, "one who has a staff of office." The term can refer to a municipal official but is more commonly used to refer to anyone who has been initiated on Wajxaquib Batz as a daykeeper. The term *vara* has been adapted to refer to the sacred bag of *tzité* seeds and rock crystals that each daykeeper maintains and uses in divination.

alaxik: The term used by Momostecans to refer to their patrilineage, especially to locally coresident members of a patrilineage represented by a *chuch kajaw*, a daykeeper from the patrilineage elected by its elders to perform offerings at the hilltop *warabal ja* and *winel* altars belonging to the *alaxik*.

alcalde: A mayor. The term can refer to the elected head of the municipal government. It can also refer to the *síndico segundo,* the Indian *alcalde* who, as the leader of the *alcaldes* of the *cantones,* mediates between the *principales* and the municipal government. The *síndico* and the other *alcaldes* of the *cantones* are appointed by the *principales. Alcalde* is also used to designate the highest post in each *cofradía,* a position that carries the responsibility of sponsoring the *cofradía's* fiesta and ensuring that all of the appropriate ceremonies and offerings are made.

alcalté: The pronunciation of *alcalde* most commonly used when speaking Quiché.

aldea: An official subdivision of a municipality represented by an *alcalde* and other officials.

almanaco: The 260-day divining calendar. See *tzolkin.*

amak: usually defined in colonial dictionaries as "hamlet," the term *amak* referred to several different kinds of communities depending on its context or modification by other terms. There were the *ch'uti amak* (little hamlet), *nima amak* (big hamlet), *amak tinamit* (group of small hamlets formerly a town or fiefdom dependent on a fortified center), and others. A detailed discussion is available in Fox and Cook (1996: 811–812).

armita: Literally, "hermitage." This is the term used by Momostecans for a *cofradía* house, which is usually a rented house in the town center. This is where the *cofrades* of a particular saint hold the saint's fiesta.

autor: The sponsor or producer of a dance performance.

auxiliatura: Also known in Guatemala as an *ayuntamiento.* This is an auxiliary government appointed by the *principales* to supplement the elected municipal corporation. The *auxiliatura* is composed of the *síndico segundo* (Indian *alcalde*) and several councilmen and a secretary from the town center, as well as the *alcaldes* and other officials of the *aldeas.*

bomba: An exploding skyrocket fired from a mortar at events like *cofradía* festivals and weddings. It is used to mark the transition points in rituals that are of general interest to a wider public that might not be in attendance. The *bombas* make a festival more lively and so please the saints and the *primeros.*

brujería: The Spanish term for witchcraft, used by Momostecans to denote the use of supernatural power (*itzinel*) to harm people.

cabawil: A sixteenth-century term denoting a stone or wooden image that served as the representation (*wachibal*) of a powerful patrilineage's tutelary god. The term is no longer understood in this way in Momos. It has been retained in folklore as the *cabwel,* a part-human and part-animal creature that ate humans and was kept in caves by a *cacique* until it was destroyed by a saint. The Momostecan *cabwel* was named Ek' (Black) and was kept in a cave in San Vicente Buenabaj.

cabecera: The nucleated center of a municipality where the municipal corporation (*cabildo*) meets, the parish church and cemetery are located, and the *cofradías* hold the annual festivals for the community's saints in their *armitas.*

cabildo: The municipal corporation. The *cabildo* was officially organized in the sixteenth century, and over the centuries has coordinated the rising power of the *cabecera* and its allied Ladino and more acculturated Maya elite at the expense of the *cacique* lineages in the rural hamlets.

cacique: The head of a lineage that has a traditional claim to elite status via descent from a pre-Hispanic conqueror. In the early colonial period these *caciques* were also called *calpuls.* Some modern *caciques,* though, are descendants of *caciques* who first attained locally recognized elite status during the colonial period through creating and managing a *parcialidad,* that is, a rural communal enterprise that linked several large extended families or lineage segments in management of an estate and in the cult of a Catholic saint. The nineteenth and twentieth centuries have seen the *caciques* lose political power to the *cabildo* and its staff of acculturated urban Momostecans.

calpul: In the pre-Hispanic period, a *calpul* was a *chinamit* or the head of a *chinamit.* During the colonial period, *chinamits* were redesignated as *parcialidades,* and eventually the main ones became *cantones.* The term *calpul* is used in Momos today to refer to a *cofrade,* because, it is said, it used to be that each *cofradía* represented a *cantón.*

calvario: Calvarios are chapels located in community cemeteries. Images of the crucified and entombed Christ are displayed there, and offerings are made to the souls of the dead on the Day of the Dead and on days Ajpu. Momostenango's *calvario* is located in the cemetery on the eastern side of the town center.

c'amal be: The term means a guide, and its most common reference in Momos is to a marriage go-between. The directorate of the *cofradías,* the five most important sodalities—Señor Resurrección (or Corpus), Santiago, María Concepción, Santa Cruz, and Cristo Crucificado (or Capitagua)—are referred to as the *c'amal be* of the *cofradías.* They mediate between the *cofradías* and their external overseers: the priest, the *principales,* and the *cabildo.*

cantón: The unofficial or traditional rural communities that descended from the colonial *parcialidades* are called *cantones.* They had their own patron saints prior to the centralization of saints in the church in the nineteenth and twentieth centuries. They generally correspond to the official *aldeas,* but a few *cantones* are located within *aldeas,* like Pueblo Viejo in Tunayac and Pologua in Pasajoc.

capitana: See *nima chichu.*

caudillo: At the end of the colonial period, and on through the nineteenth and early twentieth centuries Ladino political/military bosses came to dominate politics based on their control of regional power bases. They were called *caudillos.*

chinamit: A pre-Hispanic community composed of several intermarrying patrilineages that controlled a communal estate, maintained the cult of a *cabawil* (patron deity), and was dominated by an elite patrilineage and its head, sometimes called a *calpul.* The *chinamits* were given patron saints and renamed *parcialidades* during the colonial period, and have descended into modern times as *cantones.*

chuch axel: A woman who serves a saint as an auxiliary to the male *cofradía.*

chuch kajaw: A daykeeper or priest-shaman who has an official capacity as the representative of a corporate group like an *alaxik, cofradía,* dance team, *aldea,* or municipal corporation.

cofrade: Member of a *cofradía.*

cofradía: A sodality composed of four or more men occupying ranked positions who are appointed by the *principales* to maintain the cult of a saint for a year.

comunidad: The late nineteenth and early twentieth century term for communities that had been *parcialidades* as they adjusted to the hostility of the postcolonial liberal regimes to their collective ownership and management of estates. Some *comunidades* continued to manage a collective estate into the mid-twentieth century.

costumbre: Any particular behavior directed toward the supernatural as mandated by the tradition is a *costumbre.* When used as a proper noun, Costumbre refers to the overall practice of syncretized Maya-Catholic religion. The heart of this religion, also called Poronel, is the burning of resins, barks, candles, and liquor at altars (*porobal*) established by the ancestors, often accompanied by periods of sexual abstinence.

Costumbrista: Momostecan traditionalists who practice the Costumbre religion.

c'oxol: A dwarf spirit seen in wild places. Seeing the *c'oxol* is a sign of one's impending death. It is thought to be a treasure guardian and an assistant to more powerful *mundos.* Ordinarily the *c'oxol* is dressed in red (see K'aki' C'oxol). Dennis Tedlock (1985: 368) defines the *c'oxol* as a "spark striker" and elaborates his conception of this being in detail.

delicado: This Spanish term is generally used by Momostecans in the translation of Quiché ideas about contact with the supernatural; it connotes the combined sensitivity and danger associated with such undertakings. For example, a saint might be referred to as *delicado* to translate the Quiché terms *itzel ri tiox* (evil/powerful the saint) or *kaxlic ri tiox* (painful the saint), in a context where the idea is that one must be very careful of one's thoughts and actions and follow all of the prescribed *costumbre* in order to avoid punishment.

deputado: The deputy is the second-ranked position in a *cofradía.* In major *cofradías,* deputies often remain in service for many years and master and transmit *cofradía* lore.

Dios Mundo: The Holy World. The animistic personifiers of nature, often thought of as the spirits of mountains, caves, and springs, from whom permission is required before exploiting nature by hunting, logging, or farming are called *mundos.* The yearbearers (Mamlab) are also *mundos,* approached by *aj mesas* at their shrines on the major, direction-associated mountains. When all the *mundos* are lumped together as a single collective entity, "Dios Mundo" or "Juyup Takaj" (mountain-plain) is generally used.

dueño: A *mundo,* the supernatural owner of a mountain or other wild place who must be asked for and paid for any trespassing on his property. The *dueño del cerro* is visualized as a Ladino or gringo, often in old-fashioned (colonial period) clothing.

encomienda: A colonial period grant of service or tribute that obligated an indigenous community to the demands of an *encomendero,* a Spaniard or creole who had been thus rewarded for service to Spain.

Grasejos: This Spanish term meaning "jesters" is often pronounced as *carase'j.* It is the name of a dance of contraries performed during Lent and Holy Week. See Tzulab.

guachibal: See *wachibal.*

guaro: See *aguardiente.*

ilbal: One of the four rock crystals kept in the *vara* or divining kit of a daykeeper. The *ilbal* is held up to the eye and used to see hidden things.

juyup: A mountain or a wilderness (a *monte*). The term is the root of *ujuyubal* (mountain place), a shrine complex.

Juyup Takaj: Juyup and *takaj* are complementary opposites representing mountain and plain, and also representing wilderness and cultivation, a version of the nature/culture opposition. See Dios Mundo.

K'ak'i C'oxol: The red *c'oxol,* also called Aj Itz or Tzitzimite, depicted in the Conquest Dance. This being is the diviner for and adviser to Tecum. See *c'oxol.*

Ladino: A mestizo; a person of mixed European and Mayan ancestry who rejects Mayan identity, speaks Spanish, and identifies with the Hispanic national culture. Ladinos and Indians continue to represent castelike groups in the national society and the rural villages, with Ladinos generally occupying commercial, professional, and political positions and controlling the formal institutions of commerce and the state.

mai: A cohort or temporal grouping of the souls of the dead. A *mai* may correspond to the dead of a generation or of a century.

Mam: Literally, "grandfather." It is also used to refer to the supernatural concept of the *alcalde del mundo,* the Quichean yearbearer, one of four personified days that are seated, in turn, on directionally associated sacred mountains, in an eternal rotation as the alternating owners of the solar year.

mesa, mesabal: An altar. *Mesa* is probably a contraction of *mesabal* (lit., "broom place" or "swept place"). The *mesa* altars are special altars marked by crosses; they often have the tablelike form of a little stone bench with one or more crosses standing behind it. These are the altars for important *mundos,* including the Mams,

and they do not belong to specific *alaxiks*. Offerings may only be
made by *aj mesas*, and the *mesa* altars figure preeminently in the
cult institutions that protect town officials, in requests for rain, and
in the defense of individual clients against witchcraft.

mortoma: The lowest-ranked position in a *cofradía*. The term is
apparently a Quichean corruption of the Spanish term *mayordomo*.

mundo: See Dios Mundo.

municipio: A municipality. Momostenango is a *municipio*. A *municipio* has a *cabecera* (town center) and several *aldeas* (rural hamlets)
within its jurisdiction. It has been recognized for decades that, for
the Quiché, *municipios* are not just political units but also linguistic
and cultural units.

mu's: The Quiché term for a *Ladino*. It also has the general meaning
of something fancy or pretty and can mean a dandy. As a proper
noun, Mu's or Nabe Mu's (First Ladino) is the husband or chief
consort of Xinula in the Grasejos or Tzulab Dance.

nawal (nagual): One's spirit alter ego. For example, the *nawal* of a
drunk is the weasel and the *nawal* of Tecum is the quetzal. The
term may also refer to a transformer or to an animal that a transformer has become.

nima chichu: The great lady. This is the highest position in the
women's auxiliary in the sodality of a saint.

novena: A vow to sponsor a festival, or to perform some other significant religious undertaking, nine times.

nuevo: a new dancer or *cofrade*.

octavo: A measure of liquor; an eighth of a liter, or approximately a
pint, which, like its U.S. counterpart the fifth, is a standard size.

ojew achi': This is an archaic term for a war captain or a local feudal
lord, or both, that referred to the native conquerors of rural *chinamits* during the period of Quiché expansion from the capital at
Utatlán. In modern times this meaning has been forgotten and the
term is used as the proper noun Ojew Achi'—sometimes corrupted
to Yew Achi' or even Yegua Achi' (mare man)—to refer to the *mundo*
who opposes the saints.

paraje: A small community, often organized around a hilltop altar
complex representing one or more *alaxiks*. The *paraje* is usually
named after some feature of the local topography and is the smallest
named territorial unit of an *aldea* or *cantón*.

parcialidad: A *parcialidad* was a community composed of several

intermarrying patrilineages that managed a collectively held estate
and the cult of a saint, all under the auspices of the resident patriarch of an elite lineage. The *parcialidad* evolved from the *chinamit,*
and as the colonial period came to a close it evolved into the *cantón,* the traditional territorial subdivision of a *municipio.*

pasado: an outgoing or retiring *cofrade,* dancer, or dance sponsor at
the end of a stipulated period of service.

porobal: The generic term for a Quichean altar; literally, "a place or
thing used for burning." A *porobal* complex usually belongs to
a corporate group of some kind—for example, an *alaxik* or a
sodality—and has two components: an *ujuyubal* and an *uja'l.*
The *mesa* is a specialized *porobal.* A *porobal* is usually a mound
of stones and large pot shards with an interior or enclosed area
for burning. It may be closed with a flat stone or large shard when
not in use.

Poronel: See Costumbre.

primeros: The founders of a community, family, or sodality whose souls
continue to watch over things and send punishments to afflict their
inferior replacements for incompetent performance of *costumbre.*

principales: The elder living trustees of the community. The *principales* are men, usually in their forties and older, who have served in
the *auxiliatura* as either the *alcalde* of an *aldea* or as the *síndico
segundo.* The *principales* are a self-replicating board of directors,
since they name men to the positions that can lead up to *principal*
status. They also name the *cofrades* and oversee the *cofradías,* but
in Momos *cofradía* participation cannot lead to *principal* status.

rawas: Awas is a difficult word to translate precisely. It can mean
"taboo" and is a polite term for the genitals of either sex, as in "a
male came up to her 'taboo' *(awas),* or vagina" (Tedlock 1982: 62).
It can also refer to the hearth of a shrine (Tedlock 1982: 146). In the
context of the present work, the term is always modified by *ri* (the),
giving the compound word *ri + awas = r'awas* or *rawas.* Here it
refers to a shrine or its hearth, as in "The *rawas* was in the house,
like an oven of adobe" and "The following day was the day of the
rawas for the image." There is an implication of a magical power
greater than in ordinary *costumbre;* that is, the *rawas* is especially
delicado.

retal: Retal (or *r'etal*) is a variant of *ri etal* (the sign). A *retal* is a sign,
especially a sign sent by a supernatural power. Sometimes a sign is

clear, but often its meaning is obscure and may require divination, or just waiting to see what it portends.

ropa: Ropa is the Spanish word for "clothing." In the sodalities, the *ropa* of an image refers to all of its possessions, including cloaks, hats, blankets, jewelry, and even little toys and the like.

secreto: A secret, but with the implication of something mystical or miraculous. Important saints have *secretos*, like the ability to travel on their own or like the knob on the head of San Antonio that is seen only by the *cofrades*. A *secreto* may simply be esoteric knowledge, or it may be knowledge that once was known but has been forgotten. For example, as one informant observed, "Only the *primeros* know the *secreto* of burying thirteen wax candles in the hole before the pole is seated there." The *cofrades* know to bury the candles, but they don't know why or what effect this has. This lost knowledge is a *secreto*.

síndico segundo: Also called the Indian *alcalde*. The *síndico* is the head of the *alcaldes* of the *aldeas* and the chief officer of the *auxiliatura*. He is named by the *principales*, and when his year's service is over he becomes a *principal*.

takaj: A flat area like a plain or broad valley, but also an area that is inhabited by people and cleared for planting or planted in crops. In this sense it contrasts with *juyup*, which can mean a mountain or a cave, but also has the implication of a jungle or bush, a *monte*.

tamalito: An unflavored tamale made by boiling maize dough in a corn husk packet. Tamalitos are a greater staple in the Momostecan diet than tortillas.

tinamit: A nucleated area or town center. The ruins of an abandoned pre-Hispanic center are called *ojer tinamit* (old town).

tzolkin: This term, commonly used in Mayanist literature for the 260-day divining calendar, was coined by William Gates in 1921 as a Yucatec version of the Quiché *chol k'ij* (i.e., "ordering of the days"; see Tedlock 1982: 219). It is constructed of two simultaneous cycles, one of 20 named days and another of the numbers 1 through 13, so it repeats itself every 260 days (13 × 20). Momostecans generally use the Spanish term *almanaco* to refer to their count of the days, and many actually keep a pocket calendar in which the Quiché days are written in next to their Gregorian counterparts. The sodalities perform *costumbre* at specific altars on schedules within the cycle of numbers (e.g., days numbered 1, 6, and 8). There are also day

names that correspond to important observances, for example,
visitations with the dead and the image of Corpus on days Ajpu.

The *almanaco* returns to its starting point every 260 days, marked
in Momostenango by major observances celebrated on the last day
of the old cycle (7 Tzi') and the beginning of the new cycle (8 Batz).
This festival marks the starting and ending points for the initiation
of new diviners (*aj vara*). The following is a sample segment of this
calendar, beginning with its 7 Tzi' to 8 Batz ending-starting period:
7 Tzi' (ends one cycle), 8 Batz (starts the next cycle), 9 E, 10 Aj,
11 Ix, 12 Tziquin, 13 Ajmac, 1 No'j, 2 Tijax, 3 Cawuk, 4 Ajpu (some
informants give this day as Junajpu), 5 Imox, 6 Ik', 7 Ak'abal, 8 C'at,
9 Can, 10 Came, 11 Quiej, 12 K'anil, 13 Toj, 1 Tzi', 2 Batz (and so on
through 260 days until returning to 7 Tzi'). For an exhaustive treatment of Momostecan calendrics, including the 260-day divining
calendar and the 365-day solar calendar, see Tedlock 1982: 88–131.

tzul: Someone whose behavior is crazy, especially when it is disrespectful and involves the use of vulgar language. As a proper noun,
"Tzulab" (the plural form of *tzul*) is the name of a dance given during Lent and Holy Week.

uja'l: Literally, "its water" (i.e., the water belonging to the complex of
altars). This is the spring or streamside altar in a paired altar complex for an *alaxik* or sodality. The other altar is the *ujuyubal*. The
water is possessed by the supernatural—by a saint or the *primeros*.

ujuyubal: Literally, "its mountain place." This term refers to the hilltop (or sometimes cave mouth) altar in a paired complex with an
uja'l. The *ujuyubal* of a saint is often a cave, sometimes a cave
located in a mountain.

vara: The *vara* is a unit of measurement about a meter in length. It
is also the term for a staff carried by an official as an emblem of his
position, and is used in a derivative sense as the term for the little
bag of *tzité* seeds and rock crystals carried by a daykeeper and used
in counting and consulting the days during a divination.

wachibal: Sometimes given as *guachibal*. This term means a representation or image of something. Examples include photos, drawings,
and carved statues. The image of a saint is a *wachibal*. *Wachibal*
also refers to the *cofradía*-like cult of a saint that belongs to a lineage segment in a local community but lacks official status and
oversight by the *cabildo* and the Catholic Church.

warabal ja: Literally, "sleeping house." This refers to the *porobal* of an *alaxik* (lineage segment) where the *chuch kajaw* of the *alaxik* offers prayers and incense to the souls of the ancestors to protect the members of the *alaxik*. The image of a saint also may have a *warabal ja:* the sleeping place of the souls of the *primeros*.

winel: The *porobal* of an *alaxik* where the *chuch kajaw* makes offerings for the milpas and domesticated animals.

Xibalba: The underworld. Xibalba also refers to an evil people who inhabited the world before Jesucristo rose as the sun. They went naked and didn't bury their dead.

xinula: A Ladina. When used as a proper noun it is the name of the young woman in the Tzulab Dance and of the old woman in the Monkeys Dance.

Bibiliography

Acuña, Rene

1975   Problemas del *Popol vuh*. *Mester.* 5: 123–132.

1983   El *Popol vuh,* Vico y la *Theologia indorum.* In *Nuevas perspectivas sobre el "Popol vuh,"* edited by Robert Carmack and Francisco Morales Santos, 1–16. Guatemala: Piedra Santa.

Alvarez Arevalo, Miguel

1987   *Manuscritos de Covalchaj.* Guatemala: n.p.

Barrett, Richard A.

1991   *Culture and Conduct.* Belmont, Calif.: Wadsworth.

Bode, Barbara O.

1961   *The Dance of the Conquest of Guatemala.* Publications of Middle American Research Institute, no. 27. New Orleans: Middle American Research Institute, Tulane University.

Bricker, Victoria

1981   *The Indian Christ, the Indian King: The Historical Substrate of Maya Myth and Ritual.* Austin: University of Texas Press.

Bunzel, Ruth

1952   *Chichicastenango: A Guatemalan Village.* Seattle: University of Washington Press.

Campa, Arthur L.

1979   *Hispanic Culture in the Southwest.* Norman: University of Oklahoma Press.

Campbell, Joseph

1949   *The Hero with a Thousand Faces.* New York: Bollingen Foundation (1949); New York: MJF Books, facsimile edition, by arrangement with Princeton University Press (1996).

Canby, Peter

1994   *The Heart of the Sky: Travels among the Maya.* New York: Kodansha America.

Cancian, Frank

1967   Political and Religious Organizations. In *Handbook of Middle American Indians,* edited by Robert Wauchope, vol. 6. Austin and London: University of Texas Press.

Carlsen, Robert, and Martin Prechtel
    1991   The Flowering of the Dead: An Interpretation of Highland Maya Culture. *Man,* n.s., 26: 23-42.
Carmack, Robert M.
    1966   La perpetuación del clan patrilineal de Totonicapán. *Antropología e historia de Guatemala* 18, no. 2: 43-60.
    1973   *Quichean Civilization: The Ethnohistoric, Ethnographic, and Archaeological Sources.* Los Angeles: University of California Press.
    1977   Ethnohistory of the Central Quiché: The Community of Utatlán. In *Archaeology and Ethnohistory of the Central Quiché,* edited by Dwight T. Wallace and Robert M. Carmack, 1-19. Publications of the Institute for Mesoamerican Studies, no. 1. Albany: Institute for Mesoamerican Studies, State University of New York at Albany.
    1979   *Historia social de los quichés.* Guatemala: Seminario de Integración Social Guatemalteca, Ministerio de Educación.
    1981   *The Quiché Mayas of Utatlán.* Norman: University of Oklahoma Press.
    1995   *Rebels of Highland Guatemala.* Norman: University of Oklahoma Press.
Carmack, Robert M., Janine Gasco, and Gary H. Gossen
    1996   *The Legacy of Mesoamerica: History and Culture of a Native American Civilization.* Upper Saddle River, N.J.: Prentice Hall.
Carrasco, Pedro
    1961   The Civil-Religious Hierarchy in Meso-American Communities: Pre-Spanish Background and Colonial Development. *American Anthropologist* 63, no. 4: 483-497.
Chance, John K., and William B. Taylor
    1985   Cofradías and Cargos: An Historical Perspective on the Mesoamerican Civil-Religious Hierarchy. *American Ethnologist* 12: 1-26.
Chicas Rendón, Otto, and Héctor Gaitán A.
    1995   Recetario y oraciones secretas de Maximón. Guatemala: O. Chicas, 10a. Ave. 11-8, Zona 1; New York, N.Y.: Casa de las Velas.
Christenson, Allen J.
    1998   Scaling the Mountain of the Ancients: The Altarpiece of Santiago Atitlán, Guatemala. Ph.D. diss., University of Texas at Austin.
Coe, Michael
    1978   *Lords of the Underworld: Masterpieces of Classic Maya Ceramics.* Princeton: Art Museum, Princeton University.
Colby, Benjamin
    1976   The Anomalous Ixil—Bypassed by the Postclassic? *American Antiquity* 41, no. 1: 74-80.
Cook, Garrett
    1981   Supernaturalism, Cosmos, and Cosmogony in Quichean Expressive Culture. Ph.D. diss., State University of New York at Albany.
    1983   Mitos de Momostenango comparados con el *Popol vuh.* In *Nuevas perspectivas sobre el "Popol vuh,"* edited by Robert M. Carmack and Francisco Morales Santos, 135-154. Guatemala: Editorial Piedra Santa.

1986 Quichean Folk Theology and Southern Maya Supernaturalism. In *Symbol and Meaning beyond the Closed Community: Essays in Mesoamerican Ideas,* edited by Gary H. Gossen, 139-153. Albany: Institute for Mesoamerican Studies, State University of New York at Albany.

Cook, Garrett W., and John W. Fox

1994 Sacred Journeys and Segmentary Polities in Mayan Culture. Paper presented at the Primero Seminario de las Mesas Redondas de Palenque, September 30, 1994, Palenque, Chiapas, Mexico.

Correa, Gusavo

1960 El espíritu del mal en Guatemala. In *Nativism and Syncretism,* edited by Munro Edmonson. Publications of Middle American Research Institute, no. 19. New Orleans: Middle American Research Institute, Tulane University.

Coto, Fray Thomas de

1983 *Thesaurus verborum: Vocabulario de la lengua cakchiquel y guatemalteca, nueuamente hecho y recopilado con summo estudio, travajo y erudición.* Edited by Rene Acuña. Mexico, D.F.: Nacional Autónoma de México.

De Borhegyi, Stephan F.

1956 Development of Folk and Complex Cultures in the Southern Maya Area. *American Antiquity* 21, no. 4: 343-356.

Douglas, Mary

1973 *Natural Symbols.* New York: Pantheon.

Dundes, Alan

1963 Structural Typology in North American Indian Folk Tales. *Southwestern Journal of Anthropology* 19: 121-130.

1968 Introduction to the second edition of *Morphology of the Folktale,* by V. Propp, xi-xvii. American Folklore Society Bibliographical and Special Series, vol 9, rev. ed. Austin: University of Texas Press.

Edmonson, Munro S.

1960 Nativism, Syncretism, and Anthropological Science. In *Nativism and Syncretism,* edited by Munro Edmonson, 181-204. Publications of the Middle American Research Institute, no. 19. New Orleans: Middle American Research Institute, Tulane University Press.

1965 *Quiché-English Dictionary.* Publications of the Middle American Research Institute, no. 30. New Orleans: Middle American Research Institute, Tulane University.

1971 *The Book of Counsel: The "Popol Vuh" of the Quiché Maya of Guatemala.* Publications of the Middle American Research Institute, no. 35. New Orleans: Middle American Research Institute, Tulane University.

Eliade, Mircea

1963 *Myth and Reality.* New York: Harper and Row.

1968 *The Quest: History and Meaning in Religion.* Chicago: University of Chicago Press.

Farriss, Nancy

1984 *Maya Society under Colonial Rule: The Collective Enterprise of Survival.* Princeton: Princeton University Press.

Fischer, J. L.
  1963   The Sociopsychological Analysis of Folktales. *Current Anthropology* 4: 235–295.
Foster, George
  1960   *Culture and Conquest: America's Spanish Heritage.* Viking Fund Publications in Anthropology, no. 27. New York: Wenner-Gren Foundation for Anthropological Research.
Fox, David G.
  1973   *Lecciones elementales en quiché.* Publicaciones Especiales del Instituto Indigenista Nacional. Guatemala: Instituto Lingüístico de Verano de Centroamérica.
Fox, John W.
  1976   *Quiché Conquest: Centralism and Regionalism in Highland Guatemalan State Development.* Albuquerque: University of New Mexico Press.
  1987   *Maya Postclassic State Formation: Segmentary Lineage Migration in Advancing Frontiers.* Cambridge: Cambridge University Press.
Fox, John W., and Garrett W. Cook
  1996   Constructing Maya Communities: Ethnography for Archaeology. *Current Anthropology* 37, no. 5: 811–821.
Fox, John W., Garrett W. Cook, Arlen F. Chase, and Diane Z. Chase
  1996   Questions of Political and Economic Integration: Segmentary versus Centralized States among the Ancient Maya. *Current Anthropology* 37, no. 5: 795–801.
Freidel, David A.
  1990   The Jester God: The Beginning and End of a Maya Royal Symbol. In *Vision and Revision in Maya Studies,* edited by Flora S. Clancy and Peter D. Harrison, 67–78. Albuquerque: University of New Mexico Press.
Freidel, David, Linda Schele, and Joy Parker
  1993   *Maya Cosmos: Three Thousand Years on the Shaman's Path.* New York: William Morrow.
Furst, Peter T.
  1986   Human Biology and the Origin of the 260-Day Sacred Almanac: The Contribution of Leonhard Schultze Jena (1872–1955). In *Symbol and Meaning beyond the Closed Community: Essays in Mesoamerican Ideas,* edited by Gary H. Gossen, 69–76. Albany: Institute for Mesoamerican Studies, State University of New York at Albany.
Geertz, Clifford
  1973   *The Interpretation of Cultures.* New York: Basic Books.
Gonzalez, Gaspar Pedro
  1995   *A Mayan Life.* Rancho Palos Verdes, Calif.: Yax Te' Press.
Gossen, Gary
  1974   *Chamulas in the World of the Sun: Time and Space in a Maya Oral Tradition.* Cambridge: Harvard University Press.
  1986   Preface to *Symbol and Meaning beyond the Closed Community: Essays in Mesoamerican Ideas,* edited by Gary H. Gossen, ix–x. Albany: Institute for Mesoamerican Studies, State University of New York at Albany.

Guiteras Holmes, Calixta
1961 *Perils of the Soul.* New York: Free Press of Glencoe.
Hervieux, Jacques
1960 *The New Testament Apocrypha.* Translated by Dom Wulstan Hibberd. New York: Hawthorne Books.
Hill, Robert M. II
1992 *Colonial Cakchiqueles: Highland Maya Adaptations to Spanish Rule, 1600–1700.* Orlando: Harcourt Brace Jovanovich.
Hill, Robert M., and James Monoghan
1987 *Continuities in Highland Maya Social Organization: Ethnohistory in Sacapulas, Guatemala.* Philadelphia: University of Pennsylvania Press.
Himelblau, Jack J.
1989 *Quiché Worlds in Creation: The "Popol Vuh" as a Narrative Work of Art.* Culver City: Labyrinthos.
Holland, William R.
1964 Contemporary Tzotzil Cosmological Concepts as a Basis for Interpreting Prehistoric Maya Civilization. *American Antiquity* 29, no. 3: 301–306.
Hunt, Eva
1977 *Transformation of the Hummingbird: Cultural Roots of a Zinacantán Mythical Poem.* Ithaca: Cornell University Press.
Huxley, Aldous
1934 *Beyond Mexique Bay.* London: Chatto and Windus.
Jose Chonay, Dionisio, and Delia Goetz
1953 *Title of the Lords of Totonicapán.* Norman: University of Oklahoma Press.
Kurath, Gertrude P.
1967 Drama, Dance, and Music. In *Handbook of Middle American Indians,* edited by Robert Wauchope, vol. 6. Austin: University of Texas Press.
La Farge, Oliver
1940 Maya Ethnology: The Sequence of Cultures. In *The Maya and Their Neighbors,* edited by C. L. Hay et al., 281–291. New York: D. Appleton-Century.
1947 *Santa Eulalia: The Religion of a Cuchamatán Indian Town.* Chicago: University of Chicago Press.
1956 Etnología maya: Secuencia de las culturas. In *Cultura indígena de Guatemala: Ensayos de antropología social,* edited by Richard N. Adams et al. Publications of the Seminario de Integración Social Guatemalteca, no. 1. Guatemala: Editorial del Ministerio de Educación Público.
La Farge, Oliver, and Douglas Byers
1931 *The Year Bearer's People.* Publications of Middle American Research Institute, no. 3. New Orleans: Middle American Research Institute, Tulane University.
Las Casas, Bartolomeo de
1967 *Apologética historia sumario.* 2 vols. Edited by Edmundo O'Gorman. Mexico, D.F.: Instituto de Investigaciones Históricas, Universidad Nacional Autónoma de Mexico.

Leach, Edmund
1964   *Political Systems of Highland Burma.* Boston: Beacon Press.
León Portilla, Miguel
1988   *Time and Reality in Mayan Thought.* Norman: University of Oklahoma Press.
Lowie, Robert
1954   *Indians of the Plains.* New York: McGraw-Hill.
Mace, Carroll
1970   *Two Spanish-Quiché Dance Dramas of Rabinal.* New Orleans: Tulane University Press.
Madsen, William
1960   Christo Paganism. In *Nativism and Syncretism,* edited by Munro Edmonson, 105–180. Publications of Middle American Research Institute, no. 19. New Orleans: Middle American Research Institute, Tulane University.
Malinowski, Bronislaw
1944   *"A Scientific Theory of Culture" and Other Essays by Bronislaw Malinowski.* Chapel Hill: University of North Carolina Press.
McAnany, Patricia A.
1995   *Living with the Ancestors: Kinship and Kingship in Ancient Maya Society.* Austin: University of Texas Press.
McArthur, Harry S.
1972   Los bailes de Aguacatán y el culto a los muertos. *América Indígena* 32, no. 2: 491–513.
Menchú, Rigoberta
1984   *I, Rigoberta Menchú: An Indian Woman in Guatemala,* Edited and with an introduction by Elizabeth Burgos-Debray. Translated by Ann Wright. New York: Verso.
Mendelson, E. Michael
1958   The King, the Traitor, and the Cross. *Diogenes* 21: 1–10.
1959   Maximon, an Iconographical Introduction. *Man* 59, no. 87 (April): 57–60.
1965   *Los escándalos de Maximón.* Guatemala: Seminario de Integración Social Guatemalteca, Ministerio de Educación.
1967   Ritual and Mythology. In *Handbook of Middle American Indians,* edited by Robert Wauchope, vol. 6, 392–415. Austin: University of Texas Press.
Molina F., Diego
1983   *Las Confesiones de Maximón.* Guatemala: Artemis y Edinter.
Mondloch, James L., and Eugene P. Hruska
1975   Basic Quiché Grammar: 38 Lessons. State University of New York at Albany. Photocopy.
Oakes, Maud
1951   *Two Crosses of Todos Santos: Survivals of Maya Religious Ritual.* Bollingen Series, no. 27, Princeton: Princeton University Press.
O'Brien, Linda Lee
1975   Songs of the Face of the Earth: Ancestors' Songs of the Tzutujil-Maya of Santiago Atitlán. Ph.D. diss., University of California at Los Angeles.

Paret-Limardo, Lise
    1963   *La danza del venado en Guatemala.* Guatemala: Centro Editorial José de Pinada Ibarra, Ministerio de Educación Pública.

Parsons, Elsie Clews
    1966   *Mitla, Town of Souls.* Chicago: University of Chicago Press.

Pasinski, Tony
    1990   *The Santos of Guatemala.* Guatemala City: Didacsa Centro Científico Cultural.

Pickands, Martin
    1986   The Hero Myth of Maya Folklore. In *Symbol and Meaning beyond the Closed Community: Essays in Mesoamerican Ideas,* edited by Gary H. Gossen, 101–124. Albany: Institute for Mesoamerican Studies, State University of New York at Albany.

Price, Barbara
    1974   The Burden of the *Cargo:* Ethnographic Models and Archaeological Inferences. In *Mesoamerican Archaeology: New Approaches,* edited by Norman Hammond, 445–467. Austin: University of Texas Press.

Propp, V.
    1968   *Morphology of the Folktale.* Translated by Laurence Scott. Austin: University of Texas Press.

Radin, Paul
    1956   *The Trickster: A Study in American Indian Mythology.* London: Routledge and Paul.

Recinos, Adrián
    1950   *"Popol Vuh": The Sacred Book of the Ancient Quiché Maya.* Translated by Delia Goetz and S. G. Morley. Norman: University of Oklahoma Press.
    1957   *Crónicas indígenas de Guatemala.* Edited by Adrián Recinos. Guatemala: Imprenta Universitaria.

Recinos, Adrián, and Delia Goetz
    1953   *The Annals of the Cakchiquels.* Norman: University of Oklahoma Press.

Redfield, Robert
    1941   *The Folk Culture of Yucatán.* Chicago: University of Chicago Press.
    1958   *Tepoztlan, A Mexican Village.* Chicago: University of Chicago Press.

Redfield, Robert, and Alfonso Villa Rojas
    1964   *Chan Kom: A Maya Village.* Chicago: University of Chicago Press.

Reina, Ruben E.
    1966   *The Law of the Saints: A Pokomam Pueblo and Its Community Culture.* New York: Bobbs-Merrill.

Remington, Judith A.
    1977   Current Astronomical Practices among the Maya. In *Native American Astronomy,* edited by Anthony F. Aveni, 75–88. Austin: University of Texas Press.

Rojas Lima, Flavio
    1988   *La cofradía: Reducto cultural indígena.* Guatemala: Litografía Moderna.

Sabloff, Jeremy A., and Gordon R. Willey
  1967   The Collapse of the Maya Civilization in the Southern Lowlands: A Consideration of History and Process. *Southwestern Journal of Anthropology* 23: 311–336.

Saler, Benson
  1960   *The Road from El Palmar: Change, Continuity, and Conservatism in a Quiché Community.* Ph.D. diss., University of Pennsylvania. Ann Arbor: University Microfilms.
  1967   *Nagual,* Witch, and Sorcerer in a Quiché Village. In *Magic, Witchcraft, and Curing,* edited by John Middleton. Garden City, N.Y.: Natural History Press.

Schele, Linda
  1992   *Workbook for the XVIth Maya Hieroglyphic Workshop at Texas.* Austin: Department of Art and Art History and Institute of Latin American Studies, University of Texas at Austin.

Schele, Linda, and David A. Freidel
  1990   *A Forest of Kings: The Untold Story of the Ancient Maya.* New York: William Morrow.

Schultze Jena, Leonhard
  1954   *La vida y las creencias de los indígenas quichés de Guatemala.* Translated by Antonio Goubard Carrera and Herbert Sapper. Biblioteca Popular, vol. 49. Guatemala: Editorial del Ministerio de Educación Pública.

Shaw, Mary, ed.
  1971   *According to Our Ancestors.* Summer Institute of Linguistics Publications in Linguistics and Related Fields, no. 32. Guatemala: Instituto Lingüístico de Verano en Centro América.

Siegal, Morris
  1941   Religions in Western Guatemala: A Product of Acculturation. *American Anthropologist* 43: 63–76.

Singer, Milton
  1959   *Traditional India: Structure and Change.* Philadelphia: American Folklore Society.

Smith, Carol
  1978   Beyond Dependency Theory: National and Regional Patterns of Underdevelopment in Guatemala. *American Ethnologist* 5: 574–615.

Tarn, Nathaniel, and Martin Prechtel
  1986   Constant Inconstancy: The Feminine Principle in Atiteco Mythology. In *Symbol and Meaning beyond the Closed Community,* edited by Gary Gossen. Albany: Institute for Mesoamerican Studies, State University of New York at Albany.

Tax, Sol
  1937   The *Municipios* of the Midwestern Highlands of Guatemala. *American Anthropologist* 39: 423–44.
  1952   *Heritage of Conquest: The Ethnology of Middle America.* Glencoe, Ill.: Free Press.

Tax, Sol, and Robert Hinshaw
  1969   The Maya of the Midwestern Highlands. In *Handbook of Middle American Indians,* edited by Robert Wauchope, vol. 7. Austin: University of Texas Press.
Tedlock, Barbara
  1982   *Time and the Highland Maya.* Albuquerque: University of New Mexico Press.
  1986   On a Mountain in the Dark: Encounters with the K'iche' Maya Culture Hero. In *Symbol and Meaning beyond the Closed Community: Essays in Mesoamerican Ideas,* edited by Gary H. Gossen, 125–138. Albany: Institute for Mesoamerican Studies, State University of New York at Albany.
  1992   The Sky in Maya Cosmology. Paper given at the Maya Meetings at Texas, VIIIth Texas Symposium, Austin, March 12.
Tedlock, Dennis
  1985   *"Popol Vuh": The Definitive Edition of the Mayan Book of the Dawn of Life and the Glories of God and Kings.* New York: Simon and Schuster.
  1986   Creation in the *Popul Vuh:* A Hermeneutical Approach. In *Symbol and Meaning beyond the Closed Community: Essays in Mesoamerican Ideas,* edited by Gary H. Gossen, 77–82. Albany: Institute for Mesoamerican Studies, State University of New York at Albany.
  1993   *Breath on the Mirror: Mythic Voices and Visions of the Living Maya.* San Francisco: Harper.
Thompson, J. Eric
  1930   *Ethnology of the Mayas of Southern and Central British Honduras.* Publications of the Field Museum of Natural History, no. 274; Anthropological Series, vol. 17, no. 2. Chicago.
  1970   *Maya History and Religion.* Norman: University of Oklahoma Press.
Tozzer, Alfred M.
  1966   *Landa's "Relación de las cosas de Yucatán."* Reprint, New York: Kraus.
Turner, Victor
  1968   *Myth and Symbol.* Vol. 10 of *International Encyclopedia of the Social Sciences.* New York: Crowell, Collier and Macmillan.
  1969   *The Ritual Process: Structure and Anti-structure.* Chicago: Aldine.
  1974   *Dramas, Fields, and Metaphors: Symbolic Action in Human Society.* Ithaca: Cornell University Press.
  1977   Symbols in African Ritual. In *Symbolic Anthropology,* edited by Janet L. Dolgin, David S. Kemnitzer, and David M. Schneider, 183–194. New York: Columbia University Press.
Vogt, Evon Z.
  1961   Some Aspects of Zinacantán Settlement Pattern and Ceremonial Organization. *Estudios de Cultura Maya* 1: 131–145.
  1964   The Genetic Model and Maya Cultural Development. In *Desarollo cultural de los mayas,* edited by Evon Z. Vogt and Alberto Ruz L., 9–48. Mexico, D.F.: Universidad Nacional Autónoma de México.
  1969   *Zinacantán.* Cambridge: Harvard University Press.

Wallace, Anthony F. C.
    1966   *Religion: An Anthropological View.* New York: Random House.
Wallace, Dwight T.
    1977   An Intra-site Locational Analysis of Utatlán: The Structure of an Urban Site. In *Archaeology and Ethnohistory of the Central Quiché,* edited by D. T. Wallace and R. M. Carmack, 20–54. Albany: Institute for Mesoamerican Studies, State University of New York.
Watanabe, John
    1990   From Saints to Shibboleths: Image, Structure, and Identity in Maya Religious Syncretism. *American Ethnologist* 17, no. 1: 129–148.
Weber, Max
    1969   Major Features of World Religions. In *Sociology of Religion,* edited by Roland Robertson. Baltimore: Penguin.
Wilk, Richard R.
    1991   *Household Ecology: Economic Change and Domestic Life among the Kekchi Maya in Belize.* Tucson: University of Arizona Press.
Wolf, Eric
    1959   *Sons of the Shaking Earth.* Chicago: University of Chicago Press.

Index